web
developer's guide to
JavaScript
& VBScript

web
developer's guide to
JavaScript
& VBScript

Peter Aitken

CORIOLIS GROUP BOOKS

PUBLISHER	**KEITH WEISKAMP**
PROJECT EDITOR	**DENISE CONSTANTINE**
COVER ARTIST	**GARY SMITH**
COVER DESIGN	**ANTHONY STOCK**
INTERIOR DESIGN	**MICHELLE STROUP**
LAYOUT PRODUCTION	**PROIMAGE**
COPY EDITOR	**MAGGY MISKELL**
PROOFREADER	**CINDY LEIGH**
INDEXER	**LENITY MAUHAR**

The Coriolis Group, Inc.
7339 E. Acoma Drive, Suite 7
Scottsdale, AZ 85260
Phone: (602) 483-0192
Fax: (602) 483-0193
Web address: http://www.coriolis.com

ISBN 1-883577-97-7 : $39.99
Printed in the United States of America
10 9 8 7 6 5 4 3 2 1

"To the Buddha for all that he and his teachings have brought us."

Acknowledgments

Several talented individuals at The Coriolis Group contributed to the creation of this book, from the initial concept to dotting the final "i's:" Keith Weiskamp, Denise Constantine, Anthony Potts, David Friedel, Maggy Miskell, and ProImage. Thanks, everyone.

Contents

Chapter 6   JavaScript Methods and Functions   153

Chapter 7   Responding to User Actions   199

Introduction

The Web seems to be the hottest topic going these days, and one of the hottest topics on the Web is a new breed of developer's tool called *scripting languages*. A scripting language is a mini-programming language that you, the Web page developer, can use right in your Web documents to provide interactivity, customization, and a wide variety of other capabilities that were just not possible before. With a scripting language, your Web pages can be transformed from merely a static presentation of information to a lively and customizable experience.

The whole idea of a scripting language had its start with Netscape Communications and their JavaScript language. JavaScript is still in the final stages of development, but even so, it is becoming more and more common on the Web. Many of the really impressive pages you see probably have JavaScript working away behind the scenes!

Never one to be outdone for long, Microsoft has joined the fray with Visual Basic Script, or VBScript for short. Based on their immensely popular Visual Basic, VBScript is very different in execution, but similar in capabilities, to JavaScript. It is not quite as far along in development, and there are relatively few Web sites using it at present; but I am sure that situation won't last for long!

This book provides all the information you need to start enhancing your Web pages with JavaScript or VBScript. If you're just getting started in Web development, you'll also find a chapter on Hypertext Markup Language fundamentals and an appendix covering the basics of the Internet and the World Wide Web. More experienced readers can skip these parts and dive right into the chapters on JavaScript and VBScript. You'll find lots of sample code, numerous working examples, and detailed reference information. Remember, however, that both of these languages are still evolving, and from an author's perspective, it's next to impossible to hit a moving target dead-center. By the time you read this, details of language syntax or implementation may have changed, and you'll need to refer to the Netscape or Microsoft documentation for the latest information.

Looking for Web Sites

Throughout this book, you'll see special sidebars called *Web Watch*, which I use to call your attention to a wide variety of sites on the Web. Some of these have interesting JavaScript or VBScript programs for you to try, while others have useful software that can be downloaded. A few are totally unrelated to the book, but they are, at least in my opinion, unusual or interesting in some way. Remember, however, that the Web is not static. A site that was alive and well when I wrote the book may be long gone by the time you read it. Or, it may still exist but at another location. If you cannot find a site, I suggest that you try locating it with one of the Web search engines, such as Yahoo or Lycos (Appendix A has more information on Web searches).

On the CD-ROM

The CD-ROM contains all of the book's JavaScript and VBScript code, so you can try out my sample programs without having to do a lot of typing. There's also an array of useful software, most but not all related to Web development. You'll find a powerful programmer's editor, a full-featured graphics program, several HTML editors, and lots more. You would have to pay hundreds of dollars to purchase the equivalent commercial programs!

Appendix B provides details on the software, installation, and so on.

A Note on Shareware

Many of the utility programs provided on the CD-ROM are *shareware*. This is true also of many of the programs you'll download over the Net. Please remember that shareware is not "freeware." If you like the program and find it useful, you are required to register and pay the author a fee, usually in the $10-25 range (which you have to admit is really quite reasonable compared to the cost of some commercial software!). There's no way you can be forced to pay, but doing so not only gives you a clear conscience, it also provides shareware authors with the support they need to keep offering us so many useful programs.

Chapter **1**

Scripting the Web

What are Scripting Languages?

Because you're reading this book, it's safe to assume that you're interested in developing material for publication on the World Wide Web. It's also a good bet that you've spent a fair amount of time surfing, getting a feel for what's out there and how other developers are doing things. Have you noticed that Web pages seem to be improving these days? They have more interactive elements, permitting the user a greater degree of freedom in finding his or her own way through the material. They are also more easily customized, allowing you to see things your way. Some pages even perform tasks like numerical calculations—jobs that were usually relegated to stand-alone programs. These and many other improvements in Web pages are the work of JavaScript and, to a lesser extent, VBScript. So what are these languages?

As the names suggest, JavaScript and VBScript are *scripting* languages. You are probably aware that you

1

use a regular programming language such as C++ or Pascal to create complete application programs. In contrast, a scripting language is used within a program to extend its capabilities. If you've ever written a macro in a Lotus 1-2-3 spreadsheet or used WordBasic to perform some task in a Microsoft Word document, you have already used a scripting language. In a similar fashion, JavaScript and VBScript extend the capabilities of Web pages.

JavaScript was the first Web scripting language. Developed by Netscape Communication, it has been supported by the Netscape Navigator browsers starting with version 2.0. As of this writing JavaScript is still under development, and even though it is probably pretty close to its final form, it is not yet a "done deal." All of the scripting you see on the Web is done with JavaScript, although by the time this book is published, this won't be the case any more. Only Netscape browsers support JavaScript, although Microsoft has announced its intentions to provide JavaScript support in its browser, Internet Explorer.

VBScript is Microsoft's response to JavaScript. The VB stands for Visual Basic and, in fact, VBScript is a subset of the popular Visual Basic programming language. Because Netscape had a significant head start, VBScript was considerably behind in development and was supported only by the pre-release version of Microsoft Internet Explorer version 3.0. Plans for other companies, such as Netscape, to support VBScript in their browsers have not been announced, but my guess is that such support will be coming and may in fact be available by the time you are reading this. After all, when Microsoft puts its considerable weight behind a standard, you can be pretty sure it will get some acceptance!

NOT FOR THE WEB ONLY

The use of JavaScript and VBScript is not limited to the World Wide Web. JavaScript is relevant to any network that uses Internet technology, hypertext transfer protocol (HTTP), and hypertext markup language (HTML) documents. This includes the so-called intranets, networks internal to an organization that use Internet technology to share information among employees.

For the remainder of this book, we will assume that you have at least a fundamental knowledge of how the Internet and the World Wide Web work. If you're just getting started with the Web, or perhaps feel you could use some review on the basics, you might want to read Appendix A, *Web Basics*, before continuing.

How Do Script Languages Work?

When you view a Web page, you are actually viewing a hypertext markup language (HTML) document that is transferred over the network from the server, or host, computer to your computer (the *client*). The HTML document is loaded into your browser—Netscape Navigator, Microsoft Internet Explorer, or whatever—and displayed for your perusal. The HTML document contains text as well as special tags that control how the text is formatted while specifying the display of images, tables, buttons, and other such elements. On its own, an HTML document is pretty static, and no matter how terrific it looks, it doesn't really do anything.

A script program, either JavaScript or VBScript, is embedded within the HTML document. Your browser intercepts the script code and carries out the specified actions. Because the script languages have considerably more capability than HTML alone, the author of the document has a lot more freedom to create interactive and "smart" Web pages. From the developer's perspective then, using JavaScript or VBScript consists of placing the desired code statements inside an HTML document. The idea of separating a script program from an HTML document makes no sense—by definition, a JavaScript or VBScript program is part of an HTML document. Once could create an HTML document that contains nothing but a JavaScript or VBScript program, but it's still an HTML document!

From the end-user's perspective, the only thing required to "run" JavaScript or VBScript programs is a browser that supports the particular script—or, in techie-talk, a browser that is *JavaScript or VBScript enabled*. When you view an HTML document in a browser, the script code that it contains will either be executed immediately or in response to user actions.

JavaScript Is Not Java

Perhaps you have heard of a new programming language called Java. Is this related to JavaScript? Yes and no. A bit of history will help me to explain this less-than-decisive answer.

JavaScript has its origins in a scripting language called LiveScript that was under development by Netscape Communications. At the same time, another company called Sun Microsystems was working on a programming language called Java. Java is not a scripting language, but rather a regular programming language intended to create stand-alone applications. Unlike other languages such as C and Basic, Java is specialized for the creation of so-called *applets*, small- to medium-size programs that are intended to be downloaded from a server to the user's computer when and if they are needed for execution. Two main components make up this specialization:

- Java programs are compact. You don't want to have time to read *War and Peace* while an applet is downloading! Small programs and quick downloads are essential for maximum usability.

- Java programs are secure. Users would be hesitant to download and run a program that might be infected with a computer virus or contain programming bugs that have the potential to cause mischief. The safety of Java programs is based on a variety of design and implementation factors that make it impossible (or so they say) for unauthorized "hacked" Java programs to corrupt your system.

When Sun and Netscape started working together, they quickly realized that many of the specifications for Java would apply equally well to LiveScript. As a result, the name of the scripting language was changed to JavaScript, and many of the statements, keywords, and constructs of Java were adopted. JavaScript can be thought of as a little brother to Java, providing a defined subset of its capabilities—just those capabilities required in a scripting language. Like Java, JavaScript is a secure language that is incapable of writing to disk or other actions that could be used by a virus to damage your system. Here's a rundown of the most salient characteristics of JavaScript and how they compare to Java:

- JavaScript is an *interpreted* language; its source code (the code you write) is downloaded and translated (interpreted) into instructions the computer can understand at the time it is needed. In contrast, Java is a *compiled* language; the source code is translated into machine instructions on the server computer, and it is those instructions that you download when the applet is run.

- JavaScript is *object-based*; the programs you write utilize pre–defined objects, but you are limited in terms of creating your own objects. Java is *object-oriented*, permitting both the use of pre–defined objects and full power for creation of new ones.

- JavaScript has *loose data typing*; a JavaScript variable can hold any kind of data. Java has *strong data typing*; each variable must be declared to hold a specific type of data.

- JavaScript code is *embedded*; it is always part of an HTML file. Java applets are *independent*; they are stand-alone applications that can be accessed from HTML.

Some of these terms and explanations may not mean a great deal to you right now. That's to be expected—after all, we're just getting started!

A JavaScript Example

Enough talk—it's time to take a look at an actual JavaScript program. This is a very simple one that doesn't do anything useful, but we have to start somewhere. We'll see a more useful JavaScript program later in the chapter.

Listing 1.1 contains the full text of an HTML file that contains a JavaScript script.

LISTING 1.1   SIMPLE.HTML

```
<html>
<head>
<title>Simple JavaScript</title>
</head>
<body>
This line displayed with "normal" HTML.
<br>
<script language="JavaScript">
document.write("This line displayed with JavaScript.")
</script>
<br>
This final line with HTML again.
</body>
</html>
```

If you load this file into a JavaScript-enabled browser, you'll see the following display:

```
This line displayed with "normal"HTML.
This line displayed with JavaScript.
This final line with HTML again.
```

Not too exciting—and not really something for which you would use JavaScript in a real program—but it gives you the idea of how a JavaScript script appears. As you may have figured out, the JavaScript part of the HTML file begins with the <script ...> tag and ends with the </script> tag. The remainder of the file is "plain" HTML. We'll learn all about HTML files in Chapter 2.

...And VBScript Is Not Visual Basic

Just like JavaScript is not Java, VBScript is not Visual Basic. Actually, VBScript is a lot closer to Visual Basic than JavaScript is to Java. If you are familiar with Visual Basic programming (either the programming environment or the

Visual Basic for Applications scripting language), then you have a big head start in learning VBScript. In fact, VBScript is a subset of the full Visual Basic language, and there are a lot of things in Visual Basic that are not in VBScript. Don't let this give you the idea that VBScript is crippled or feeble—it contains those language elements that are needed for Web scripting and, like JavaScript, lacks those capabilities, such as reading and writing files, that could be used by unscrupulous individuals to create scripts that would either cause mischief on your system or would read private information from your disk for transmittal elsewhere.

VBScript is similar to JavaScript in many ways—it is interpreted, loosely typed, object-based, and embedded. You would never mistake one for the other, because their syntax and keyword sets are quite different.

What You'll Need

To develop and test JavaScript or VBScript programs, you'll need a minimum of two tools. First, you need an editor to create and edit the HTML files in which your script programs will be embedded. We'll talk about specialized editors in the next chapter. For now, you can use the NotePad utility that comes with Windows 95. Secondly, you need a JavaScript- or VBScript-enabled browser to test your scripts. As I mentioned earlier, only Netscape Navigator fits the bill for JavaScript, and only Microsoft Internet Explorer 3.0 works for VBScript. It's a sure bet, however, that many other browsers will support JavaScript and/or VBScript in the very near future.

Web Watch

For a plethora of information about anything Web-related, check into Netscape's home page at http://home.netscape.com. You can download and purchase software (including Netscape Navigator), find out about the latest development tools, and link to other sites that are related to Web development. Microsoft's internet resource page is also full of interesting information and downloads: http://www.microsoft. com/internet/.

Here is the basic procedure you'll follow:

1. Open your editor and write the HTML and JavaScript or VBScript code.

2. Save the file with the desired name and the .HTML extension (for example, MY_PROGRAM.HTML).

3. Open the browser and use its File Open or equivalent command to load the file you saved in step 2.

4. Examine the display and behavior of the HTML file. Does it display as you planned? Do the scripts work as they are supposed to?

5. Return to step 1 and make any necessary additions and corrections.

It's as simple as that. As we work through the book, we'll cover some specialized tools and techniques that make the process of developing Web pages easier. Remember, however, that the real key to creating great pages is *you*. It's your creativity and imagination, coupled with a complete understanding of JavaScript/VBScript and HTML, that will combine to create successful and even impressive Web pages.

GO FOR THE GOLD

Netscape Navigator Gold combines all the capabilities of the popular Netscape Navigator browser with a powerful HTML editor. It's ideal for Web page developers because you can use one program to both write and test your HTML files. We think it's a great program that will become the tool of choice for many Web developers, which is why we devoted an entire chapter to showing you how to use it (Chapter 3). Navigator Gold was in beta testing when this book was being written; it should be released by now. Check the Netscape home page (see the Web Watch above) to obtain a copy.

Your First JavaScript Program

Before we move on to the ins and outs of HTML, let's take a look at a real JavaScript program—one that does something useful. (I'll get to VBScript next.) It's a simple program, to be sure, but that's just what you need at this point. Going through the motions of an activity is an important part of learning it. Actually performing the steps of typing a JavaScript program into your editor, loading it into a browser, and seeing it work will give you a leg up for the rest of the book. Here's what to do:

1. Open your editor, using Windows NotePad if you don't have another preferred editor, and type in the code shown in Listing 1.2.

2. Save the file with the name LIST0102.HTML.

3. Open your JavaScript-enabled browser.

4. Use the File Open (or equivalent) command to open LIST0102.HTML. In Netscape Navigator, the command is Open File on the File menu; in Netscape Navigator Gold, it is Open File in Browser.

5. Enter a 4- or 6-digit ZIP code in the entry box and click outside the box. You'll see a warning message displayed, as shown in Figure 1.1. Try entering a correct ZIP code and see what happens.

This program is a simple example of something that JavaScript is commonly used for, the validation of user input data. It verifies that a ZIP code entered by the user contains exactly 5 digits. A lot of the more interesting uses of the Web involve gathering information from the user. Online ordering of merchandise is just one example. You can save a lot of hassles if you can catch and correct errors in data entry *before* the data is sent from the client to the server. This is what data validation means. JavaScript will enable you to verify, for example, that a valid State abbreviation was entered in an address, or that a credit card number has the correct number of digits. Even better, all this is done (like all JavaScript processing) locally, on the client machine, requiring no transfer of data between client and server.

Look at the code, take it for a spin, and try to figure out how the code is working. No, we certainly don't expect you to understand all the details. A lot of this code is "plain" HTML, which you may already understand (and if you don't, Chapter 2 will fix that). Let's briefly review the JavaScript components of this document.

First, we have a function named **CheckZip**. Its code is located between the line <!-- and the line //-->. As in other programming languages, a function is a group of code statements that has been assigned a name. This code is executed, or run, only when specifically requested. The code in this function checks the ZIP code that the user entered. If it is not 5 characters long, a warning message is displayed and the focus is set back to the text box so the user can modify the entry. If the ZIP code is the proper length, another message is displayed.

The second and final JavaScript part of the document is the line that begins <INPUT and ends this.value)"> (it may be broken into two lines in the listing). This line displays a input element where the user can enter data—in this case, a ZIP code. The details in the line specify that:

- The element is a text box.

- Its name is "zip."

- It is 10 characters wide.

- It is initially blank.

- When the focus is removed from the text box, the function CheckZip is called.

That's all for now. If you need to learn about HTML, you should continue with the next chapter. Those of you who are already HTML wizards can move on to Chapters 3 or 4.

LISTING 1.2   A SIMPLE JAVASCRIPT PROGRAM.

```
<html>
<head>
<title>My First JavaScript Program</title>
<script language="javascript">
<!--
function CheckZip(form, entry)
{
if (entry.length != 5)
{
alert("A ZIP code must be 5 numbers!!")
form.zip.focus()
}
else
{
alert("My, what a nice ZIP code!")
}
}
```

```
//--
  >
</script>
</head>
<body>
<form  name="TestForm">
<hr>
<h2>Input validation</h2>
<br>

Here's a ZIP code field. Try entering an improper ZIP, such as four
or six numbers. Then move the focus off the field by clicking
elsewhere in the document.

<br><br>
<b>ZIP code:</b>
<INPUT  TYPE="text" VALUE="" NAME="zip" SIZE=10
 OnBlur="CheckZip(this.form,this.value)">
<br>
<br>
<hr>
</form>
</body>
</html>
```

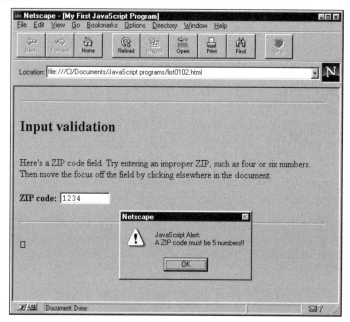

Figure 1.1

The test JavaScript program after entering an incorrect ZIP code.

Your First VBScript Program

For our first VBScript program, let's try something a bit different, something that demonstrates how scripting languages can be used to create interactive Web pages. The general procedure is similar to that described above for the JavaScript program:

1. Use your text editor to enter the code shown in Listing 1.3.

2. Save the file with the name LIST0103.HTML.

3. Open your VBScript-enabled browser, which most likely will be Microsoft's Internet Explorer version 3.

4. Load the file you just created.

You'll see a brief message and a button labeled "Click me." When you click the button, a message is displayed in a dialog box, as shown in Figure 1.2.

The code for this program is shown in Listing 1.3. Some of the elements are identical or similar to the JavaScript example presented earlier, while other aspects are quite different. We have a function, or as it is called in VBScript a Sub, located on three lines starting with Sub ... and ending with End Sub. Note that the name of the Sub is Button1_OnClick. The name of the Sub

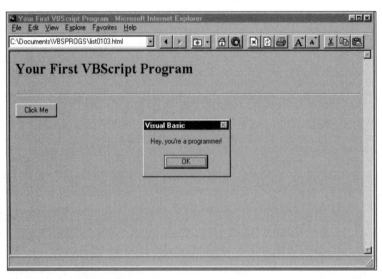

Figure 1.2
The VBScript program after clicking the button.

defines its function. In this case, the Sub will be executed when an object named Button1 is clicked by the user. There's only a single line of code within the Sub, calling the VBScript function MsgBox ("Message Box") to display a message on the screen.

Later in the code we see an <INPUT ... > tag. You may recognize this as a standard HTML tag that defines a button to be displayed on the screen. This button is assigned the name Button1 and the value "Click Me". It is this tag that causes the browser to display the button shown in the figure.

When the HTML file is loaded into a VBScript enabled browser, clicking the button causes the message box to be displayed. This link between the button and the Sub is managed automatically. All that's required on the part of the programmer is to assign the Sub a name that connects it with an object and a user action. If you have any experience with Visual Basic programming, you'll recognize this as an *event procedure*, a section of code that is executed automatically in response to a user action.

LISTING 1.3   A SIMPLE VBSCRIPT PROGRAM

```
<HTML>
<HEAD>
<TITLE>Your First VBScript Program</TITLE>
<SCRIPT LANGUAGE="VBS">
<!--
Sub Button1_OnClick
MsgBox "Hey, you're a programmer!"
End Sub
-->
</SCRIPT>
</HEAD>
<BODY>
<H2>Your First VBScript Program</H2>
<HR>
<FORM>
<INPUT NAME="Button1" TYPE="BUTTON" VALUE="Click Me">
</FORM>
</BODY>
</HTML>
```

Which Language Is for You?

Some readers may be delighted that there will be two powerful scripting languages available for enhancing Web pages. Others may be dismayed, wanting to select a single scripting language to learn and use. Which one is better? Which will have more support? These are valid questions, and I am afraid that I don't have any definite answers for you.

At present there is no doubt that JavaScript has a big head start. It is estimated that 50 to 90 percent of Internet users rely on Netscape Navigator, and JavaScript is already being used to enhance hundreds of Web pages. The JavaScript language itself is more mature, as well. I have no doubt that JavaScript will be an important part of Web development for the fore-seeable future.

On the other hand, VBScript comes from Microsoft and...well, Microsoft is Microsoft! Despite all the jokes about the 900 pound gorilla sitting wherever he wants to, the folks at Microsoft generally come out with pretty damn good products and VBScript is no exception. A good product, coupled with Microsoft's power in the marketplace and their demonstrated desire to see VBScript become widely adapted, leave little room for doubt that VBScript is here to stay. These factors, along with VBScript's close relationship with Visual Basic and Visual Basic for Applications, may eventually give it the edge.

Microsoft has licensed JavaScript from Netscape, so it seems likely that future versions of Internet Explorer will support JavaScript. Microsoft has announced that the VBScript binary (the part that a developer needs to support VBScript) will be made available without licensing fees, so we can also expect VBScript support to show up in non-Microsoft browsers (although whether Netscape will climb on board remains to be seen).

Is one language more powerful than the other? It's impossible to say because they are both still under development. In any case, the question is of limited value because a scripting language does not exist in isolation. The final Web pages you are able to create will depend less on which scripting language you use than on factors such as the plug-ins, Java applets, and ActiveX controls that are available and used to their full capacity. If you want to become an accomplished Web developer, you will have to learn a lot more than JavaScript or VBScript!

Onward!

Chapter 2 provides a concise introduction to Hypertext Mark Language (HTML), something you need to know to use either JavaScript or VBScript. If you already know HTML, you can skip this chapter, of course. Chapter 3 shows you how to use Navigator Gold, the combined browser and HTML editor from Netscape that is an excellent tool for developing Web pages that use JavaScript. Unfortunately, Microsoft has not yet released a comparable development tool for VBScript, although you can be sure that one is on the way!

The remainder of the book is divided into two sections, one on JavaScript and one on VBScript. You'll note that I have devoted more pages to JavaScript than to VBScript. There's a simple reason for this, and it is not because I favor JavaScript or because there's more to JavaScript than to VBScript. No, it's just because JavaScript is further along in development, so there's more information available to write about. You may wonder about the wisdom of writing on a topic that is as incomplete as VBScript. Shouldn't I wait until things are more settled? I don't think so. In the rapidly changing world of software technology you can't sit and wait or you'll be left behind in the dust. Learn as much as you can as soon as you can, and when the full VBScript specification becomes available, you'll be just that much further ahead of your competition!

*Hypertext Markup
Language, or
HTML, is the
language of the
Web. You need to
know at least the
basics of HTML if
you're going to
make the most of
JavaScript and
VBScript.*

Key Topics:

- **The relation–ship between HTML and the Web.**

- **HTML versions and support.**

- **The most useful HTML formatting and navigation tags.**

Chapter **2**

Hypertext Markup Language

What Is HTML?

HTML may sound mysterious and forbidding, but it's really quite simple. Whenever you view a Web page in your browser, you're viewing an HTML document. The text you're viewing is part of the document. Information on how to format the text and what pictures to display is also part of the document. Links to other Web pages are part of the HTML document, too. And, most relevant to this book, any JavaScript or VBScript code that you execute is part of the document.

An HTML document (which, by tradition, is in a disk file identified by the .HTM or .HTML extension) is a plain text file that contains, in addition to its textual content, a variety of special codes. These are the codes that control the way that the document's text is formatted, which pictures are displayed, where links point to, and so on. Let's look at an example:

```
<center>
This line will be centered on the page.
<p>
This line, too.
</center>
```

The first line is an HTML code. As you can probably guess, it centers text on the page. In effect, it instructs the browser "starting here, center everything on the page until told to stop." The third line is a code, too. It specifies the start of a new paragraph. The last line is the "stop centering" code. From this example we can learn three things:

1. HTML codes are enclosed in angle brackets.

2. Some, but not all, HTML codes come in pairs.

3. The second code in a pair—the one that turns something "off"—starts with a slash (/).

THE CODES ARE IN CHARGE

It's important to realize that the final display format of an HTML document is totally under the control of the codes. Non-HTML code formatting that you place in the document, such as blank lines and indents, will have no effect on the final display. For example, without the <p> code in the above example, the two lines of text would be displayed on the same line.

At this point, you've seen a few HTML codes. There are a lot more of them, and some are a bit more complex than these, but you should have enough of the basic idea now that HTML will not be such a mystery. There's a lot more to learn, of course, and I'll be filling in the blanks in the remainder of this chapter.

Note, however, that I am making no attempt to cover HTML completely. After all, this is a book about JavaScript and VBScript! My goal is to provide those readers who don't already have a working knowledge of HTML with sufficient information to get them started as script programmers. Certain advanced parts of HTML are not relevant to this task; other tasks that can be accomplished by HTML can now be more efficiently accomplished with JavaScript or VBScript. Entire books have been written on HTML, and you should consult one of them if you want the whole picture. One that I have found particularly useful is Urban LeJeune's *Netscape and HTML Explorer*, published by The Coriolis Group.

Before we move on, let's take a look at a real Web page and its associated HTML file. Listing 2.1 shows the HTML file for the first page on the Coriolis Group's Web site at http://www.coriolis.com, and Figure 2.1 shows part of the page as viewed in a browser. (At least this describes the page as of February, 1996. It is likely to have changed by the time you read this). It isn't necessary for you to understand all the details, but it might be useful to see a "real" HTML file and the resulting display. If you examine the HTML codes, you'll

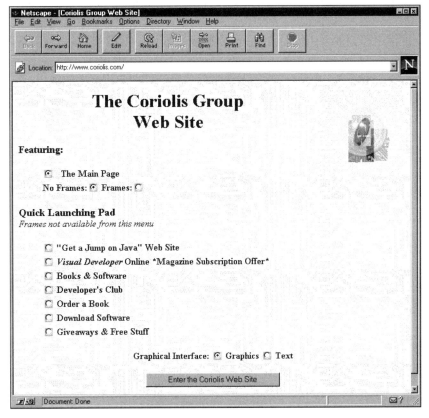

Figure 2.1

The opening page of The Coriolis Group's Web site (http://www.coriolis. com) as seen in a browser.

probably be able to figure out which ones correspond to the various elements on the display.

In case you're wondering, the Coriolis Group is a publisher of computer books (including this one), as well as the *Visual Developer Magazine.* I won't claim to be completely objective, but their site is pretty neat and I suggest you drop by for a visit once in a while. You can also take a look at my JavaScript page which has some JavaScript examples and links to other JavaScript resources on the Web.

Listing 2.1   The HTML file for the opening page of the Coriolis Group's" Web site.

```
<html>

<head>
<title>Coriolis Group Web Site</title>
<meta name="GENERATOR" content="Vermeer FrontPage 1.0">
</head>

<body background="/gifs/vdm01.jpg">
<img width=150 height=150 src="/gifs/vdm21g.jpg" alt="Coriolis Ball"
 align=right>
<h1 align=center><B>The Coriolis Group<br>
Web Site</B></h1>
<form action="http://165.247.175.230/cgi-bin/main.cgi" method="POST">
<h3><B>Featuring: </B></h3>
<ul><table border=0 COLS=2>
<td><input type=radio name=selection value=0 CHECKED></td><td><b>The
 Main Page</B></td><tr>
<td colspan=2><b>No Frames:<input type=radio checked name="noframes"
 value="1"> Frames:<input type=radio name="noframes" value="0"></b></
 td>
</table>
</ul>
<font size=+1><b>Quick Launching Pad</b></font><br><i>Frames not
 available from this menu</i>
<ul>
<table border=0 COLS=2>
<td><input type=radio name=selection value=1></td><td><B>"Get a Jump
 on Java" Web Site</B></td><tr>
<td><input type=radio name=selection value=2></
 td><td><STRONG><I>Visual Developer </I></STRONG><STRONG>Online
 *Magazine Subscription Offer*</STRONG></td><tr>
<td><input type=radio name=selection value=3></td><td><B>Books &amp;
 Software</B></td><tr>
<td><input type=radio name=selection value=4></td><td><B>Developer's
 Club</B></td><tr>
```

```
<td><input type=radio name=selection value=5></td><td><B>Order a
  Book</B></td><tr>
<td><input type=radio name=selection value=7></td><td><B>Download
  Software</B></td><tr>
<td><input type=radio name=selection value=6></td><td><B>Giveaways &
  Free Stuff</B></td>
</table>
</ul>
<center><b>Graphical Interface: <input type=radio checked
  name="graphics" value="1"> Graphics <input type=radio
  name="graphics" value="0"> Text</b><br>
<br><input type=hidden name="page" value="main">
<input type=submit value="Enter the Coriolis Web Site"></center>
</form>
</body>

</html>
```

The Browser Is in Control

If you load an HTML file into a regular editor or word processor, you'll see both the text and the codes. It requires a special program called a *browser* to intercept and interpret the HTML codes and display the document as its creator intended. Your Web browser is just such a creature. The exact way that each HTML code is interpreted, especially the text—formatting codes, is browser dependent. You'll see differences, usually minor cosmetic ones, in the way the same HTML file is displayed by two different browsers.

Creating HTML Files

Since HTML files are plain text files (sometimes called *ASCII* files), you can use just about any editor or word processor to create them. The NotePad utility that comes with Windows 95 will work just fine, for example. So will any word processor, including as Microsoft Word or WordPerfect. If using a word processor, you must remember to save the file in text format and not in the word processor's native document format (which contains a variety of non-HTML codes). In Word, for example, you would select Text Only With Line Breaks from the Save As type list in the Save As dialog box.

But surely there's a better way. With a regular editor or word processor, entering all those HTML codes manually will get a bit tiring. Computers are supposed to automate the boring tasks, and HTML coding is no exception. There's a whole swarm of HTML editors available—some good, some not-so-good, and a few terrific. Some of these are stand-alone programs, while others operate in conjunction with a commercial word processor. I have provided a selection of HTML editors on the CD-ROM for you to try out (see Appendix B for details on the software). For more information and downloads, see the next Web Watch.

Web Watch

If you're interested in information and tools related to Web page development, point your browser at The Web Designer at http://www.kosone.com/people/nelsonl/nl.htm. This page contains a cornucopia of links and resources related to Web page design, including HTML editors and page designers, information on "netiquette" (unwritten rules of Net behavior), and the Ten Commandments of HTML (which should be required reading for everyone!). This page definitely rates its own bookmark in my browser.

HTML Versions

Like everything else that is computer-related, HTML comes in versions—version 1.0, version 2.0, and so on. HTML 2.0 is the newest standard for the language, but next-to-nobody uses version 2 anymore—they're all using version 3.0 (also called HTML+), which is not yet a standard. What does this mean?

As a programming language develops, people find it useful to develop a standard, or specification, for the language. The standard consists of a detailed description of all the language's components and how they work: keywords, variable naming, statement syntax, and so on. Having commonly agreed–upon standards, the widespread use and dissemination of a language is simplified. If you are creating a Web page using the HTML 2.0 standard, for example, you know that all of the features of the page can be used by any browser that supports the HTML standard. Conversely, a programmer who is writing a browser knows that a program capable of supporting HTML 2.0 will be useable with almost all existing HTML documents.

But guess what happens about 2 milliseconds after a standard is agreed upon—or in some cases, even before. People want to improve it, increasing the flexibility and adding capabilities that aren't included in the standard. Company A wants this feature, so they add it to their programs; company B wants another feature, so they add it to their programs. You'll start hearing about unofficial standards like "Netscape HTML 2.0 Extensions" and "Microsoft HTML 2.0 Extensions." This means simply "HTML 2.0 plus some extra features that the gang at Netscape (or Microsoft) wanted." Eventually, most, if not all, of these extensions will be incorporated as part of the next official HTML standard.

In the meantime, things can get a bit messy because company A's browser doesn't support the extensions of company B's browser, and so on. For example, if you surf the Web much at all, you've probably seen pages that have a notice saying something like "This page looks best with Netscape Navigator" or "This site designed for Microsoft Internet Explorer." This means that the HTML document uses a specific set of extensions; to get their benefit, you'll need to use the appropriate browser. Fortunately, part of the basic HTML specification requires that unrecognized HTML codes simply be ignored, so unsupported extensions won't cause serious problems. A good HTML programmer will make sure that extensions are not used for anything essential, so the document can still be viewed in any browser.

Web Watch

For more information about HTML, take a gander at http://www.w3.org/hypertext/WWW/MarkUp/. For specific reference information on the proposed HTML+ standard, surf on over to http://www.w3.org/hypertext/WWW/MarkUp/HTMLPlus/htmlplus_1.html. For material on HTML 2.0 extensions, go to http://home.netscape.com/assist/net_sites/html_extensions.html. For the scoop on HTML 3.0 extensions, wander over to http://home.netscape.com/assist/net_sites/html_extensions_3.html. And finally, you'll find a useful HTML style guide at http://www.w3.org/pub/WWW/Provider/Style/.

So, what can the new HTML versions do that HTML 2.0 could not? The enhancements include tables, figure captions, mathematical equations, text flow around images, and superior hyperlink abilities. Here, I'll be be dealing with the HTML that Netscape Navigator uses—which is only logical, since this is the only browser that supports JavaScript at the present (although Internet Explorer will soon). I'll bet that most, if not all, of the Netscape extensions to HTML will become part of the new standard and therefore supported by other browsers. If you're using a non-Netscape browser and find that some of these codes don't work, you'll know that you've just run into an HTML incompatibility. Not to worry. As mentioned earlier, unsupported codes are just ignored.

Remember that this chapter makes no attempt to present the complete HTML specification—that would be a small book in itself! My goal is to provide you with sufficient familiarity with HTML that you will be able to use and explore JavaScript and VBScript.

The Basic HTML Document

Every HTML has a certain basic, minimum structure. Which means that you'll be starting all of your HTML editing projects with this basic framework. In fact, some of the specialized HTML editors automatically insert it for you whenever you start a new document. Let's take a look at the basic HTML document.

Listing 2.2 The basic framework of an HTML document.

```
<HTML>
<HEAD>
<TITLE>Title goes here</TITLE>
</HEAD>
<BODY>
<!-Comment->
Document contents go here.
</BODY>
</HTML>
```

Working from the outside inward, we have the following:

- The HTML document itself is marked by <HTML> ... </HTML> codes. Anything outside of these codes is ignored by the browser—or at least it's supposed to be ignored. Some browsers don't obey this rule, and text outside the <HTML> ... </HTML> codes is displayed in the document like any other text. If this rule were universally followed, you could put comments, reminders to yourself, and other such material outside these codes—but as things stand now, you had better not.

- The header, delineated by <HEAD>...</HEAD>, contains information that is relevant to the HTML file but is not displayed as part of the document. You'll see later that a great deal of JavaScript and VBScript code is placed in the header. Strictly speaking, the header section is not required, but most HTML documents still have one.

- The body of the document is enclosed in <BODY>...</BODY> codes. It's here that all the elements that will be displayed in the document are placed. Some JavaScript and VBScript code goes in the body as well.

- The document title is enclosed in <TITLE> ... </TITLE> codes and must be placed in the header. The title is displayed in the document window's title bar, not in the document itself. If you omit the title, then the title bar will display the HTML file name.

- A comment is any text placed inside an HTML code that begins with <!-- and ends with -->. Comments are ignored by the browser, and you can use them to include any information or reminders that may be useful when you edit the file at a later time. Because any unrecognized code will be ignored, you could actually use any non-valid HTML code as the holder for comments, but this format has become standardized.

Formatting Your Text

Character Formatting

Character formatting refers to those formatting elements that apply to individual characters in your document. There are four basic character formatting codes, as follows:

\<B\> ... \</B\>	Boldface
\<U\> ... \</U\>	Underline
\<I\> ... \</I\>	Italics
\<TT\> ... \</TT\>	Typewriter style

Typewriter style, in case you're wondering (as I was), simply means a fixed–width font where each letter is given the same amount of horizontal space regardless of its actual width. Most browsers use the Courier font for \<TT\> style. You can mix and overlap these character formats to your heart's desire, as shown in these examples:

```
<B><U>Bold and underlined</U></B>
<B><U>This is bold and underlined,</U> this just bold.</B>
<I>Italics, <U> underlined italics, </I> just underlined.</U>
```

Several other character formatting codes can be very useful at times, as shown in Table 2.1.

Table 2.1   Character formatting codes.

\<BIG\>...\</BIG\>	**Enclosed text should be displayed using a larger font than normal text.**
\<SMALL\>...\</SMALL\>	**Enclosed text should be displayed using a smaller font than normal text.**
\<SUB\> ... \</SUB\>	**Enclosed text should be displayed as a subscript using a smaller font than normal text.**
\<SUP\> ... \</SUP\>	**Enclosed text should be displayed as a superscript using a smaller font than normal text.**

You need to be aware that these codes, like some other HTML codes, fall more into the category of requests than orders. If normal text is already quite small, for example, the \<SMALL\> code may have no effect. All codes must be interpreted by a browser, and the browser settings, along with system display parameters and font availability, can all place certain limitations on what can be displayed.

Another way to change the size of text (font size) is with the <FONT SIZE> tag. A total of 7 defined font sizes are available, with the default size being 3. The seven font sizes in Netscape Navigator are displayed in Figure 2.2. For example, the following results in all of the text between the tags being displayed in size 5:

```
<FONT SIZE=5>All of this text <P>
And this text too. <br>
Is displayed in size 5. </FONT>
```

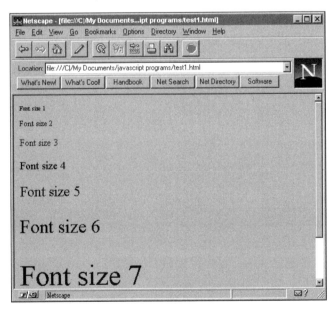

Figure 2.2

The seven available font sizes.

Lines and Paragraphs

As I have already mentioned, HTML pays no attention to white space and other formatting in your document. If you want to start a new line of text or a new paragraph, you must use the proper code. Use <br> to start a new line, <p> to start a new paragraph. The difference between these two codes is that when you use <p>, a blank line is inserted between the end of the previous paragraph and the start of the new one. In contrast, <br> does not insert any vertical spacing. Note that <p> and <br> are among the rare HTML codes that are not paired.

Headings

HTML supports six levels of headings corresponding to the codes <H1> through <H6> (with the corresponding </H1> through </H6>, of course). Level 1 is the top level and is displayed in the largest font. Lower levels are typically displayed in successively smaller and less obvious fonts. Figure 2.3 shows how the six heading styles, along with "normal" text, look in Netscape Navigator 2.0.

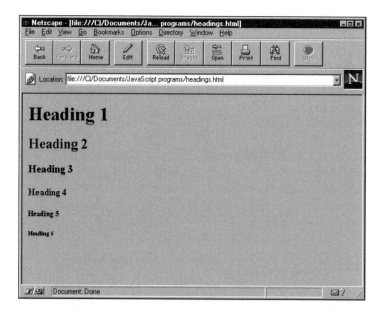

Figure 2.3

The six heading styles.

Note that the heading styles do not require <p> codes to be set apart on their own lines. Headings always start on a new line, which is also true for the text that follows them. The heading codes provide visual formatting only. Headings have no other special meanings, such as organizing an outline.

To center text on the page, enclose it in <CENTER> … </CENTER> tags. Each of these codes, in addition to controlling centering, starts a new line, so the centered text is separated from preceding and following text.

Inserting Pictures

HTML provides a variety of options for displaying images in a document. The image must already exist in its own disk file. Traditionally, HTML documents could display only images in the GIF (graphical interchange format) format. The new Netscape Navigator Gold (covered in Chapter 3) also permits display of JPG format files, and support for additional files may be added in the future. If the pictures you want to display are in another format, such as TIFF or PCX, you'll have to convert them to a supported format. Many graphics programs provide conversion capability, including the basic but useful Paint Shop Pro included on this book's CD-ROM.

How can images be used? An image can be displayed full-size on a page along with text and other elements. It can also be displayed full-size on its own page or as a small thumbnail. For any image, "full-size" means the image's native size. You can also define an image as a hyperlink. When the user clicks on the image, they are taken to another location, document, or page.

To display an image full-size as part of an HTML page, use the IMG tag:

```
<IMG SRC = "filename">
```

This is the most basic form of the IMG tag. You can include several optional subtags to control various aspects of how the image is displayed. They are described in the following paragraphs.

To specify a text message to be displayed in place of the picture, use the ALT tag:

```
ALT = "alt-text"
```

The specified text is displayed if the picture file is not available, or if the file is being viewed on a text-only browser or a browser with in-line image display turned off.

Use the ALIGN tag to control the relationship between the picture and the surrounding text. Without an ALIGN setting, text that follows the image in the HTML file is displayed starting at the bottom of the picture. There are several ALIGN settings you can use to obtain wrapped text, floating images, and so on. They are described in Table 2.2.

Table 2.2 ALIGN settings.

ALIGN =	Picture	Text
left	At left margin	Wraps to right of picture
right	At right margin	Wraps to left of picture
top	At left margin	Next line displayed to right of picture aligned at top. Subsequent lines displayed below picture.
bottom	At left margin	Next line displayed to right of picture aligned at bottom. Subsequent lines displayed below picture.
center	At left margin	Next line displayed to right of picture aligned at center. Subsequent lines displayed below picture.

The top, bottom, and middle ALIGN settings are typically used to provide a caption for the picture. Here's an example.

```
This text displayed above picture. This text displayed above picture.
  This text displayed above picture. This text displayed above
  picture.<p>
<IMG SRC="bigben.gif" ALIGN=center>
This line displayed as the caption. <P>
This text displayed below picture. This text displayed below picture.
  This text displayed below picture.
```

> **CENTERING PICTURES**
> You can use the <CENTER>...</CENTER> tags to center a picture on the page. Captions specified with the top, bottom, and center ALIGN tags will be placed to the right of the image.

Browsers will have a default setting for the amount of space that is left between a picture and surrounding text. If you want to control this spacing, use the VSPACE and HSPACE tags. The measurements are in pixels. Here's an example:

```
<IMG SRC="mypic.gif" VSPACE=20 HSPACE=25>
```

Most browsers will display a border around the picture just by default. To control the width of the border, use the BORDER tag. The border width is specified in pixels:

```
<IMG SRC="mypic.gif" BORDER=10>
```

What about image size? The default for images calls for display at their native size, but you're not limited to this. By using the HEIGHT and WIDTH tags, you can specify the exact size, in pixels, that an image will have when displayed. Here's how:

```
<IMG HEIGHT=pixels, WIDTH=pixels SRC=filename>
```

When you specify HEIGHT and WIDTH, the browser will display the image at the specified size. By using a small size, you can get the small "thumbnail" images that you see used in many pages.

Many HTML authors use the HEIGHT and WIDTH tags even when they are not changing the display size of an image. In other words, they specify HEIGHT and WIDTH settings that are the same as the image's native size. Why bother doing this? It results in faster page display. If the image size is specified in the IMG tag, the browser does not have to load the image in order to know how much space to leave for it. It can quickly draw the image border and continue displaying other page elements, coming back later to fill in the image itself.

HTML browsers treat images as if they were just large characters. For example,you can have two or more images display on the same line. To display three images (each 100 pixels square) on one line, you would write the following:

```
<IMG WIDTH=100 HEIGHT=100 SRC="image1.gif">
<IMG WIDTH=100 HEIGHT=100 SRC="image2.gif">
<IMG WIDTH=100 HEIGHT=100 SRC="image3.gif">
```

To control the spacing between images on a line, use the special code for a space, . (Remember, in HTML, white space is ignored - that's why we must use a special code for spaces). The following displays the same three images with four spaces between each pair:

```
<IMG WIDTH=100 HEIGHT=100 SRC="image1.gif">    
<IMG WIDTH=100 HEIGHT=100 SRC="image2.gif">    
<IMG WIDTH=100 HEIGHT=100 SRC="image3.gif">
```

One final optional IMG tag that you may run across is the ISMAP tag. This tag specifies that the image is a map—that specific regions of the images are hotlinks to other files or locations. A separate text file is used to specify the coordinates of the regions and the locations to which they point. This is an advanced HTML topic that will not be covered further here.

Web Watch

If you're interested in learning more about using map images, you'll find information and a tutorial at http://www.cs.bgsu.edu/~jburns/ imagemap.html.

Hyperlinks

Much of the magic of a Web document comes from its hyperlinks, or hotlinks. A link is a section of text or a picture that you click to go somewhere else. The target can be another page in the same file, another HTML file, or a completely different Web site. Each link has two parts: an *anchor*, which is what you click; and a *resource*, which is where you go. Text anchors are identified by being displayed in a different color and often underlined. Image anchors are often identified by having the mouse cursor change when positioned over the link.

To create an anchor, you use the <A> ... </A> tags. The basic format goes like this:

```
<A HREF="#link-target"> anchor-text </A>
```

There are two parts to this anchor tag. *Link-target* identifies the destination where the user is to be taken when the link is clicked. The character must be placed before the *link-targe*t text. *Anchor-text* is the link text displayed in the document—this is the text that is underlined and displayed in a different color.

If the target lies within the same document, you identify it with a slightly different format of the anchor tags:

```
<A NAME="target-tag"> target-text </A>
```

In this tag, *target-tag* identifies the resource. In other words, it must match the *link-target* in any links that point to this location. The *target-text* is the destination text. It does not have to be the entire destination, of course. It may be just the first line of a destination page—or, more commonly, just a heading. Tagging text as a link destination does not change its display formatting in any way.

Let's look at an example. The following HTML code will display a line of text with the word "here" highlighted as a link. Clicking the link will take you to the heading "Introduction to JavaScript." The anchor and the resource are linked by the identifier "JS-intro." Note that the link identifier has no other function than to tie the anchor and the destination together. You can use any text you like, as long as it's unique.

```
<HTML>
<BODY>
<H2>Introduction</H2>
If you want to learn more about JavaScript, click
<A HREF="#JS-intro">here</A>.
<P>
<P>
<P>
<P>
<P>
<A NAME="JS-intro"><H3>Introduction to JavaScript</H3></A>
blah blah blah blah
</BODY>
</HTML>
```

Linking to a destination in another document is not much harder. In fact, it's easier because no HTML codes are required to identify the destination. All that's necessary is to identify the document in the HREF subtag. If the document is on the local disk, you identify its filename. Here's a hotlink that will display the local file DETAILS.HTML:

```
<A HREF="details.html"> link-text </A>
```

If you do not specify a path for a local file, the browser will assume it is in the same directory as the parent file (the one containing the link).

When creating Web pages, you'll often want a link to point to a file on another site. In this case, you must specify the destination file's URL. The following link will display the file DETAILS.HTML located in the Documents directory at the Web site www.coriolis.com:

```
<A HREF="http://www.coriolis.com/documents/details.html/"> link-text
 </A>
```

So What Is URL?

It's a Uniform Resource Locator. If you're not familiar with the term, you might want to read Appendix A, Web Basics.

Of course, in order for links to other sites to work, the computer must have a properly configured and operating connection to the Web. Note that if you specify a URL with a location and directory but no file name, such as http://www.coriolis.com/documents/; the browser will automatically load the file named INDEX.HTML if it exists in the specified location.

What about using an image as a hotlink? Simple enough - all you do is replace the *link-text* with an image tag, as shown here:

```
<A HREF="details.html"> <IMG SRC="image-file"> </A>
```

This line will display the image whose file name is specified by *image-file*; clicking on the image will link you to the file DETAILS.HTML.

Backgrounds and Colors

The best Web sites combine interesting content with a pleasing or innovative appearance. The overall visual appeal of a site is strongly influenced by the document background and the text colors.

Cool Backgrounds

If you've done any Web surfing, you've undoubtedly noticed that lots of pages have interesting backgrounds—patterns that are displayed behind the text and images, as if the document had been printed on fancy paper. Backgrounds can be very effective, lending appeal and a touch of elegance to your pages. They can also be overdone, distracting from the document contents and sometimes making it difficult to read. If you're careful in selecting a background, however, it can be an effective tool.

A background is nothing more than a small graphics image that is repeated, or tiled, to cover the document background. If you don't want the boundaries between individual tiles to be obvious to the viewer, you must select a background image whose edges will blend well. Most often this will be a semi-abstract repeating pattern. You generally want muted colors with minimal contrast. Avoid patterns that include both light and dark areas, because it makes any superimposed text difficult to read, no matter what text color you use.

Web Watch

You'll find a cool assortment of backgrounds that you can use in your pages at http://www2.netscape.com/assist/ net_sites/bg/backgrounds. html. Another great source of backgrounds is http://the-tech.mit.edu/KPT/ bgs.html. You can download these backgrounds to your local hard disk or use them directly off the site. The latter site also has a short tutorial on creating your own backgrounds.

To specify the background for a document, add the BACKGROUND tag to the BODY HTML code:

```
<BODY BACKGROUND = background-file>
```

If the file is on your disk, simply specify the file name—with path, if necessary:

```
<BODY BACKGROUND = purptile.jpg>
```

If it's located remotely at a Web site, you must specify the complete URL. For example, this line specifies one of the backgrounds located at the MIT site that we mentioned in the previous Web Watch:

```
<BODY BACKGROUND = http://the-tech.mit.edu/KPT/Backgrounds/Orig1/
 purptile.jpg>
```

What if you don't want a background pattern, only a solid color? Then simply omit a BACKGROUND setting and set the BGCOLOR attribute to a hexadecimal number specifying the color. How does a number represent a color? That's our next topic.

HEXADECIMAL COLOR REPRESENTATIONS

Any color that you view on your screen is made up of different proportions of the three primary colors: red, green, and blue. If we specify the amount of each primary color with a number, then a set of three numbers can be used to identify any possible screen color. HTML permits each of the primaries to have 256 different values, from 0 (off) to 255 (maximum). With 256×256 ×256 or over 16 million different colors available, you should be able to find the one you want!

Rather than use normal decimal numbers, colors are represented in hexadecimal notation. Zero is represented by 00, and 255 by FF. The three components of the final color are combined into a single 6-digit hexadecimal number in the order red, green, blue (RGB). Thus, a color with the following makeup:

Red = 10

Green = 5F

Blue = 0E

is represented by the number 105F0E.

PICK A COLOR, ANY COLOR

How can you determine the hex number for a specific color, and vice versa? Netscape Navigator has a handy tool that can help. Select General Preferences from the Options menu, click the Colors tab, then click one of the Choose Color buttons. In the dialog box that is displayed, click the Define Custom Colors button. You'll see a color selector where you can pick any color by clicking with the mouse (Figure 2.4). The corresponding RGB values will be displayed in the boxes below the colors. You can also type values into the Red, Green, and Blue boxes to view the corresponding color.

To specify a specific background color, determine the hexadecimal representation of the desired color and set the BACKGROUND attribute accordingly:

```
<BODY BGCOLOR = "105F0E">
```

Setting Text Color

The color of text in a document is also specified as hexadecimal RGB values. Three aspects of text color are under your control:

TEXT   The color of "normal" text

LINK   The color of hotlink text

VLINK   The color of visited hotlink text (a link you've visited)

These attributes are included in the BODY tag. For example, here's how to get white text, red links, and green visited links:

```
<BODY TEXT="FFFFFF" LINK="FF0000" VLINK "FFFF00">
```

Remember that all browsers have their own internal default settings for colors. If you don't call out specific background and text colors in your document, the browser's defaults will be used. In fact, most browsers have a setting that

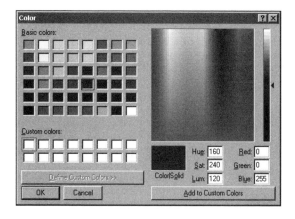

Figure 2.4

You can use Netscape's Color dialog box to determine the RGB values for a specific color.

forces their own colors to be used even when the HTML document specifies its own colors. This is useful for individuals with color vision disorders, avoiding a text/background combination that looks great to most people but ends up totally unreadable.

When choosing text colors, remember that all 3 colors (text, links, and visited links) must be clearly visible against your selected background color or pattern. Some page designers have gone a bit bonkers with colors, resulting in pages that are visually quite striking at first glance, but difficult to use.

Web Watch

If you're having trouble converting decimal color values to hex, try the online decimal to hex converter at http://www.lne.com/Web/Examples/rgb.html. For a color index and brief HTML color tutorial, take a look at http://www.infi.net/wwwimages/colorindex.html. Another color resource page is http://www.ohiou.edu/~rbarrett/webaholics/ver2/colors.html, which also provides a nice demonstration of Netscape tables.

Other HTML Goodies

Horizontal Lines

You can display a shaded horizontal line across the page with the <HR> tag. The default line is shaded and extends the full width of the page. To control the thickness of the line, use the SIZE tag:

```
<HR SIZE=pixels>
```

You can specify the line length either as a percentage of the page width or in terms of pixels:

```
<HR WIDTH=x%>
<HR WIDTH=pixels>
```

For an unshaded line, use NOSHADE:

```
<HR NOSHADE>
```

To align the line at the left or right margins as opposed to the default center, use the ALIGN tag:

```
<HR ALIGN=left>
<HR ALIGN=right>
```

Figure 2.5 illustrates some of the lines you can create with the <HR> tag. Each line is displayed below the corresponding tag text.

Including Your Email Address

If you would like people visiting your page to be able to send you email, you can do so using the so-called *mailto* protocol. This is a special type of hotlink that does not link to another document or location when clicked. Rather, it displays the browser's email window with your address already filled in. All the user has to do is type his or her message and click the "send" button. Here's how it's done, using my address:

```
<A HREF="mailto:paitken@acpub.duke.edu>SEND PETER MAIL.</A>
```

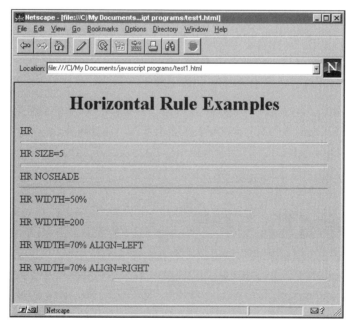

Figure 2.5

Examples of using the <HR> tag to display horizontal lines.

In the document, the phrase "Send Peter mail" will be displayed as a hotlink. Clicking it displays the Mail dialog box, as described above.

Web Watch

Bored with nothing to do? Slide on over to http://www.uroulette. com:8000/ to be connected to a completely random Web site. You'll come across some really weird and boring sites this way, but once in a while you'll stumble across a real gem.

Lists

Sometimes your documents will contain information that needs to be displayed in a list. HTML provides capabilities to display both numbered and unnumbered lists. A numbered list is referred to as an *ordered* list, while an unnumbered list (commonly known as a bulleted list) is called an *unordered* list. To create an ordered list, use the following syntax:

```
<OL>
<LI>First list item
<LI>Second list item
<LI>Third list item
</OL>
```

For an unordered list, the syntax is the same except that you use the <UL> ... </UL> tags to enclose the list. Each list item is started on a new line. You can use other HTML formatting codes within a list item, including <p> and <br>.

Wrapping Up HTML

That's it for my coverage of HTML. There's a good bit more to HTML, and I'll occasionally touch on it throughout the remainder of the book. If you've mastered the material in this chapter, then you're ready to start learning JavaScript or VBScript (or both!) and writing real scripts. If you're anxious to get started, skip ahead to Chapter 4. However, Chapter 3 is important for those who want to learn how to use Netscape's Web page editor, Navigtor Gold.

*Here's the lowdown
on using the
Navigator Gold
Editor to create
Web pages and
JavaScript
programs.*

Chapter **3**

Key Topics:

- **What you
  see is what
  you get.**

- **Formatting
  text and
  links.**

- **Adding
  pictures to
  your pages.**

Using Netscape Navigator Gold

What Is It?

If you haven't heard of the Netscape Navigator browser, I suggest that you go back to your cave in the Himalayas and resume meditating on your navel. It's entirely possible, however, that you don't know about a new version of the program called Navigator Gold. It's basically the same old browser with support for JavaScript, Netscape HTML enhancements, frames, and all the other goodies. What's added is a Web page editor that you can use to design and publish Web pages, including pages with JavaScript programs. It's a pretty neat program and has become my tool of choice for creating Web documents.

Gold is a WYSIWYG (what you see is what you get) editor, which means that you apply formatting and other aspects of document appearance exactly as you would in a Windows word processor. For example, to boldface a word, you select the word and click the "Boldface" button on the toolbar. The screen displays the document's final appearance. All those pesky HTML codes are inserted automatically but hidden from view (although you can view them if you want to).

If you are experienced with using a Windows word processor, many of the editing operations in Gold will be quite familiar to you. When you start Netscape Gold, it displays its browser window. The editor is a totally separate part of the program with its own menus and toolbars. To open the editor while you're in the browser, pull down the File menu and select either New Document (to start a new HTML document) or Open File in Browser (to work on an existing HTML document). If you want to edit the document that you are viewing in the browser, select Edit Document. You can use the standard Windows methods to switch between the editor and the browser.

Opening and Saving Documents

Once the editor has been started, you can also use its own commands for starting and opening documents, although this task may have been performed when you opened the editor from the browser window (see previous section). To start a new, blank HTML document, select New Document from the File menu or click the New Document button on the toolbar (pressing Ctrl+N works, too). You'll receive a blank editing screen ready for you to start entering material.

To open an existing HTML document for editing, select Open File from the File menu, click the Open File to Edit button, or press Ctrl+O. Then use the dialog box that is displayed to select the desired file.

You can also open a file at a remote location for editing. This is a somewhat more involved procedure and will be covered later in the chapter.

To save a document, select Save from the File menu, click the Save button, or press Ctrl+S. The first time you save a newly created document, you'll be prompted to enter a name for it. Once a document has been named, the name is displayed in Gold's title bar. If you have already named a document and want to assign it a new name, use the Save As command on the File menu. Files are normally saved with the HTML extension—which you should not change unless you know what you are doing.

TOOLBAR TIPS

Not sure what a toolbar button does? Rest the mouse pointer on it for a couple of seconds without clicking, and a brief description of the button's function will be displayed. To control which toolbars are displayed, pull down the Options menu and select the corresponding Show...Toolbar command to hide or display the toolbar.

Online Help That's Really Online

Like most Windows programs, Navigator Gold offers online help information. You can select different Help topics from the Help menu; here are some of the things that are available:

Help Menu Command	Contents
Software	Information on upgrading to a newer version of Navigator.
Web Page Starter	A site on Netscape's server that provides information and tools to help in creating Web pages with Gold.
Handbook	Instruction manual for using the program.

Release Notes	Information about features and known bugs in Gold.
Frequently Asked Questions	Answer to common questions.

Netscape Gold's help information is online in a very real sense. It is not installed on your hard disk along with the program. Rather, it resides on Netscape's server computers. When you select a help topic, you connect to the appropriate Web page to view the information. At first, this way of providing help information sounds terrific—you're always guaranteed the latest and most up-to-date information. I've found that there are some problems with it, however.

You can get help only when you are connected to the Web, of course. If you're working on a non-networked laptop, or if you use a modem and your teenager is on the phone, you're out of luck. Data transfer can be slow, too. Modem connections are inherently slow, and Netscape's servers are often so busy that response is slow or nonexistent.

The solution I suggest is to download the help files you use most often, using the browser's File Save As command. By adding these files to your Bookmarks list, you'll have instant local access to the information. Still, I hope that a future release of Netscape Gold provides local help files along with the online option.

Entering and Formatting Text

In the realm of text editing, Gold works in a fashion similar to any standard Windows word processor. Text that you type is inserted in the document at the location of the insertion point, which is marked by a blinking vertical line. To move the insertion point to a new location, click with the mouse or use the arrow keys on your keyboard. To bring another part of the document into view, use the PgUp and PgDn keys or the on-screen scroll bars.

SELECTING TEXT

Many formatting operations require that the text be selected prior to being formatted. You can select text with the mouse by simply dragging over the text; selected text is displayed in reverse video. You can also select with the keyboard by holding the Shift key down while moving the insertion point. If you select text, then press any typing key. The selection will be erased and replaced by the new text. Press Ctrl+A to select the entire document. To "unselect" text, click anywhere in the document or press an arrow key.

You have several options for deleting text. Press Backspace or Del to delete the character to the left or right of the insertion point, respectively. For larger amounts, select the text and then press Backspace or Del. If you accidentally delete the wrong text, press Ctrl+Z or select Undo from the Edit menu to get it back. The Undo command can, in fact, reverse most editing actions. You'll find that it's a real a lifesaver in some situations. To reverse an Undo operation—that is, to restore the changes that you undid—press Ctrl+Shift+Z or select Edit Redo.

Line and Paragraph Breaks

If the text reaches the right margin of the page while you're typing, it will automatically wrap to the next line. Text that is automatically wrapped always adjusts to fit the width of the window. Thus, when a user later views your document with a wider or narrower window size, the text will automatically adjust to the proper line length.

To force the start of a new line, select New Line Break from the Insert menu or press Shift+Enter. To start a new paragraph, press Enter. A new line break starts the new line immediately below the first one; a new paragraph also starts a new line, but a blank line is inserted above it.

GUARANTEED UNBREAKABLE

A nonbreaking space looks like a regular space but will not be used to break a line at the right margin. Thus, two words separated by a nonbreaking space will always be displayed on the same line. To insert a nonbreaking space, select it from the Insert menu. The HTML code for a nonbreaking space is .

If you type an ampersand (&) in your text, it is represented in the HTML source code by &amp. This permits the browser to distinguish between ampersands that are to be displayed as part of the page, and ampersands that signal the start of a special character code.

Text Alignment

Text can be aligned three different ways with respect to the page margins:

- Aligned left with a ragged right margin (the default).

- Aligned right with a ragged left margin.

- Centered with ragged left and right margins.

Alignment applies to entire paragraphs. To change alignment, position the insertion point anywhere in the paragraph and click the appropriate Alignment button on the toolbar. Note that lines of text separated with a New Line Break (Shift+Enter) are still part of the same paragraph. You must press Enter to start a new paragraph.

WHERE ARE THE MARGINS?

You may wonder where Gold has hidden the margin settings. There aren't any—not as part of the document, anyway. Since a Web page is destined to be viewed on-screen by many people using different browsers with different window sizes, the notion of fixed margins does not make a whole lot of sense. If you print a Web document, however, margins make a great deal of sense and can be set using the Page Setup command on the File menu.

Paragraph and Character Styles

The Gold editor makes it easy to assign the predefined HTML paragraph styles to your text. Place the editing cursor in the paragraph or select multiple paragraphs. Next, pull down the style list at the left end of the toolbar and select the desired style. You can also right-click a paragraph to display the context menu, then select Paragraph/List Properties to display a dialog box that will let you change the style as well as other aspects of formatting, such as alignment.

Another way to change character styles, in addition to using the buttons on the toolbars, is via the context menu. Select the text to be affected, then open the context menu and select Character Properties. In the dialog box, you can change text color, style, etc.

Other Layout Elements

An HTML document can contain a variety of other elements that help you arrange text on the screen:

- A horizontal line, or rule, provides a visual break between sections of a page.

- A non-breaking space looks like a regular space but will not be broken at the end of a line of text. In other words, the two words separated by a non-breaking space will always be displayed on the same line.

- A line break starts a new line without starting a new paragraph. There will be no extra vertical space left between the new line and the previous one.

- A break below an image provides some vertical space between the image and the following text.

To insert any of these items in your document, select from the Insert menu. You can also insert a line break by pressing Shift+Enter.

THE CLIPBOARD

You can use the Windows Clipboard to move and copy text in the Gold editor in a fashion similar to any other Windows program.

Making Lists

Gold makes it easy to create the two types of lists provided by HTML: ordered (numbered) lists and unordered (bulleted) lists. To create a list, select the paragraphs to be included in the list, then click either the Bullet List or Numbered List button on the toolbar. Each paragraph will be given its own number or bullet. To "unlist" text and change it back to a regular paragraph, follow the same procedure—select the list items, then click the button to return to normal text.

You can also create a list as you type. Without selecting any text, click one of the List buttons to make the current paragraph a list item. Each time you press Enter, the new paragraph becomes part of the list. After typing the last list item, press Enter, then click the appropriate List button to turn the list off.

Viewing and Editing the HTML Source

Behind your nicely formatted document in the Gold editor is an HTML document containing text and codes. You can view this source and edit it if desired by selecting Document Source from the View menu. Viewing the HTML source can be a useful learning tool, since you'll be able to see what codes the Gold editor used to implement the document features you added using the editor. Editing the source, on the other hand, is something you should do only if you are familiar with HTML.

When you select View Document Source, the HTML source is displayed in its own window. You can switch back to the main editing window while leaving the source window open. Changes you make, however, will not be reflected in the open source window. You have to close it and re-open it to see the effects of changes you made in the editing window. Note that you cannot make changes in the source window—this is for viewing only, not editing. To edit the source code directly, you need to use an external editor, as I'll explain later.

Inserting Pictures

If the image you want to insert is on your disk, use the Insert Image command to place it in your HTML document. First, position the document cursor at the location where you want the image; then select Image from the Insert menu. The dialog box is shown in Figure 3.1.

In the Image File Name box, type the path and name of the image file. It's usually easier to click the Browse button to select the file from a list of available image files. You have the option of specifying an alternate image or text to be displayed if the primary image is not available or the page is being viewed in a text-only browser. If the selected image file is not located in the document directory, you can select the Copy Image to the Document Location option if you want all of the document's files to be together in the same directory.

In the Alignment section of the dialog box, select the desired image/text alignment. The Preview box on the right shows you the effect of the selected alignment.

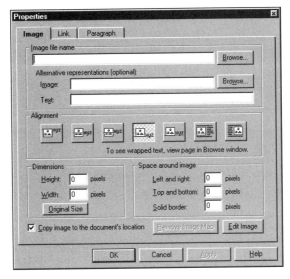

Figure 3.1

The Insert Image dialog box.

If you want to change the default border and spacing settings, enter the desired values in the boxes in the Space Around Image section.

Another way of adding images to a document is by drag-and-drop. You'll need to have the Netscape browser open to do this. Begin by selecting New Browser from the editor's File menu or by clicking the Open Browser button. You'll also have to size the browser and editor windows so they are both visible on-screen. Then, open any document—either local or remote—in the browser. Find the picture you want, point at it with the mouse, and drag it to the desired location in the editor.

WHAT A DRAG!

Dragging with the mouse is easy. Point at the screen item to be dragged, then press the left mouse button and hold it down. Move the mouse until the pointer is over the "drop" location and release the mouse button. Many programs, including Netscape Gold, change the appearance of the mouse pointer while a drag-and-drop operation is in progress. When the pointer is over a screen region where you are not permitted to drop the item, the pointer displays as a "not" symbol (a circle with a diagonal line through it).

When you add an image by the drag-and-drop image, Netscape transfers a copy of the image file from its original location to the document directory. The HTML code inserted in the document is essentially the same as the code in the source document, including an alternative text. You can later modify the image placement using the methods described in the next section.

Modifying Images

There are two aspects of modifying an image that has been placed in an HTML document. To modify the image itself—add elements, change colors and contrast, etc.—you'll need an image editor such as Adobe PhotoShop or Corel PhotoPaint to edit the image file. You can also use the PaintShop program provided on the companion CD-ROM. You should refer to your graphics program documentation for information on how to use it.

KEEP THE ORIGINAL!

Whenever you are going to modify an image, it's a good idea to keep a copy of the original file under a different name. If you don't like the changes you make, you have the option of going back to the beginning and starting again.

To modify the image placement, alternate text, etc., you will be working with the image's properties. To display the properties dialog box for an image, you can select the image by clicking it (a black border will display around it), then select Image from the Properties menu. Another way is to right-click the image to bring up the context menu, as shown in Figure 3.2. Then, select Image Properties. This displays the same dialog box you used to insert the image in the first place, as shown earlier in Figure 3.1. Modify any of the properties as needed; the new settings will take effect when you close the dialog box.

CONTEXT MENUS

If you right-click on almost any element of a document in the editor, a context menu will pop up listing commands that are appropriate for the item you clicked. These commands are always available on the main menus and toolbar as well, but many users find the context menus to be quicker.

Figure 3.2

Right-clicking an image brings up the context menu.

Creating Links

Links are the heart of any hypertext document, and Gold makes adding them easy. There are two methods of doing so. For the first one, you need to know the URL of the target. Then:

1. Position the editing cursor at the location where you want the link, or select the existing text that will become the link.

2. Select Link from the Insert menu. The dialog box shown in Figure 3.3 will be displayed.

3. In the first text box, type the link text that you want displayed in the document. If you selected text before displaying the dialog box, it will already be entered for you.

4. Type the target URL in the second text box. If the target is a local file, you can click the Browse button to find the file.

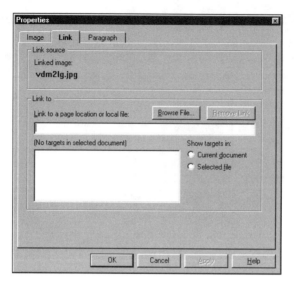

Figure 3.3

Inserting a link into a document.

That's all there is to it! The second method is even easier, but cannot be used all the time. You need to arrange the browser and editor windows so they are both visible on the screen, then display in the browser a document that contains the link you want to place in the new document. Next, simply point at the link in the browser and drag it to the desired location in the editor. You can edit the link text using the usual editor techniques.

Inserting HTML Tags

The Gold editor does not support all HTML capabilities. Using frames and creating tables are two of the most obvious examples. For certain document tasks, you'll just have to insert the HTML codes yourself. To insert a single HTML code, select HTML Tag from the Insert menu. The dialog box shown in Figure 3.4 will be displayed. Enter the desired tag, including the enclosing angle brackets, then click OK. To verify the syntax of your tag before inserting it, click the Verify button. The effects of tags you insert yourself do not display in the document in the editor—you'll need to switch to the browser to view their results. In the editor, each tag is displayed as a small yellow triangle, so you'll know exactly where they are.

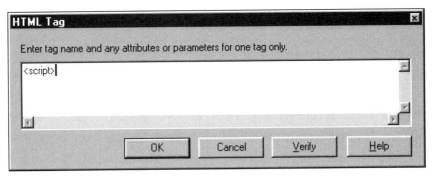

Figure 3.4

Inserting an HTML tag in a document.

I'll warn you ahead of time not to expect very much from the Verify function. It will catch some syntax errors but not others. Just because the Verify function does not object to your tag is no guarantee that it is correct!

To delete a HTML tag, place the editing cursor just to the right of it, then press Backspace. To edit a tag, double-click it to open a dialog box with the tag displayed, then edit it as usual.

Adding JavaScript Code

In the editor, JavaScript code is displayed in red text. There are two methods for adding JavaScript to a document. The first method starts by typing the JavaScript code into your document as regular text. Then:

1. Select all of the code.

2. Right click the code and select Character Properties from the context menu.

3. In the dialog box, turn on the Client option in the JavaScript section.

4. Click OK.

The second method requires the use of an external editor, which I'll explain in the next section. I have found this second method to be preferable; and since you'll need an external editor for other tasks anyway, you might as well use it for JavaScript, too.

Using External Editors

Gold lets you define links to two external editors—one for text and one for images. You can then start these programs from within Gold to perform editing tasks that are impossible or inconvenient in Gold. To define your external editors, select Editor Preferences from the Options menu. A dialog box will be displayed with a section titled External Editors. You can specify your HTML source (text) editor and image editor by typing the full paths to their executable files in the text boxes, or by using the browse buttons to locate the file.

Once your editors are defined, you can open your text editor by selecting Edit Document Source from the View menu. You would think that the folks at Netscape would have arranged it so that the document is automatically loaded into the text editor, but no—you have to open it yourself. Once it's loaded, however; things work smoothly. As you switch back and forth between the Gold editor and your own text editor, you will be reminded that the file has been changed so you can reload it.

An external text editor is necessary because the Gold editor does not provide you with any means of editing the HTML document header. Since this section is where most of your JavaScript functions will go, you clearly need some means of editing here. An external editor is also handy for adding JavaScript code to the body of the document, as mentioned earlier.

To edit an image, right-click the image and select Edit Image from the Context menu that is displayed. Your image editor will start and load the image for editing. Needless to say, you must use an image editor that can deal with the .JPG and .GIF files used in HTML files.

Testing Your Document

Even though Gold is a WYSIWYG editor, the real proof of the pudding will be trying your document out in a browser. This is easy enough—just click the Netscape icon on the toolbar or select Browse Document from the File menu. The Netscape browser will start, if necessary, and load the document. It will appear just as it would to any user accessing it from your Web site. You can try out the links, too.

Netscape's Web Page Starter

Netscape provides a Web page specially designed to help you create your own Web documents. Click the Web Page Starter button on the editor's toolbar to connect to this site. You can use predefined page templates to begin the process, or use the Page Wizard to walk you through the steps of starting a page. You can also download resources such as clip art, animated GIF's, and special bullets and rules to use in your document. The instructions given on the page are quite clear, so I won't bother describing how to use it. (They'll probably change it by the time you read this anyway!) Particularly if you're just getting started designing Web pages, I think you'll find this resource quite useful. Once you have used the site to create a page, all you have to do is download it and add your personal touches.

Document Information

If you select Document from the Properties menu, you'll see a dialog box with three tabs that allow you to specify a variety of information about the document. Some of this information can be useful to the users of your document, so it's a good idea to pay some attention to what you are inserting here. The entries are described here:

Location
:   The location of the current document on your local disk.

Title
:   The text that you desire to appear in the window title when the document is browsed. Although optional, it's a good idea to specify a title for your documents since this is how most Web search tools locate specific Web pages.If you want readers to be able to locate your page easily, select a useful title that conveys what your page is all about.

Author
:   The name of the document's author. This information can be helpful to readers who've found your document by using a Web search tool and must now select from a list.

Description
:   A brief description of the contents of your document. This information can be helpful to readers searching for a specific topic.

Creation date	The date you first saved the current document.
Last updated	The date you last made changes to the current document.
Other Attributes	In this section you enter keywords that Internet searching services such as Yahoo can use to help users locate your document. Type the category name (obtained from a catalog server) that best fits your document. Classification names is another (optional) method used by searching services to locate documents.

Editing a Remote Document

You are not limited to editing HTML documents on your local hard disk. You can edit a remote document—one that you obtain from a server site. However, you don't edit the remote document directly. Rather, you download a copy of it and edit the copy.

The ability to edit remote documents can be useful in several situations. Perhaps it is a document for which you are responsible. If you need to make changes, you can complete the editing and then upload the changed copy to the server. If you find a site whose page is particularly appealing, you can edit the document in order to see how various effects were created and use parts of it in your own documents. Of course, you must be aware of copyright restrictions if you plan to take advantage of this option.

To edit a remote document, select Open Location from the File menu. In the dialog box that is displayed, enter the document's URL and click Open in Editor Window option. When you click OK, another dialog box will be displayed informing you that you must save the remote document locally before making any changes. You'll find two options available in this dialog box:

Adjust links ...	This option ensures that any links in the document to other files in the same directory are relative when saved locally. These links will work locally if you've also saved the remote files to which they point. Links to files outside the document's directory are absolute and will remain pointing at their original targets. Turning off this option results in

lack of modification for local link path names, which means that links local to the saved document may no longer work.

Save images ...   This option saves a copy of any image files used by the document in the same local location as the document. Because images are not located within the document itself, turning off this option means that the HTML document (but not the image files) is saved locally. Leaving this option turned on means that a document's images are always kept in the same directory as that document.

Unless you have special reasons for doing otherwise, I recommend that you leave both of these options on and then click the Save button. Next, you will have to specify a folder and name for the downloaded file. The document (and local images, if the Save Images option is selected) will be downloaded to the specified folder, and the HTML document will be opened in the editor.

Here's where we start getting into the nuts and bolts of JavaScript. You'll learn all about the data types, statements, keywords, expressions, and other elements of JavaScript.

JavaScript

Key Topics:

- **JavaScript and HTML.**

- **Data types and variables.**

- **Program control with loops and conditional statements.**

- **Creating functions and objects.**

From Square One

Like any programming language, JavaScript has a lot of details. I've heard it said, "The devil is in the details." Then again, I've also heard, "God is in the details." I don't know where these quotations originated, but if either one of them is true—or both!—we're still stuck with learning the details. I'll try to make it as painless as possible by including interesting (I hope!) demonstration programs.

Web Watch

If you're looking for a pithy quotation to use in a report, love letter, or birthday card, meander over to http://www.columbia.edu/acis/bartleby/bartlett/ for an online version of Bartlett's Familiar Quotations. Want something a bit less pithy? Try http://cruciform.cid.com/~werdna/fun.html for quotations from Dave Barry, Star Trek, and Dan "Potatoe" Quayle.

If you have experience programming in C or C++, then a lot of JavaScript's details will look familiar to you. JavaScript is, in fact, based on C. There are differences, however, so you need to pay attention!

JavaScript and HTML

You already know that JavaScript programs exist only within HTML files. Each section of JavaScript code within an HTML file must be set off with special tags that identify it as script:

```
<SCRIPT>
JavaScript statements go here
</SCRIPT>
```

You can include a script language specifier as part of the first script tag:

```
<SCRIPT LANGUAGE="JavaScript">
```

The language specifier is optional, possibly because JavaScript is the only scripting language available. I always stick it in, though—just to be safe.

JavaScript code also needs to be hidden from browsers that don't support it. This is accomplished by placing the code inside HTML comment tags:

```
<!--
JavaScript code goes here
-->
```

Without these comment tags, a browser that is not JavaScript-enabled will display the JavaScript code on the document page—not a good thing!

Look Before You Leap

I have always found that examples are a powerful learning tool. By themselves, examples are not enough, but combined with reasonably clear explanations and definitions, they can be a terrific help. Imagine, for example, explaining what a tree is like to someone who has no knowledge of trees. How much easier your job would be if you could show them an actual tree along with your explanation!

Following the same approach, I am going to show you a JavaScript program that demonstrates the major components that make up the language. Then, as you read the remainder of the chapter, you will have a better idea of what I'm talking about. I don't pretend that this program does anything useful—after all, it's just a demonstration! The code is presented in Listing 4.1. I have numbered the lines so I can refer to them in the explanation that follows.

You'll notice that in this and most other programs I have omitted the comment tags. Since you are learning JavaScript it is a safe assumption that you are using a JavaScript-enabled browser. You cannot make this assumption when you are writing scripts for real Web pages, so be sure to include those comment tags!

Listing 4.1 A simple JavaScript demonstration program, DEMO1.HTML.

```
1.   <HTML>
2.   <HEAD>
3.   <script language="javascript">
4.   function Reverse(obj)
5.       {
6.       var t1, t2 = ""
7.       t1 = obj.value
8.       for (var count = t1.length - 1 ; count >= 0 ;  count--)
9.            t2 += t1.charAt(count)
10.      obj.value = t2.toUpperCase()
11.      }
12.  </script>
13.  </HEAD>
14.  <BODY>
15.  <form NAME="form1">
16.  <H2>JavaScript Example</H2>
17.  Click on this box then type in your name:<br><br>
18.  <input type="text" name="text1" length="40" value="" ><br><br>
19.  Now, click this button and see what happens:
20.  <input type="button" name"button1" value="Reverse!"
21.      onclickReverse(document.form1.text1)"><br>
22.  </form>
23.  </BODY>
24.  </HTML>
```

What does this program do? It displays a box for entering text and a button to click, as shown in Figure 4.1. When you click the button, the text in the box is reversed to read backwards and converted to upper case.

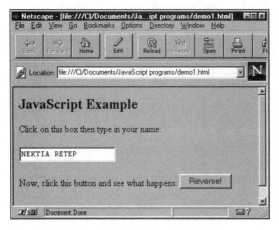

Figure 4.1

The demonstration program in action.

Now let's look at the parts of the program. Some of these components you should already understand from your knowledge of HTML (you *did* read Chapter 2, didn't you?), such as lines 1, 2, 14, and 17.

Lines 4 through 11 define a function named **Reverse**(). A function is a section of code that can be called from elsewhere in the program. I'll explain the contents of the function soon.

Lines 15 and 22 contain tags defining the beginning and end of a form. Most of the interesting things you can do in JavaScript and HTML must be done on forms. A document can have multiple forms, as will be explained later.

Line 18 creates and displays a JavaScript object. This is the box for text entry as seen in the figure. The code specifies that:

- The object is type "text"—that is, a text box.

- The object's name is "text1."

- The size of the object (length in characters) is 40.

- Its initial value, or contents, is a blank string.

Lines 20 and 21 create and display another object. These two lines should really have been a single line, but needed to be broken into two lines to fit the page width. This object is the rectangular button that the script displays, and the details are as follows:

- The object type is "button"—a rectangular button that can display a caption.

- The object's name is "button1."

- Its value—the caption displayed on it—is "Reverse!"

- When the user clicks the button, the function **Reverse**() is to be executed. The text box object (text1) is passed to the function.

Now we can talk about the code in the function. Line 6 creates two variables, named t1 and t2; the value of t2 is set to an empty string. In line 7, the value of t1 is set to one of the properties of the object that was passed to the function—in this case, the value property, which provides the text that the user entered into the text box.

Lines 8 and 9 are a loop or section of code that executes repeatedly. Here, we loop once for each character in the variable t1, taking characters one at a time from the end of t1 and adding them to t2. The result, of course, is to reverse the order of the characters.

Finally, we come to line 10. Since the variable t2 contains text, it is a JavaScript string object. Line 10 uses the string object's **toUpperCase**() method to convert the text to upper case, then assigns the result to the value property of the object that was passed to the function. What this does is display the reversed, upper case text in the original text box.

In this short and rather dumb program, you have seen most of JavaScript's main components at work. Now that you know what these parts look like, you'll be better able to make sense of the following brief overview of JavaScript:

- JavaScript has objects that provide certain functionality to the program.

- Objects have properties, which contain information or data.

- Objects also have methods, which perform actions.

- Some JavaScript objects can automatically respond to events, such as user input.

- JavaScript code can be set apart in named functions. A function can be executed in response to a user event.

That about sums it up. But an overview is just that—an overview. We still have all those pesky details to handle. For the remainder of this chapter (and the next couple of chapters, too), we'll be doing just that.

The JavaScript Object Model

JavaScript is an *object-based* language. Note that I did not say object *oriented*. There is a distinction between the two that will make a difference to you only if you have some experience programming with a truly object–oriented language such as C++ or Smalltalk. I'll talk briefly about the differences in a bit, but first we need to deal with the more general question—what's an object?

In truth, that's not an easy question! I could say "an object is a construct with properties and methods," but I don't think that gives a clear idea of the concept. Perhaps it's easier, rather than trying to explain what an object is, to explain how they came to be.

In the days before objects, programs had data and programs had functions (also called *procedures*), and the two were totally separate. Data was stored in variables, and all a variable could do was to hold a chunk of data—a string, for example, or a number. If you wanted to do something with the data, you had to write a function yourself or find one in your language's library. If you had some string data and wanted to find out something about the data—its length, for example—you had to pass the string to a function and get the result back as the function's return value. Likewise, to manipulate the string in some way, such as changing it to all upper case, you also needed a function.

This method of programming, called *procedural* programming, works perfectly well and has been used to write thousands of terrific programs. But still, some computer scientists thought that there might be some advantages in doing things differently. The notion of removing the separation between variables and functions seemed promising. What if we had some entity that could do both—contain data like a variable, and manipulate it like a function? Thus, the idea of objects was born.

Programmers create objects based on the needs of the program. Since there are many tasks that are common to most programs, object-based languages such as JavaScript provide a collection of built-in objects. The objects you use in your programs will include some of these built-in objects and may also include objects that you create yourself.

The concept of an object will be easier to understand with an example. I spoke earlier about using variables and functions to work with string data. Let's see how this works with a JavaScript object. Suppose that you have a variable named X to which you assign some string data:

```
X = "JavaScript"
```

X is not just a simple variable in JavaScript, but a String object (one of JavaScript's built-in object types). If you want to determine the number of characters in the string, you do not need to pass the data to a function. You can use one of the object's properties:

```
Y = X.length
```

After this statement executes, the variable Y has the value 10. Likewise, to manipulate the data—say, convert it to upper case—you use one of the object's methods:

```
Z = X.toUpperCase()
```

After this statement, the variable Z contains "JAVASCRIPT."

I hope this simple example has given you a feel for what objects are. You can look forward to many more details, but hopefully you will be able to understand them better now that you have at least a faint view of the "big picture." Not all objects have to do with user data—there are some that are related to the document and others to the browser—but they all share the same basic idea.

Data in JavaScript

Almost all of the JavaScript programs you will write are going to deal with data in one form or another. JavaScript can work with four types of data (values):

- Numbers such as 123, -0.45, and 0.

- Strings, or text, such as "JavaScript" and "Internet."

- The Boolean (logical) values true and false.

- The special value null.

The data you work with in JavaScript will be represented either as a variable or as a literal.

Variables

A *variable* is a named storage container for a value. Once you create a variable, you use its name to refer to it in code. JavaScript variable names must adhere to the following rules:

- The first character in the name must be a letter or the underscore (_) character.

- Subsequent characters can be letters, numbers, and the underscore.

It's a good idea (a *really* good idea, in fact) to use descriptive variable names. In other words, the name of the variable should describe the value that it holds. If your program uses the prime interest rate in its calculations, for example; you wouldn't get into trouble calling the variable Prime_Rate. You could just as easily call it XY, Bushels_Of_Corn, or Rush_Limbaugh_Is_A_Twit, and JavaScript wouldn't care one bit. When you or someone else reads or modifies the code, however; you'll have a lot better chance of understanding what's going on if you used Prime_Rate.

> ### A CASE OF EASE-SENSITIVITY
> For reasons totally beyond me, JavaScript variable names are case-sensitive (as is the language as a whole). Thus, the variable Total is a different variable than total or TOTAL. This is a real pain in the tail lights, but we have to live with it, so be careful. If you select a variable name style, such as all caps or initial cap only, and stick with it, you'll be less likely to have problems.

JavaScript is a *loosely typed* language, which means that it does not have different types of variables for different types of data. If you've ever programmed in C, Basic, or another traditional language, I'm sure you're familiar with all the different variable types: one type for integers, another for floating points, still another for strings. JavaScript makes it so much easier. There's only one type of variable, and you can put any value your heart desires into it. Furthermore, JavaScript is pretty smart when strings and numbers are mixed. Usually what happens is that the number is converted to a string. Thus, if you write:

```
X = "The distance is " + 100 + " miles."
```

The result is that the variable X contains the string "The distance is 100 miles."

Before you can use a variable, you have to declare it. This is done with the **var** keyword, as follows:

```
var Prime_Rate
```

This statement creates a variable named Prime_Rate. You can optionally initialize a variable to some value when you declare it:

```
var Prime_Rate = .06
```

Multiple variables can be declared with a single var keyword:

```
var Prime_Rate = .06, Amount = 5000, Months_To_Pay
```

VAR BE GONE?

Strictly speaking, declaring variables with var is required only if the variable is being declared inside a function and another variable of the same name has been declared outside the function. It is good practice, however, and it helps to prevent pesky errors, to use **var** all the time. Even the folks who created JavaScript say it is "good style" to use **var**, and you wouldn't want to be unstylish, would you?

Literals

A *literal* is a value typed directly into the program's source code. Type numbers just as you normally would:

```
100
0.12
-15.7
```

Number literals can also be entered in floating point notation (sometimes called *scientific* notation). This notation expresses a number as a floating point value multiplied by 10 raised to a power, and is particularly useful for very large and very small numbers. For example, you could write the value 1234 as follows:

```
1.234E3
```

which means 1.234 times 10 to the third power, or 1.234 times 1000. Similarly, you can write 0.00000567 as 5.67E-7. The "E" can be either upper or lower case.

In addition to the standard decimal (base 10) notation, integer numbers can be expressed in octal (base 8) or hexadecimal (base 16) notation. A leading 0 on an integer literal means octal notation, while a leading 0X means hexadecimal notation. Recall that octal notation uses only the digits 0-7, while hexa-decimal notation uses the standard digits 0-9 as well as the letters A through F.

HEXAWHATSIS?

Unlike our everyday number system, which expresses numbers in powers of 10, hexadecimal uses powers of 16 and octal uses powers of 8. You can refer to just about any computer encyclopedia or beginner's programming book if you need more details.

Strings can be enclosed in either single or double quotes:

```
"Hello, world"
'corned beef'
"100"
```

If a string contains either a single or double quote, you must enclose it in the other type of quotation:

```
"Henry's uncle"
'He said \"hello" to me.'
```

If you must use a quotation mark in text that is enclosed in the same type of mark, precede it with a backslash. This signals JavaScript that the quotation mark is to be treated as part of the text:

```
'He said "That is Henry\'s uncle" to the waiter'
"He said "hello\" to me."
```

For Boolean values, use the keywords **true** and **false**. Likewise, for the null value, use the **null** keyword:

```
DataSaved = false
Total = null
```

Special Characters in String Literals

JavaScript defines several *escape characters* that can be included in string literals. If you've done any C programming, these will be familiar to you:

\b   backspace

\f   form feed

\n   new line

\t   tab

\r   carriage return

To be honest, I do not know exactly why these special characters are supported in JavaScript, because they have no effect on the display. Thus, the JavaScript statement:

```
document.write("Hello, \t\n there")
```

results in exactly the same display as

```
document.write("Hello, there")
```

In other words, the escape characters are just ignored. Perhaps they are supported in order to facilitate interactions between JavaScript and C programs, but that's just a guess. In any event, the only practical effect of these characters is that if you want to include a backslash in a string literal, you must precede it with another backslash, thus:

```
MyFolder ="c:\\aitken"
```

JavaScript also permits you to create data arrays. (These will be covered later in the chapter.)

DOCUMENT.WRITE? WRONG!

It's difficult to present JavaScript details without getting ahead of myself, using language features I have not explained yet. The **document.write()** statement used in the above code is a perfect example. **Document** is one of JavaScript's objects, and **write** is one of the document object's methods. You'll learn all about it soon. For now, suffice it to say that this statement displays whatever expression is within the parentheses on the browser screen.

Expressions and Operators

When you manipulate data in a JavaScript program, much of what you do will involve expressions and operators. In this section, I'll show you what they are and how to use them.

Expressions

You've already learned that JavaScript supports three kinds of values: numbers, strings, and logical (Boolean) values. An *expression* is anything in JavaScript that evaluates to a value. We have, therefore, three kinds of expressions:

- Arithmetic expressions evaluate to a number.

- String expressions evaluate to a string.

- Logical expressions evaluate to **true** or **false**.

We can see that any literal (number, string, or logical) is an expression. Likewise, any variable that has been assigned a value is also an expression.

UNDEFINED VERSUS NULL

If you have declared a variable but not assigned a value to it, its value is undefined. This is not the same as **null**, which must be explicitly assigned to a variable. After this statement:

var x, y = null

the variable x is undefined and y is NULL. If you try to display the value of an undefined variable, you get nothing. In contrast, a null variable displays "NULL." An undefined or NULL variable does not evaluate to a value and is therefore not an expression.

Another way to define an expression is to say it is anything that can be placed on the right side of an assignment statement. The equal sign is the assignment operator; when you write the following (called an *assignment statement*),

```
x = expression
```

you are saying, "assign the value of *expression* to x." Note that an assignment statement is itself an expression. Thus, assuming the variables x and y have already been declared, the statement

```
x = y = 7
```

results in both x and y being assigned the value 7. The literal 7 is an expression, with the value 7 (of course). The assignment statement y = 7 is also an expression with the value 7.

Arithmetic Operators

The *arithmetic operators* perform arithmetic operations on numerical expressions. The four standard operations are indicated by the usual symbols: addition (+), subtraction (-), multiplication (*), and division (/). The modulus operator, %, returns the remainder when the two integer operands are divided. For example, the expression

```
14 % 5
```

evaluates to 4, and the expression

```
6 % 3
```

evaluates to 0.

String Operators

This section should really have been called String Operator, because there is only one of them. The *concatenation operator* (+) combines two strings into a single string value. If you execute the statement

```
x = "Java" + "Script"
```

the result is that x contains "JavaScript." You'll note that the same symbol is used for concatenation as for addition. JavaScript knows what to do based on the difference in the values. If they are both number values, addition is performed. If one or both of them are string values, concatenation is performed.

Increment and Decrement Operators

The increment and decrement operators are used to increase or decrease the value of a variable by 1. They are indicated by ++ and --, respectively. They can be used in two ways: when placed before a variable name, in *prefix* mode, the variable is incremented or decremented and then its value is returned. For example, if the variable x holds the value 5, then after executing the statement

```
y = ++x
```

both y and x are equal to 6. In *postfix* mode, the value is returned before the variable is incremented or decremented. After executing this statement (again starting with x equal to 5):

```
y = x++
```

y will be equal to 5 and x will be equal to 6. The decrement operator works the same way; with x starting with the value of 5,

```
y = --x
```

results in both x and y equal to 4. In contrast,

```
y = x--
```

gives y equal to 5 and x equal to 4.

Assignment Operators

You've already seen the basic assignment operator =, which assigns the value of the expression on the right side of the operator to the variable on the left side. There are also some "shorthand" assignment operators that save you some typing in certain situations shown in Table 4.1. The general form is

```
x <op>= y
```

where y is any expression and <op> is any one of the standard arithmetic operators (+ - * / or %). This syntax means exactly the same as

```
x = x <op> y
```

Thus, to add 10 to the value of x and store the new value in x, you could write

```
x += 10
```

which does the same thing as the long form:

```
x = x + 10
```

Likewise, to divide x by (y+z) and store the value in x, you would write:

```
x /= (y+z)
```

Table 4.1   The full set of shorthand arithmetic operators.

SHORTHAND	MEANS
x += y	x = x + y
x -= y	x = x - y
x *= y	x = x * y
x /= y	x = x/y
x %= y	x = x % y

Bitwise Operators

The so-called *bitwise operators* treat their operand as binary numbers—in other words, as a series of 1s and 0s. These operators make sense only for integer operands. The bitwise operators utilize binary representation, but the values they return are standard JavaScript numbers.

BINARY SCHMINARY

Binary notation represents a number in terms of powers of 2. The only digits used are 0 and 1. In binary, counting from decimal 1 to 10 goes like this: 1, 10, 11, 100, 101, 110, 111, 1000, 1001, 1010.

The bitwise logical operators compare the digit (0 or 1) in each position of their two operands; the digit in the corresponding position of the result is determined as follows:

- Bitwise AND (&): result is 1 only if both operands are 1. Result is 0 if either or both operands are 0.

- Bitwise OR (|): result is 1 if one of the operands is 1, or if both are 1. Result is 0 only if both operands are 0.

- Bitwise exclusive OR (^). Result is 1 if the operands are different (one is 0, the other is 1). Result is 0 if operands are both 0 or both 1.

Here are some examples. JavaScript stores integers with 32 bits, but I've shortened them to 8 bits to make the examples more readable. If x is assigned the decimal value 75 and y the decimal value 25, we are dealing with these binary numbers:

```
01001011      (decimal 75)
00011001      (decimal 25)
```

Then the three bitwise operators work like this:

```
z = x & y
    01001011
&   00011001
    00001001      (decimal 9)
z = x | y
    01001011
```

```
|    00011001
     01011011    (decimal 91)
z = x ^ y
     01001011
^    00011001
     01010010    (decimal 82)
```

The bitwise shift operators have the effect of shifting a binary value's 1s and 0s to the left or to the right. What exactly is shifting? First, you must think of a binary number as having a certain number of *positions*—in JavaScript's case, 32. The first digit on the right is in position 0, the next one is in place 1, and so on up to position 31. Shifting moves digits the specified number of positions either left or right. Shifting left by one, for example, would result in the digit in position 0 moving to position 1, the digit in position 1 moving to position 2, and so on. Digits that "fall off" at one end are discarded. For left shifting, blank spaces that are created at position 1 are filled with 0s. For right shifting, blank spaces that are created at the leftmost position are filled with the digit that was there originally. Let's look at some examples. Again, I have shrunk JavaScript's 32 bit format to 8 bits for the sake of clarity:

```
00110100    shifted left 1     01101000
00110100    shifted left 2     11010000
10110100    shifted right 2    11001101
00110100    shifted right 2    00001101
```

The shift operators are written like this:

```
x >> y       Shift x right by y positions
x << y       Shift x left by y positions
```

Why, you may be asking, does left-shift always insert 0s in blank spaces at position 1 while right-shift makes copies of the digit that was originally in position 31 (or, in the above truncated examples, position 7)? The reason is that the highest order bit in a binary representation is the *sign bit*. A 1 in that position indicates a negative number, while a 0 indicates a positive number. By filling blank spaces with the original sign digit, you are assured that the shifted number retains the sign of the original number before shifting. This type of right-shift is known in official parlance as *sign-propagating right shift*.

But wait! Just in case you aren't already confused enough, JavaScript provides a second right-shift operation called zero-fill right-shift. With this operation, zeros are used to fill blank spaces no matter what the original sign might have been. *Zero-fill* right-shift is indicated by three right angle brackets:

```
x >>> y
```

As with the arithmetic operators, JavaScript provides shorthand notation for certain uses of the bitwise logical and shift operators shown in Table 4.2.

Table 4.2   Shortcut notations for bitwise operators.

SHORTCUT NOTATION	MEANS THE SAME AS
x <<= y	x = x << y
x >>= y	x = x >> y
x >>>= y	x = x >>> y
x &= y	x = x & y
x ^= y	x = x ^ y
x |= y	x = x || y

Logical Operators

The *logical* operators perform operations on logical, or Boolean, values. Recall that there are only two possible logical values, true and false. In effect, the logical operators allow you to take two or more logical values and combine them to create a single yes/no, true/false answer. You do this every day without realizing it. For example, "I will go to dinner with you, only if it's that fancy French place and you pick up the tab." You are stating two conditions here, and both of them must be true for the final answer to be true. Congratulations, you've just encountered the AND operator, symbolized in JavaScript by &&. Thus, the expression

```
LogicalExpr1 && LogicalExpr2
```

evaluates as true only if both LogicalExpr1 and LogicalExpr2 are both true. Expressing the original question this way, we have:

```
GoToDinner = FrenchPlace && PickUpTab
```

There's also the OR operator (||) which evaluates as true if either one, or both, of its operands are true. "I will lend you $50 if you will pay me back by Friday, or if you promise to never ask for a loan again." The expression

```
LogicalExpr1 || LogicalExpr2
```

is false only if both LogicalExpr1 and LogicalExpr2 are false; otherwise it is true. Again:

```
LendMoney = PayBackByFriday || NeverAskAgain
```

There's one more logical operator, NOT. This operator takes only a single operand, and it simply reverses its value from true to false or vice versa. Thus,

```
!LogicalExpr1
```

evaluates as true if LogicalExpr1 is false, and evaluates as false if LogicalExpr1 is true. For example, "I'll go to dinner with you if it's that fancy French place and you promise not to talk about that stupid JavaScript project." In techie notation:

```
GoToDinner = (FrenchPlace) && !(TalkAboutJavaScript)
```

When would you use these logical operators? They are most frequently used in combination with the comparison operators, to be covered next.

THE TRUTH ABOUT TRUE

Computers represent all data internally as numbers. In JavaScript, as in every other programming language I've ever encountered, the logical value false is represented by 0. **True** is represented by the value 1 (some other languages use -1). JavaScript "knows," however, when a variable is holding a logical value. For example, if you execute these two lines:

var x = true

document.write(x)

you'll get "true" displayed in the document, not "1". If you use a logical value in an arithmetic expression, the internal numerical representation is used. Thus, after these statements:

var x = true

var y = 10 + x

the variable y will have the value 11.

Comparison Operators

The comparison operators, which let you perform comparisons (no kidding!) between values, are shown in Table 4.3. They return logical values: **true** if the comparison is true, **false** if not.

Table 4.3 Six comparison operators.

OPERATOR	COMPARISON PERFORMED
==	Equal to
!=	Not equal to
>	Greater than
<	L ess than
>=	Greater than or equal to
<=	Less than or equal to

You use these operators by placing them between the two expressions you want to compare:

```
Expression1 <op> Expression2
```

This statement is itself an expression that evaluates to true or false depending on the specific comparison operator used and the values of the two expressions; some examples are shown in Table 4.4.

Table 4.4   Expressions evaluated.

EXPRESSION	EVALUATES AS
5 < 10	true
6.02 >= 6.0	true
5 != 10/2	false

When comparing string values, "greater than" and "less than" are determined by the ASCII value of the characters in the string. ASCII (American Standard Code for Information Interchange) values are the numbers that the computer uses internally to represent letters, punctuation marks, and other characters. Fortunately, ASCII values follow alphabetical order so comparisons based on ASCII values usually make intuitive sense. I say "usually" because there is one gotcha: since all the upper case letters have lower ASCII values, they are considered to be "before" the lower case letters. Thus,

```
Z < a
```

evaluates as **true**. To be exact, the upper case letters have values 65 through 90 (A through Z), and the lower case letters are 97 through 122. As long as you are aware of this potential problem, you will have no trouble performing true "alphabetic" string comparisons.

CARELESS COMPARISONS

The simplest way to avoid string comparison errors is to be sure that the two strings being compared are both the same case—all upper case or all lower case. Any JavaScript variable that contains a string value has the built-in ability to temporarily convert itself to either all upper case or lower case. You'll learn more about this when we talk about JavaScript objects and methods; for now I'll just show you how to do it. If SV1 and SV2 are the string variables that you want to compare, you would write

SV1.toUpperCase() < SV2.toUpperCase()

or

SV1.toLowerCase() < SV2.toLowerCase()

Either way, you are guaranteed a true alphabetical comparison regardless of the case of the original values. Note that using toLowerCase() or toUpperCase() does not actually change the string stored in the variable—it simply returns a copy of the string value with the case changed.

Conditional Expressions

A *conditional expression* has one of two values depending on whether a specified condition is **true** or **false**. By *condition* I mean a logical expression—one that evaluates as one of the two values, true or false. You write a conditional expression like this:

```
(condition) ? val1 : val2
```

If *condition* is true, the expression evaluates to the value of *val1*. If *condition* is false, the expression evaluates to the value of *val2*. Here's an example of using the conditional expression to compare the values of the variables x and y and assign the larger one to the variable z:

```
z = ( x > y ) ? x : y
```

In the same manner, we could assign the logical value true or false to the variable PastDue depending on whether the balance owed is greater than 0:

```
PastDue = (BalanceOwed > 0) ? true : false
```

Operator Precedence and Parentheses

Funny things can happen sometimes when an expression contains two or more operators. Let me illustrate with this expression:

```
4 + 6 / 2
```

Seems clear, right? Four plus 6 is 10, and 10 divided by 2 is 5. Case closed! But is it really? What if you do the division first. Then we have 6 divided by 2 is 3, and 3 plus 4 is 7. Which answer is correct?

In JavaScript, the second one is correct. Why? Because the division operator has higher *precedence* than the addition operator. When an expression is encountered, JavaScript scans the entire line before doing anything. Operations with the highest precedence are performed first, those with the second highest are performed second, and so on down the precedence hierarchy. From highest to lowest (operators on the same line have the same precedence), this is:

- logical NOT (!), increment (++), decrement (--)

- multiply (*), divide (/), modulus (%)

- addition (+), subtraction (-)

- Shift (<<, >>, >>>)

- Relational (<, <=, >, >=)

- Equality (==, !=)

- Bitwise AND (&)

- Bitwise exclusive OR (^)

- Bitwise OR (|)

- Logical AND (&&)

- Logical OR (||)

- Conditional (?:)

- Assignment (all of them)

If the precedence of the operators in an expression does not give the evaluation you desire, you can use parentheses to modify the evaluation order. When an expression contains one or more pairs of parentheses (and they must always be in pairs), JavaScript starts with the innermost parentheses and evaluates its contents first. Then JavaScript works outward until the entire expression has been evaluated. Thus, if you write

```
(4 + 6) / 2
```

you'll get the result 5, because the parentheses force the addition to be performed before the division. Likewise, with the expression

```
(4 * (6 + 3)) / 2
```

the addition is done first, then the multiplication, and finally the division.

You can insert parentheses in an expression even if they are not necessary to change the order of evaluation. This can be useful for complex expressions where parentheses can make the line easier to read.

Statements

A JavaScript statement is simply a way to tell the computer to do something. For the most part, the statements available in JavaScript control the execSåion of the script—they control which lines of code are executed, when they are executed, and how many times they are executed. If you have any familiarity with C or C++, these statements will look very familiar to you. If you have used another language, such as Basic or Pascal, the actions and logic of the statements will be familiar, even though the syntax will be new.

While

The **while** statement executes a group of one or more JavaScript statements, as long as a specified logical condition is true. The general syntax is like this:

```
while (condition)
    {
    statements
    }
```

When execution reaches the **while** statement, *condition* is evaluated. If it is true, all of the statements within the braces are executed, execution loops back to the **while** statement, and the process starts again. You'll often hear this referred to as a *while loop*, since execution loops back repeatedly. Here's a simple example that counts down from 4 to 1 on the browser screen:

```
var z = 4
while (z > 0)
    {
    document.write(z-- + "<br>")
    }
```

Note that I added the HTML code <br> to the expression being displayed so that each value of z would display on a new line. Without this, the output would have been 4321 on a single line.

If *condition* is false, execution skips over the statements in the braces and continues with the first statement following the closing brace. A moment's thought about the logic of the **while** statement reveals two things:

1. If *condition* is false the first time it is evaluated, then the statements in the braces will not be executed at all.

2. If *condition* is initially true and nothing happens inside the loop to change it to false, the statements will be executed over and over, endlessly.

To terminate a while loop early, you can use either the break or the continue statement. These are covered later.

For

The **for** statement is another loop that provides the capability to execute a group of statements repeatedly. It is similar in concept to the **while** loop, but has a very different syntax:

```
for (initial ; condition ; update)
    {
    statements
    }
```

The elements *initial, condition,* and *update* are all expressions, with *condition* being a logical expression. Here's how a **for** loop works:

1. When execution first reaches the **for** statement, *initial* is evaluated. It is usually used to assign an initial value to a counter variable. You can use var to declare a new variable as part of *initial*.

2. The expression *condition* is evaluated. If **true**, proceed with #3. If false, the loop terminates and execution passes to the first statement following the closing brace.

3. All of the statements in the loop are executed.

4. The expression *update* is evaluated.

5. Return to step #2.

To illustrate, here's a **for** loop that does exactly the same thing as the while loop presented earlier—count down from 4 to 1 on-screen.

```
for (var z = 4 ; z > 0 ; z--)
    {
    document.write(z + "<br>")
    }
```

The three elements inside the parentheses are optional. You can omit *initial* if the counter variable is assigned its initial value elsewhere in the program. Similarly, you can omit *update* if the counter is updated by code within the loop. Here's how:

```
var z = 4
...
for (; z > 0 ; )
    {
    document.write(z-- + "<br>")
    }
```

You can even omit *condition*, in which case it is always considered to be **true**. This results in an "infinite" loop and can be used only when a **break** statement within the loop is used to terminate it (more on **break** soon). Note: when one or more of the **for** loop's expressions are omitted, the separating semicolons must still be included.

In these examples, I have included only a single statement inside the loop. JavaScript places no limits on how many statements a loop can contain. Practically speaking, however, I suggest that you avoid overly-large loops because they make the code more difficult to read and debug. It's impossible to assign a precise number to "overly-large." A dozen statements is certainly okay, and a hundred is definitely too many. Use common sense. If a loop is too big to view all at once in your code editor, then it's too big!

if...else

The **if...else** construct is used to execute a group of statements depending on whether one or more conditions are **true** or **false**. You would not use **if...else** to execute statements multiple times. This construct is reserved for those times when you want to execute the statements once or not at all. The syntax is:

```
if (condition)
    {
    block1
    }
```

```
else
    {
    block2
    }
```

If *condition* is true, the statements in block1 are executed (once) and those in block2 are not executed. If *condition* is false, then the reverse holds. The **else** part of the statement is optional; if there are no statements to be executed if *condition* is **false**, then simply omit the else statement and its associated block of code.

The braces surrounding the statements following the **if** and **else** are required only for multiple statements. If there is only a single JavaScript statement to be executed, you can (but are not required to) omit the braces. Here's an example:

```
if (z == 4)
    document.write("Z equals 4")
else
    document.write("Z does not equal 4")
```

Break and Continue

Break and **continue** statements can be used only within a **while** or a **for** loop. They are used to terminate the loop entirely (**break**) or to start the next iteration of the loop (**continue**). Expressed another way, when **break** is encountered, execution passes immediately to the first statement following the end of the loop; when **continue** is encountered, execution passes to the first loop statement (the **while** or **for**), skipping any statements between the **continue** and the end of the loop.

Let's look at an example. Remember how earlier we used a **while** loop to print the numbers from 4 to 1 on the screen? This is the method we used before:

```
var z = 4
while (z > 0)
    {
    document.write(z-- + "<br>")
    }
```

Using break, here's how it would look:

```
var z = 4
while (true)
    {
    document.write(z-- + "<br>")
```

```
    if (z == 0)
        break
}
```

Note first that we used the logical literal **true** for the **while** statement's condition. This means the **while** loop will execute forever if left to itself. Within the body of the loop, we use an **if** statement to test the value of z, exiting the loop with **break** once z has reached 0.

The following code illustrates the use of **continue**. Before I tell you, try to figure out what this code will do.

```
var z = 10
while (z > 0)
    {
    z--
    if (z == 6)
        continue
    document.write(z + "<br>")
    }
```

Have you figured it out? It will display the following on the screen:

```
9
8
7
5
4
3
2
1
```

Note that the number 6 is omitted from the sequence. The code in the loop uses an **if** with a **continue** to go back to the start of the loop, skipping the **document.write()** statement, when z is equal to 6.

Comments

A comment is not really a statement, since it is ignored by JavaScript and has no effect on the operation of the program. Comments are used by the programmer to explain what the script does and how it works. You create a single line comment by starting with two slash characters:

```
// This is a comment.
```

Multiple line comments start with /* and end with */, like this:

```
/* All of this text
is one
big comment. */
```

I suggest that you get in the habit of using comments liberally. Your code may seem perfectly clear to you when you write it, but when you (or worse yet, someone else) need to modify or debug it sometime down the road, you will be glad of some plain English explanations of what's going on. You can also use comments as an aid during program development, commenting out program statements to see the effect they are having.

With

With comes in handy when you want to do more than one thing with an object. I know, I know, we haven't covered objects yet, but the concept of the **with** statement is pretty simple, so I'll present it here and then go into more detail later. Actually, you've already been introduced to a JavaScript object, **document**, and one of its methods, **write**. When you want to use one of an object's methods, you write the object name followed by a period and the method name:

```
document.write("Hello, world.")
```

The **with** statement provides a kind of shorthand that is useful when you want to do a number of things with the same object. In effect, the **with** statement specifies a default object for statements in a block. The syntax is as follows:

```
with (object)
    {
    statements
    }
```

For any statement within the braces that requires an object reference, you can omit the object name and the default *object* will be used. For example, instead of writing

```
document.write(W)
document.write(X)
document.write(Y)
document.write(Z)
```

you could write the following:

```
with (document)
{
write(W)
write(X)
write(Y)
write(Z)
}
```

That's all there is to the **with** statement. It's not too helpful for small sets of statements, but if you need to execute a dozen or more methods for a given object, you can save a bit of typing.

Other JavaScript Statements

There are several other statements, but I won't be covering them here. You already met the **var** statement, which is used to declare variables, earlier in the chapter. The **for..in** statement is used with object properties, and I'm going to wait to cover that until after you know a bit more about objects. The **function** and **return** statements are used with functions, and they deserve a whole section of their own—coming up next!

Functions

Functions are an important part of JavaScript. In fact, they are central to any programming language used today. A function permits you to create a self-contained section of code that performs a specific action, then assigns that code a name. Whenever you want to execute the code, you refer to it by name in your program—this is referred to as *calling* a function. You can pass data to the function, and the function can return data to the calling program.

There are numerous advantages to using functions. With sections of code that you'll use over and over again in different parts of a program, you can just write the code only instead of repeating it each time you need it. In addition, code inside a function is isolated from the rest of the program, minimizing the chance of errors and other unwanted interactions. Finally, when we get to JavaScript events, you'll see that functions are the only practical way to connect code to user actions.

Let's look at an example. Here's the code for a function that adds three numbers and returns the result. Generally, you will not use functions for such simple tasks, but it serves perfectly well as an example.

```
function SumOf(a, b, c)
{
var sum
sum = a + b + c
return sum
}
```

Let's break this function into its component parts.

1. Every function definition starts with the keyword **function** followed by the name of the function—in this case, SumOf. Rules for function names are the same as for variable names, and within a script each function name must be unique.

2. Following the function name is a pair of parentheses enclosing the function's *parameters*. The parameters represent the data that the calling program passes to the function. You can have any number of parameters, separated by commas. Some functions take no parameters, in which case the function name is followed by empty parentheses.

3. The function code is enclosed in braces. A function can contain any JavaScript statements except another function definition.

4. Inside the function code, the **return** keyword is used to specify the value returned by the function to the calling program. Some functions do not return a value, in which case the **return** keyword is simply omitted.

How do you execute, or call, a function? A function that returns a value is an expression, so the function can be used anywhere you would use any other expression. When you call a function, you use its name followed by parentheses containing the *arguments*, specific values passed to the function parameters.

For example:

```
x = SumOf(1, 2, 3)
```

When this line executes (assuming the **SumOf**() function has been defined as above), here's what happens:

1. Execution passes to the **SumOf**() function.

2. The first argument, in this case 1, is placed in the function's first parameter, a. The second and third arguments are placed in the second and third parameters b and c, respectively.

3. The function code declares a variable named sum, adds the values passed in the three parameters, assigns the result to sum, then returns the value of sum to the calling program.

4. Execution returns to the calling program. The returned value is assigned to the variable x.

ARGUMENT VERSUS PARAMETER

Confusion sometimes arises about the meanings of these two terms. A parameter is a placeholder in a function definition for a value to be passed to the function. In the above definition of SumOf(), a, b, and c are parameters. An argument is a specific value passed to a function when a program calls it. Above, 1, 2, and 3 are arguments. Many people aren't aware of this distinction, and use the terms interchangeably.

What about a function that does not return a value? First, let's look at an example. This function takes a single argument, then displays that argument in the document centered and surrounded by asterisks. Here's the code:

```
function FancyDisplay(message)
{
document.write("<Center>***************************<br>")
document.write("***" + message + " ***<br>")
document.write("***************************<br></Center>")
}
```

To call it, all that is required is this:

```
FancyDisplay("ANNOUNCEMENT")
```

When using functions, remember that JavaScript is case-sensitive. You must use the exact same capitalization when calling a function as you did in the function definition. Also, be sure to pass the correct number of arguments. JavaScript, at least in the beta version I am using, does not require a function call to include the same number of arguments as there are parameters in the function definition. If you pass too many arguments, the extra ones will be ignored. If you pass too few, then the function parameters that did not receive values will be undefined during that execution of the function.

BY VALUE ONLY

JavaScript function arguments are always passed by value. This means that a copy of the argument is made and passed to the function, and the code inside the function cannot modify the original argument. For example, here's a function that modifies its argument:

```
function foo(x)

{

x = 100

}
```

Suppose you call it like this:

```
var num = 5

foo(num)
```

After the call to foo(), num still has the value 5. Because only a copy of num was passed to the function, code inside the function could not change the contents of the original variable num. This differs from many other languages which permit function arguments to be passed by reference, in which case code inside the function can change the argument's value.

Where Do I Put My Functions?

Your function should be placed in the header section of the HTML file; that is, between the <Head> and </Head> tags. As with any JavaScript code, functions need to be identified as JavaScript with the appropriate tags. Here's an example:

```
<HEAD>
<script language="JavaScript">

function FancyDisplay(message, x)
{
document.write("<Center>*****************************<br>")
document.write("***    " + message + x + "    ***<br>")
document.write("****************************<br></Center>")
}

function AnotherFunction(x, y, z)
{
...
}

function StillAnotherFunction(a, b, c)
{
...
}
</script>
</HEAD>
```

Technically, functions could be placed in the body of the HTML file. This is not a good idea, however, because of the way an HTML file is processed. When a browser loads a file, it processes the contents from the top down as they are loaded. When a call to a function is encountered, the browser can know about the function only if it has already been loaded. The only way to ensure that all function definitions have been loaded before any function calls occur is to place the definitions in the header section.

Local Variables

One of the convenient features of functions is that variables declared inside a function are local. Within a given function, each variable that is declared in the function is separate and distinct from any other variable(s) of the same name that are declared in other functions, or in JavaScript code outside a function (variables declared outside a function are global variables). This independence of variables frees you from having to worry about duplicate variable names, and also prevents unwanted interactions between global and function code. To summarize the relationship between global and local variables:

- All variables that you use in global code (code outside of functions) must be declared globally (outside of any function). In global code, variables declared inside functions might as well not exist.

- Within a function, a locally declared variable takes precedence over a global variable of the same name. You can access global variables inside a function as long as there is no local variable declared with the same name. Within a given function, variables declared in other functions are not accessible.

Creating Your Own Objects

The objects that are built into JavaScript (which will be covered in detail in the next chapter) demonstrate the power of an object based language. What about creating your own objects? This, too, is possible, and opens a wide range of possibilities. Perhaps the most commonly needed type of user-defined object is an array, so I'll cover those first. Then I'll explain creating more general types of objects.

Arrays

JavaScript does not include explicit support for arrays, but its object model makes it easy for you to create your own arrays. Since arrays are very useful in many programs, it's a good idea for you to know how to create and use them.

WHAT'S AN ARRAY?

An array is an indexed collection of data elements, or variables. If you have an array named data with 10 elements, you have in effect 10 distinct variables, data[0], data[1] ... data[9]. You can use these individual elements like any other variable:

data[5] = 100

```
data[6] = "Particulate matter"

document.write(data[8])
```

The advantage of arrays comes when the array subscript (the number in the brackets) is itself a variable, permitting you to use program loops to step through arrays and similar tasks that would be cumbersome with ordinary variables.

I will show you two approaches to creating an array, both of which involve a JavaScript function. The first method creates an array and fills it with the arguments passed to the function.

WHAT'S THIS?

A very important keyword in JavaScript is "this." Once you get used to it, you'll find yourself using it all the time. Whenever it is used in code, the this keyword always refers to the current object. For example, the code

```
this.length
```

always refers to the length property of the current object. It's not always obvious what object is current, but as you gain experience, you'll develop a feel for it.

First, define a function as follows:

```
function initArray() {
     this.length = initArray.arguments.length
     for (var i = 0; i < this.length; i++)
      this[i+1] = initArray.arguments[i]
     }
```

To create and initialize an array, you could write the following:

```
newArray = new initArray(1, 2, 3, 4)
```

The result is an array named newArray containing 4 elements that contain the values 1, 2, 3 and 4. You can use the function as many times as needed:

```
anotherArray =  new initArray("Apple", "Oranges", "Grapes")
```

Let's look at how this works. The **new** statement in JavaScript specifies that a new object be created. The code in the associated function determines the details of the object. Step by step, here's what happens:

1. The variable on the left side of the = sign will become the array name. When the **new** keyword specifies that a new object is being created, the function initArray() is called.

2. Within the function, the **this** keyword refers to the current object—the new object just created. This object has the **length** property, and we set this equal to the number of arguments passed to the function. This value is obtained from the **length** property of the function's **arguments** array.

3. A **for** loop steps through the function arguments array, assigning each one in turn to the corresponding element in the newly–created object. Note that the two arrays are out of step—arguments[0] is assigned to this[1], and so on. Why? Because the first element of the new array, this[0], is used to hold the array's length property.

Once you've created an array using this function, you can assign new values to the array elements as needed. For example,

```
myArray[2] = "Pomegranites"
```

Now let's take a look at a complete program that creates and uses an array. ARRAY1.HTML in Listing 4.2 uses the above function to create and initialize an array. The array contents are displayed, then one of the array elements is changed and the contents printed again. The program displays the following in your document:

```
3 The Coriolis Group
The Wild and Crazy Group
```

Note that the first value displayed is "3," illustrating how an array object's length property is stored in element 0 of the array.

Listing 4.2   ARRAY1.HTML demonstrates how to create and initialize an array in one step.

```
<HTML>
<HEAD>
<SCRIPT>
```

```
function initArray() {
      this.length = initArray.arguments.length
      for (var i = 0; i < this.length; i++)
       this[i+1] = initArray.arguments[i]
      }
</SCRIPT>
</HEAD>
<BODY>
<SCRIPT>
var myArray = new initArray("The", "Coriolis", "Group")
for (var i = 0; i < 4; i++)
   document.write(myArray[i])
document.write("<br>")
myArray[2] = "Wild and Crazy"
for (var i = 1; i < 4; i++)
   document.write(myArray[i])
document.close()
</SCRIPT>
</BODY>
</HTML>
```

What about expanding an array once it has been created? For example, after creating the array myArray in the above example with 3 elements, could you then write the following?

```
myArray[4] = "something else"
```

In my experiments this does work, although the **length** property (myArray[0]) is not updated to reflect the new array element. You could set the **length** property yourself, I suppose, but because this method is not mentioned in the JavaScript documentation, it is probably wise to keep arrays at their "official" size and not tempt fate.

A second approach to creating arrays is to create an empty array of a specified length, initializing the array elements to 0 if desired. A function to do this is shown here:

```
function initArray(ArrayLength)
    {
     this.length = ArrayLength
     for (var i = 0; i < this.length; i++)
      this[i+1] = 0
    }
```

To demonstrate this function, I have written a JavaScript program that displays a calculator on screen. Rather than the standard algebraic calculator that is a common project for beginning JavaScript programmers, I have created a calculator that use Reverse Polish Notation, or RPN. If you've ever used a Hewlett Packard calculator, you already know what RPN is. Calculators that use RPN are favored by most scientists and engineers over algebraic calculators. Their operation is based on the concept of a last-in, first-out stack. We use the array to implement the stack. In an algebraic calculator, you press the keys corresponding to the way you would write down the problem. For example, to multiple 2 times 4 then add 3, you would press

```
2 x 4 + 3 =
```

An RPN calculator lacks an = key, having an Enter key instead which serves to place the entered number on the stack. The same problem would be keyed as follows:

```
2 ENTER 4 x 3 +
```

Pressing Enter places the number in the display on the top of the stack. Pressing an operator key performs the specified operation between the number in the display and the number on the top of the stack. The result of the calculation is placed in the display and on the stack.

The calculator is shown in Figure 4.2, and its code is presented in Listing 4.3.

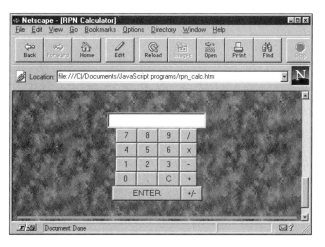

Figure 4.2
The RPN calculator.

Listing 4.3   RPN_CALC.HTML implements a Reverse Polish Notation calculator in JavaScript.

```
<html>
<head>
    <title>RPN Calculator</title>
    <meta name="Author" content="Peter G. Aitken">
    <meta name="GENERATOR" content="Mozilla/2.0GoldB2 (Win32)">
<script>
< -- hide script from old browsers.
function initArray(ArrayLength)
    {
        this.length = ArrayLength
        for (var i = 0; i < this.length; i++)
        this[i+1] = 0
    }
function AddDigit(Digit)
{
    if (NewNum)
        {
document.forms[0].display.value = Digit
    HasDecimal = false
    NewNum = false
        }
else
    document.forms[0].display.value += Digit
}
function AddDecimal()
    {
    if (NewNum)
        {
                                                    " "

        HasDecimal = true
        NewNum = false
        }
    else if (!HasDecimal)
        {
                HasDecimal = true
        document.forms[0].display.value += "."
        }
    }
function Clear()
    {
    document.forms[0].display.value = ""
    HasDecimal = false
    }
function EnterKey()
    {
    if (document.forms[0].display.value != "")
        {
```

```
        //Put display value on the stack.
        PutOnStack(document.forms[0].display.value)
        //Add decimal point if needed.
        if (!HasDecimal)
            document.forms[0].display.value += "."
        //Add zeros.
        var x = document.forms[0].display.value.length
        for (var i = 0; i < 16 - x; i++)
            document.forms[0].display.value += "0"
        //Set flags.
                NewNum = true
        HasDecimal = false
        }
    }
function ChangeSign()
    {
    var temp
    temp = document.forms[0].display.value
    if (temp.charAt(0) == "-")
        document.forms[0].display.value = temp.substring(1,
  temp.length)
    else
        document.forms[0].display.value = "-" + temp
    }
function Calc(op)
    {
    var result
    //Need at least one value on the stack.
    if (StackPtr > -1)
        {
        if (op == '+')
                {
                result = eval(Stack[StackPtr])
                result += eval(document.forms[0].display.value)
                document.forms[0].display.value = result
                }
         if (op == '-')
                {
            result = eval(Stack[StackPtr])
                result -= eval(document.forms[0].display.value)
            document.forms[0].display.value = result
                }
      if (op == 'x')
        {
            result = eval(Stack[StackPtr])
         result *= eval(document.forms[0].display.value)
            document.forms[0].display.value = result
        }
      if (op == '/')
        {
            result = eval(Stack[StackPtr])
```

```
                var y = eval(document.forms[0].display.value)
                if (y != 0)
                        {
                        result /= eval(document.forms[0].display.value)
                        document.forms[0].display.value = result
                        }
                else
                        alert("Cannot divide by zero!")
                }
            NewNum = true
                HasDecimal = false
                PutOnStack(result)
                }
        }
    function PutOnStack(value)
        {
        //Puts a value on the stack, checking for overflow.
        if (StackPtr >= 39)
            alert("Stack Overflow")
        else
            Stack[++StackPtr] = value
        }
    // end hiding. -->
    </script>
    </head>
    <script><!-- hide script
    var HasDecimal = false
    //Variable to serve as stack pointer.
    var StackPtr = -1
    //Flag for new number entry.
    var NewNum = true
    //Initialize a 40 element array for the stack.
    var Stack = new initArray(40)
    // end hiding--></script><input type="text" name="display" value=""
      length=20>
    <br>
    <input type="button" name="7" value="  7  " onClick = "AddDigit(7)">
    <input type="button" name="8" value="  8  " onClick = "AddDigit(8)">
    <input type="button" name="9" value="  9  " onClick = "AddDigit(9)">
    <input type="button" name="/" value="  /  " onClick = "Calc('/')">
    <br>
    <input type="button" name="4" value="  4  " onClick = "AddDigit(4)">
    <input type="button" name="5" value="  5  " onClick = "AddDigit(5)">
    <input type="button" name="6" value="  6  " onClick = "AddDigit(6)">
    <input type="button" name="x" value="  x  " onClick = "Calc('x')">
    <br>
    <input type="button" name="1" value="  1  " onClick = "AddDigit(1)">
    <input type="button" name="2" value="  2  " onClick = "AddDigit(2)">
    <input type="button" name="3" value="  3  " onClick = "AddDigit(3)">
    <input type="button" name="-" value="  -  " onClick = "Calc('-')">
```

```
<br>
<input type="button" name="0" value="  0   " onClick = "AddDigit(0)">
<input type="button" name="." value="   .   " onClick =
  "AddDecimal()">
<input type="button" name="clear" value="  C   " onClick = "Clear(>
<input type="button" name="+" value="  +  " onClick = "Calc('+')">
<br>
<input type="button" name="Enter" value="    ENTER     " onClick =
  "EnterKey(>
<input type="button" name="Sign" value=" +/-  " onClick =
  "ChangeSign()">
</form></p></center>

</body>
</html>
```

Creating Other Types of Objects

The procedure for creating other types of objects is similar to what you already
learned for arrays:

1. Define the object type by writing a function.

2. Create an instance of the object with the **new** keyword. The defining
    function must specify the object's name and its properties and methods.
    We'll cover methods later. For example, to define an object that can be
    used to store and manipulate information about a book collection, you
    could write the following function:

```
function book(title, author, category)
{
this.title = title
this.author = author
this.category = category
}
```

This function defines an object named car that has three properties: title, author,
and category. Now you can create an object called myBook as follows:

```
myBook = new book"JavaScript Guide", "Peter Aitken", "Computer
  Programming")
```

This statement creates an instance of the book object named myBook and
assigns it the specified values for its properties. The value of myBook.title is
the string "JavaScript Guide," and so on. You can create any number of book
objects by calls to **new**.

An object can have a property that is itself another object. For example, you could define an object called person as follows:

```
function person(fname, lname)
{
this.lname = lname
this.fname = fname
}
```

Next, create an instance of person as follows:

```
pAitken= new person("Peter","Aitken")
```

You do not have to rewrite the definition of book to include an author property that takes a person object. For example, if you create an instance of book like this:

```
myBook = new book("JavaScript Guide", pAitken, "Computer
  Programming")
```

you'll be able to access the individual properties of the person object as follows:

```
myBook.author.fname
myBook.author.lname
```

One nice flexibility feature of JavaScript objects is the ability to add a property to a previously defined object. For example, the statement:

```
myBook.pubDate = "1996"
```

adds a property named pubDate to the object myBook, and assigns it a value of "1996." Be aware that this does not affect any other objects of type book, only the instance named myBook. To add the new property to all objects of the same type, you have to add the property to the definition of the book object type before creating instances of the object.

DEFINING METHODS

To create a method for a user-defined object type, you must write a function that carries out the desired actions, including it as a method definition in the object type definition. As an example, here's a function to display the information about a book object:

```
function display()
{
var buf
buf = this.title + " by " + this.author.fname + "" +
  this.author.lname
document.writeln(buf)
}
```

Note that we use the **this** keyword to refer to the object to which the method belongs. To make this function a method of the book object, add the statement

```
this.display = display
```

to the object definition of book. Now the complete definition of book looks like this:

```
function book(title, author, category)
{
this.title = title
this.author = author
this.category = category
this.display = display
}
To use the display() method for a particular instance of book:

myBook.display()
anotherBook.display()
```

Now (finally) we can start looking at JavaScript, you'll notice that many of these objects look suspiciously like HTML statements.

Key Topics:

- **JavaScript's object hierarchy.**

- **Getting user input.**

- **Working with links.**

- **Controlling the screen.**

Objects

The Object Hierarchy

This section is divided by object functionality. We'll look first at objects that you use to get user input, then we'll review hyperlink-related objects and screen control objects. We'll finish off with miscellaneous objects that don't happen to fit into one of these categories. But first, let's look at the overall object hierarchy.

In any HTML/JavaScript document, the top banana is the **document** object. A **document** object is defined by the <BODY> ... </BODY> tags in the file and whatever is between them. A given document object is defined by a particular URL. All other objects are subsumed within the **document** object.

One level below the document object is the **form** object. A document can contain one or more forms (a document can contain no forms, but formless documents are limited to the static display of text and pictures—not very interesting from the developer's standpoint). The **forms** property of the **document** object provides an indexed array of all the **form** objects within the **document**. The notation

```
document.forms[x]
```

provides access to the *x*th form in the document, and the notation

```
document.forms.length
```

returns the total number of forms in the document. As with all JavaScript arrays, elements are 0-based. If a document has 4 forms, **document.forms.length** will return 4 and you can access the forms as **document.forms[0]** through **document.forms[3].**

Each individual **form** can contain other objects of various types (described later in the chapter). These objects are usually related to user input and include boxes for entry of text, option buttons, and the like. Each **form** object has a **length** property that returns the number of objects on the form, and an **elements** property that provides an indexed array of these objects. Thus, the notation

```
document.forms[0].length
```

returns the number of objects on the first form in the current document, and

```
document.write(document.forms[1].elements[1].value)
```

returns the **value** property of the second object on the second form in the document. (Remember, the first form and the first object have index 0).

Getting User Input

First, I need to say a word about the format used to present the details of the JavaScript objects. I have typically split the object code over several lines for the sake of clarity. In a real program, it would all be on one line. Text in *italics* represents a placeholder for something we supply—some text, for example. Elements enclosed in square brackets are optional; we do not include the brackets in the code.

All of the user input objects start with the INPUT keyword, followed by the **type** parameter which specifies the particular object. This is followed by a variable number of additional parameters specific to the object.

You'll note several mentions of *submitting* forms in the discussion of objects. This is a process in which information that a user enters into an HTML page is sent to the server computer where the page originated. I'll bet you've seen this in your Web wanderings whenever you have filled out a survey or questionnaire, participated in an auction, or placed an order. We'll cover submitting forms later in the book; for now, it's enough that you know what the term means.

Button

The **Button** object displays a rectangular button with a caption in the document, much like the Command Buttons that you see in all Windows dialog boxes. The user can click the button with the mouse and trigger actions that are specified by the programmer. The syntax for a **Button** object is as follows:

```
<INPUT
type = "Button"
name = "name"
value = "text"
[onClick = "handler"] >
```

- *name* is a string literal specifying the object's **name** property. You use this name to refer to the object in code.

- *text* is a literal specifying the text to be displayed on the Button (its **value** property).

- *handler* specifies the JavaScript code that is executed when the Button is clicked. This is usually, but not necessarily, the name of a function to execute. Note that specifying an onClick handler is optional, but a **Button** object without one is pretty useless—yes, it will display; it just won't do anything.

PROPERTIES

There are two properties, **name** and **value**. These properties provide access in code to the values set with the identical keywords when the Button is defined.

METHODS

The Button object has a single method, **Click()**. Executing the **Click()** method has the same effect as the user clicking the Button.

EXAMPLE

Please see Listing 5.1 later in this chapter for an example of using a **Button** object.

Checkbox

The **Checkbox** object displays a small square box with an adjacent label. The user can click the box to turn it on or off. The box displays an "X" when the option is on, and the box is empty when the option is off. The syntax is:

```
<INPUT
type = Checkbox"
name = "name"
value = "Value"
[CHECKED]
[onClick = "handler"]
> text
```

- *name* is a string literal specifying the object's **name** property. You use this name to refer to the object in code.

- *value* specifies the value to be returned to the server when the form containing the Checkbox is submitted.

- CHECKED, if included, specifies that the Checkbox be initially displayed with an X (that is, "on"). Otherwise the Checkbox is initially off.

- *handler* specifies the JavaScript code that is executed when the Checkbox is clicked.

- *text* is the text that is displayed next to the Checkbox. Note that *text* is not actually part of the Checkbox definition, but is regular HTML text. If you want the label to be displayed to the left of the Checkbox, place *text* just before the Checkbox tag.

PROPERTIES

- *checked* property returns **true** if the Checkbox is checked, **false** if not. You can also set the state of the Checkbox by setting the **checked** property to true or false in code.

- *defaultChecked* property returns true if the default state of the Checkbox is "on"; in other words, if the CHECKED option was specified in the Checkbox tag.

- *name* property returns the value of the name attribute assigned in the Checkbox tag. You can also set this property to assign a different name attribute to the object.

- *value* property is used to obtain or change the object's value attribute.

METHODS

There is only a single method for the Checkbox object, **Click()**. Executing this method has the same effect as the user clicking the object.

Form

The **Form** object is central to many of the things you'll probably want to do with HTML and JavaScript. User-input objects, such as Text and Checkbox, must be placed on a form. You also use forms to post data to or retrieve data from a server.

A **Form** is delimited by <Form> and </Form> tags. The opening <Form> tag includes a variety of parameters that specify details of the form's behavior. Between the tags you place the HTML text and codes and other objects that will display on the form. The syntax of the <Form> tag's parameters is shown here.

```
<Form
name = "formname"
target = "windowname"
action = "serverURL"
method = method
enctype = "enctype"
[onSubmit = "handler"] >
```

- *name* is a string literal specifying the object's **name** property.

- *windowname* is the name of the browser window or frame where responses to form input are to be displayed. This parameter is required only if you want any data that is returned from the server to be displayed in a window other than the one where the form is displayed. This parameter can refer to an existing window, to a frame name specified in a <FRAMESET> tag, or to one of the literal frame names **_top**, **_parent**, **_self**, or **_blank**. It cannot be a JavaScript expression such as parent.frame.name.

- *serverURL* specifies the URL of the server where form input information is to be sent.

- *method* specifies how information is sent to the server. This parameter has two possible values. GET appends the data to the URL (on most servers, this information is placed in the environment variable QUERY_STRING). It is POST that sends the information as a body of data that will be available on *stdin*; the length of the data body will be placed in the environment variable CONTENT_LENGTH. The default is GET.

- *enctype* specifies the form's MIME encoding. The available settings are "application/x-www-form-urlencoded" and "multipart/form-data."

- *handler* specifies the JavaScript code to be executed when the form is submitted. The handler code can control whether the form is submitted or not by returning true or false, respectively. Typically, the handler code consists of the **return** keyword followed by a call to a verification function (which you write) that returns the desired value:

```
< FORM ... onSubmit = "return VerifyData(this)">
```

PROPERTIES

A Form object has the properties **action**, **encoding**, **method**, and **target** that correspond to the same items set in the Form tag. There is also the **elements** property, which provides a zero-based indexed array of all the objects on the Form (Text, Checkbox, etc.), and the **length** property, which returns the number of objects on the form.

METHODS

The only method for the Form object is **Submit**, which submits the form to the server. Executing this method in code has the same effect as clicking a Form's Submit button.

Password

The **Password** object is identical to a **Text** object except that its value is hidden by displaying asterisks in place of the typed characters. Also, it has no event handlers. As its name implies, it is used to permit the user to enter a private password without the worry of prying eyes. Use standard HTML syntax to define a Password object:

```
<INPUT
 TYPE="password"
 NAME=name
 [VALUE="value"]
 SIZE=size>
```

- *name* is a string literal specifying the Password object's name.

- *Value* is an optional string literal specifying the Password object's initial contents.

- *Size* is an integer value specifying the Password object's width, in characters.

PROPERTIES

- *defaultValue* property reflects the value set in the VALUE attribute (if any).

- *name property* reflects the object's name attribute.

- *value property* returns the current contents of the object.

METHODS

The **focus**() method sets the focus to the object.

The **blur**() method removes the focus from the object.

The **select**() method selects, or highlights, the text displayed in the object.

Radio

The **Radio** object is used to display a set of two or more option buttons on a form. The user can select one and only one of the options. Each of the Radio buttons in a group is given the same name, distinguished from each other by an index. The user clicks a button to turn it on, which automatically turns off the button in the group that was on previously. The syntax for creating a Radio object is:

```
<INPUT
 TYPE="radio"
```

```
NAME"name"
VALUE="value"
[CHECKED]
[onClick="handler"]> text
```

- *name* is the name of the Radio object group.

- v*alue* is the value returned to the server when the button is selected at the time the form is submitted.

- CHECKED is an optional argument that specifies that the button is to be selected (turned "on").

- *Handler* is the JavaScript code to be executed when the button is clicked.

- *Text* is the identifying text displayed next to the button.

To create a group of Radio buttons, define two or more Radio objects that have the same NAME attribute but different VALUE and *text* arguments. If you define a group with *n* members and the NAME *radioName*, you can then access them individually in code as follows:

```
radioName[0]
...
radioName[n-1]
```

PROPERTIES

- **checked** is used to turn a button on in code.

- **defaultChecked** is used to determine if a button's CHECKED attribute was defined.

- **length** returns the number of buttons in the Radio object.

- **name** reflects the NAME attribute.

- **Value** reflects the VALUE attribute.

METHODS

The **click()** method has the same effect as if the user had clicked the button.

EXAMPLE

The following code displays four radio buttons to permit the user to select their preferred programming language. Their selection is displayed in a text box.

```
<form name="form1">
Please select your preferred programming language: <p>
<INPUT type="radio" name="language" value="C"
 onClick="form1.lang.value = 'C'" > C<br>
<INPUT type="radio" name="language" value="C++"
 onClick="form1.lang.value = 'C++'" > C++<br>
<INPUT type="radio" name="language" value="Pascal"
 onClick="form1.lang.value = 'Pascal'" > Pascal<br>
<INPUT type="radio" name="language" value="Basic"
 onClick="form1.lang.value = 'Basic'" > Basic<p>
<INPUT type="text" name="lang" value="" ><br>
</form>
```

Reset

The **Reset** object displays a button on a form which, when clicked, resets all form elements to their default values. These are the same values as when the form was first loaded.

```
<INPUT
 TYPE="reset"
 NAME="name"
 VALUE="buttonText"
 [onClick="handler"] >
```

- *name* is the name of the Reset object.

- *buttonText* is the text to display on the button.

- *handler* is the JavaScript code to execute when the button is clicked.

The *handler* code is not required to clear the form—this is accomplished automatically. Use a handler if you want some other action performed when the Reset button is clicked.

PROPERTIES

- **name** and **value** properties reflect the NAME and VALUE attributes, respectively.

METHODS

The **click()** method has the same effect as the user clicking the button.

Select

Use the **Select** object to display a scrolling list or a selection list. The user can select one item from a selection list, or multiple items from a scrolling list. In the latter case, pressing Shift while clicking permits selection of multiple adjacent items from the list, and pressing Ctrl while clicking permits selection of multiple non-adjacent items.

```
<SELECT
 NAME="name"
 SIZE="size"
 [MULTIPLE]
 [onBlur="BlurHandler"]
 [onChange="ChangeHandler"]
 [onFocus=" ChangeHandler"] >
 <OPTION VALUE = "value_1" [SELECTED]> text_1
 ...
 <OPTION VALUE = "value_n" [SELECTED]> text_n
 </SELECT>
```

- *name* is the name of the **select** object.

- *size* is its vertical size—the number of items it can display without scrolling.

- MULTIPLE specifies a scrolling list. If omitted, a selection list is created.

- *BlurHandler, ChangeHandler,* and *ChangeHandler* are JavaScript code to be executed when the related event occurs.

- *Value1* through *value_n* and *text_1* through *text_n* are the value and associated text for each of the individual items displayed in the list.

- The optional SELECTED specifies that the associated list item is to be highlighted when the list is displayed.

The code to create a Select object consists of three parts:

1. A <SELECT ...> tag that specifies the object's name, size, type (single or multiple selections) and the event handlers for each of the object's three supported events.

2. A series of two or more <OPTION ...> tags, one for each item to be displayed in the Select object.

3. A </SELECT> tag marking the end of the object definition.

Within a Select object containing n items, the individual list items (the ones defined by the <OPTION> tags) are accessible in the indexed array **options[x]** where the index x ranges from 0 to *n-1*. The index of the currently selected item is available in the Select object's **SelectedIndex** property. Therefore, you obtain the value property of the selected item with the following code, which assumes that the Select object's NAME attribute is mySelect:

```
myselect.options[myselect.selectedIndex].value
```

PROPERTIES

The Select object itself has properties, and the individual OPTION items have their own properties. The Select object's properties are:

- **length** returns the number of items in the Select object.

- **name** reflects the Select object's NAME attribute.

- **options** accesses an indexed array of <OPTION> items.

- **selectedIndex** reflects the index of the currently selected option—or of the first selected option, if multiple options are selected.

Each OPTION item has the following properties:

- **defaultSelected** reflects the item's SELECTED attribute.

- **index** reflects the index of the item.

- **length** reflects the number of options in the parent Select object.

- **name** reflects the parent Select object's NAME attribute.

- **selected** allows you to determine whether an option item is selected, and can also be used to programatically select an option item.

- **selectedIndex** reflects the index of the selected option (same as the Select object's property of the same name).

- **text** reflects the text displayed in the list—that is, the text that follows <OPTION> tag.

- **value** reflects the VALUE attribute of the item.

METHODS

The Select object has no methods.

EXAMPLE

The first example shows another method of letting users select their preferred programming language (compare with the example for the Radio object). It displays a selection list with 4 language names displayed. When the user selects one, its value is displayed in a text box.

```
<form name="form1">
Please select your preferred programming language: <p>
<SELECT NAME="myselect" SIZE="5"
  onChange="document.form1.lang.value=myselect.options[myselect.
      selectedIndex].value">
<OPTION VALUE="C"> C
<OPTION VALUE="C++"> C++
<OPTION VALUE="Pascal"> Pascal
<OPTION VALUE="Basic"> Basic
</SELECT>
<INPUT TYPE="text" NAME="lang" VALUE="">
</form>
```

The second example is a complete program and can be loaded into the Netscape browser and run. It uses a multiple selection Select object to present a list of food items from which the user can select. When selection is completed, clicking a button displays the names of the selected items in a TextArea box.

Listing 5.1 Using the Select object to obtain multiple selections from the user.

```
<HTML>
<HEAD>
<script language="javascript">
function ReviewChoices()
  {
  var i, s
  s = "You selected "
```

```
  for (i = 0; i < document.form1.myselect.length; i++)
      {
      if (document.form1.myselect.options[i].selected)
        {
        s += document.form1.myselect.options[i].text
        s += ", "
        }
document.form1.output.value = s
      }
  }
</script>
</HEAD>
<BODY>
<form name="form1">
Hold down Ctrl and click to select the desired food items: <p>
<SELECT NAME="myselect" SIZE="8" MULTIPLE >
<OPTION> Onion Soup
<OPTION> Shrimp Cocktail
<OPTION> Country Pate
<OPTION> Breast of Chicken
<OPTION> Porterhouse Steak
<OPTION> Sauteed Vegetables
<OPTION> Vanilla Ice Cream
<OPTION> Fruit Cocktail
</SELECT>
<p>Then click the button to review your choices.
<INPUT TYPE="button" NAME="review" VALUE="Review Choices"
 onClick="ReviewChoices()"><br>
<TEXTAREA NAME="output" WRAP="virtual" ROWS=2 COLS=40> </TEXTAREA>
</form>
</BODY>
</HTML>
```

Submit

The **Submit** object displays as a button which, when clicked, causes the form to be submitted.

```
<INPUT
 TYPE="submit":
 NAME="name"
VALUE=" ext"
[onClick="handler""
```

- *name* is the **Submit** object's name.

- *text* is the text displayed on the **Submit** button.

- *handler* is the JavaScript code to be executed when the button is clicked.

When a **Submit** object is clicked, the contents of the form it is on are submitted to the URL, identified by the form's **Action** property. A new page is always loaded when a form is submitted. This will be the same page unless a different one is specified.

PROPERTIES

The **name** and **value** properties reflect the **Submit** object's NAME and VALUE attributes, respectively.

METHODS

The **Click** method has the same effect as the user clicking the Submit button.

Text

The **Text** object displays a text box for display and input of data on an HTML form. It is identical to the standard HTML **Text** object with the addition of event handlers.

```
<INPUT
  TYPE="text"
  NAME="name"
  VALUE="value"
  SIZE="size"
  [onBlur="BlurHandler"]
  [onChange="ChangeHandler"]
  [onFocus="FocusHandler"]
  [onSelect="SelectHandler"] >
```

- *name* is the name of the Text object.

- *value* is the text displayed in the text box.

- *size* is a value specifying the width, in characters, of the object.

- *BlurHandler, ChangeHandler, FocusHandler,* and *SelectHandler* represent the JavaScript code that will be executed when the related event occurs to the Text object.

PROPERTIES

The **defaultValue** property reflects the Text object's VALUE attribute— its initial value when first created. The **value** property is used to retrieve and set its current contents. The **name** property reflects the object's NAME attribute.

METHODS

The **focus()**, **blur()**, and **select()** methods have the same effect as if the associated event had been performed by the user.

Textarea

A **Textarea** object is similar to a Text object except it can contain multiple lines of text. It permits the user to enter larger pieces of data.

```
<TEXTAREA
 NAME="name"
 ROWS=rows
COLS=cols
WRAP="off|virtual|physical"
[onBlur="BlurHandler"]
 [onChange="ChangeHandler"]
 [onFocus="FocusHandler"]
 [onSelect="SelectHandler"] >
text
</TEXTAREA>
```

- *name* is the name of the Textarea object.

- *rows* and *cols* specify the size of the object, in characters.

- *Text* is the text to display in the Textarea object.

- The setting of Wrap controls the wrapping of text lines when they reach the right edge of the Textarea object:

    - *off:* Lines are displayed as typed with no wrapping

    - *virtual:* Lines are wrapped as needed on the display but are submitted as types.

    - *Physical:* Lines are wrapped both for display and submitting.

- *BlurHandler, ChangeHandler, FocusHandler,* and *SelectHandler* are the JavaScript code fragments that will be executed when the related event occurs to the Textarea object.

PROPERTIES

- **defaultValue** reflects the VALUE attribute, the contents of the object when it was first created.

- **name** reflects the object's NAME attribute.

- **value** is used to set and retrieve the current contents of the Textarea object.

METHODS

The **focus()** and **blur()** methods are used respectively to give the focus to and remove the focus from the **Textarea** object. The **select()** method selects (highlights) the contents of the object. Use **select()** in conjunction with **focus()** to move the focus to the **Textarea** object and select its entire contents in preparation for user input.

EXAMPLE

See the example under the **Select** object for a demonstration of using the Textarea object.

Working with Hyperlinks

Anchor

A section of text that can be the target of a hypertext link, an anchor can also be a link object, serving as the target of one link and the source of another. To define an anchor object, use standard HTML syntax:

```
<A [HREF="locationOrURL"]
NAME="name"
[TARGET="window"]>
anchorText
</A>
```

- *locationOrURL* identifies a destination anchor or URL. If this optional attribute is present, the anchor object is also a link object.

- *name* specifies the tag that becomes a valid hypertext target within the current document.

- *window* specifies the window into which the link is loaded. This attribute is required only if *locationOrURL* is specified.

- anchorText specifies the text to display at the anchor.

You can reference the anchor objects programmatically by using the anchors array. This array contains an entry for each <A>...</A> tag in the document that contains a NAME attribute. The order of anchor objects in the array is the same as their order in the document. The first anchor is **document.anchors[0]**, the second is **document. anchors[1]**, and so on. The anchors array is read-only. If an anchor object is also a link object, the object has entries in both the anchors and links arrays. Note that you can also define an anchor using the String object's anchor method.

PROPERTIES

The **anchor** object has no properties. The anchors array has one property, **length**, which returns the number of elements in the array. Thus the array elements range from **document.anchors[0]** to **document.anchors[document. anchors.length - 1]**.

METHODS

None.

Link

A link is text or an image that serves as a hypertext link. When the user clicks the link, the link target is loaded into its target window. A link can also be an anchor object. To define a link, use standard HTML syntax with the addition of the **onClick** and **onMouseOver** event handlers:

```
<A HREF="locationOrURL"
[NAME="name"]
[TARGET="window"]
[onClick="ClickHandler"]
[onMouseOver="MouseOverHandler"]>
text
</A>
```

- *locationOrURL* identifies the target of the link.

- *name* specifies the tag that becomes an available hypertext target within the current document. If this attribute is present, the link object is also an anchor object.

- *window* specifies the window that the link is loaded into; *window* can specify an existing window, a frame name specified in a <FRAMESET> tag, or one of the literal frame names **_top**, **_parent**, **_self**, or **_blank**. It cannot be a JavaScript expression such as **parent.frameName** or **windowName.frameName**.

- *text* is the text displayed as the link in the document.

Each **link** object is also a **location** object and has the same properties (see the entry for **location** object for more information). You can also define a link using the **string** object's **link** method. You can access a document's **link** objects using the **links[]** array, which contains an entry for each link in the document. The order of **link** objects in the array is the same as their order in the document. The first link is **document.links[0]**, the second is **document.links[1]**, and so on. The links array is read-only. If a link object is also an anchor object, the object has entries in both the anchors and links arrays.

When the user clicks a link object and displays the destination document, the destination document's referrer property will contain the URL of the source document (the one containing the original link).

PROPERTIES

The **link** object has the following properties. Most of these are in common with the location object and permit extraction of various parts of the target URL.

- **hash** specifies the anchor name, if present, in the target URL. The hash is the optional part of the URL following the hash symbol (#) that identifies a specific location within the document.

- **host** specifies the hostname:port portion of the target URL. If the URL does not include a port, then the **host** property is identical to the **hostname** property.

- **hostname** specifies the host and domain name, or IP address, of the target URL.

- **href** specifies the entire target URL.

- **pathname** specifies the URL/path portion of the target URL.

- **port** specifies the communications port specified in the target URL, if present.

- **protocol** specifies the protocol at the beginning of the target URL, including the colon. For example, http:.

- **search** specifies the query portion of the target URL, if present. This is a string beginning with a question mark in the URL.

- **target** reflects the TARGET attribute specified in the link tag.

The links array has one property, **length**, which reflects the number of links in the document.

METHODS

None.

Location

A **location** object represents a complete URL. You use the object's properties to extract specific portions of the URL. You do not create location objects, but rather make use of the location object that is associated with each **document** object. To use a location object, use the following syntax:

```
[windowRef.]location.propertyName
```

- windowRef is the value returned when the window was created, or one of the keywords top or parent.

- propertyName is one of the properties listed below.

The **location** object is contained by the **window** object. If you reference a **location** object without specifying windowRef, the location object represents the current location. If you do specify windowRef, the location object represents the location (URL) of the specified window. Be careful not to confuse the **location** object with the **location** property of the **document** object. You cannot change the value of the location property (**document.location**), but you can change the value of the **location** object's properties.

PROPERTIES

Each URL can contain the following components:

```
protocol//hostname:port pathname search hash
```

The protocol and hostname parts are required, and the other components may or may not be present. The following properties permit extraction of specific parts of the URL:

- **hash** specifies the anchor name, if present, in the target URL. The hash is the optional part of the URL following the hash symbol (#) that identifies a specific location within the document.

- **host** specifies the hostname:port portion of the target URL. If the URL does not include a port, then the host property is identical to the host-name property.

- **hostname** specifies the host and domain name, or IP address, of the target URL.

- **href** specifies the entire target URL.

- **pathname** specifies the URL/path portion of the target URL.

- **port** specifies the communications port specified in the target URL, if present.

- **protocol** specifies the protocol at the beginning of the target URL, including the colon. For example, http:.

- **search** specifies the query portion of the target URL, if present. This is a string beginning with a question mark in the URL.

URL TYPES

When you specify a URL, you should use standard URL formats and JavaScript statements. Here is the syntax for specifying some of the common URL types:

URL type	Protocol	Example
JavaScript code	javascript:	javascript:history.go(-2)
Navigator info	about:	about:cache

World Wide Web	http:	http://www.coriolis.com/
File	file:	file:///javascript/calculat.html
FTP	ftp:	ftp://ftp.coriolis.com/pub/ javascript
MailTo	mailto:	mailto:paitken@acpub.duke. edu
Usenet	news:	news://news.duke.edu/comp.lang. javascript
Gopher	gopher:	gopher.myhost.com

The javascript: protocol evaluates the expression after the colon (:), if present, and loads a page pointed to by the string value of the expression. If the expression evaluates to undefined, no new page loads.

The about: protocol provides information on Navigator and has the following syntax:

about:[cache|plugins]

about: by itself has the same effect as choosing About Netscape from the Navigator Help menu.

about:cache displays statistics about the disk cache.

about:plug-ins displays information about plug-ins that have been configured. This is the same as choosing About Plug-ins from the Navigator Help menu.

Controlling the Screen

Frame

A frame is an independently scrollable section of a window. Using frames, a page can display two or more different URLs on the same page. For example, you could display a table of contents or an index in one frame and the textual material in another. Frames can display different URLs and can also be targeted by other URLs, all within the same screen. A set of frames makes up a page.

You use standard HTML syntax to define a frame object. Frame objects are created within <FRAMESET ...> </FRAMESET> tags, which have the following components:

1. An opening <FRAMESET tag that specifies the frame sizes and, optionally, the JavaScript code to be executed when the window containing the frames is loaded and unloaded.

2. A series of two or more <FRAME...> tags that each define the contents and name of an individual frame.

3. A closing </FRAMESET> tag.

The syntax is as follows:

```
<FRAMESET
ROWS="rowHeightList"
COLS="columnWidthList"
[onLoad="LoadHandler"]
[onUnload="UnloadHandler"]>
[<FRAME SRC="locationOrURL" NAME="name">]
...
[<FRAME SRC="locationOrURL" NAME="name">]
</FRAMESET>
```

- *rowHeightList* is a comma-separated list of values specifying the heights of the frames. The default unit is pixels. You can append an optional suffix to use another measurement unit. Most commonly, the % symbol is used to define frame sizes as percentages of the total window size.

- *columnWidthList* is a comma-separated list of values specifying the widths of the frames.

- *LoadHandler* and *UnloadHander* are JavaScript code to be executed when the specified event occurs. While these event handlers are specified in the <FRAMESET> tag, they are actually event handlers for the window object.

- Each <FRAME> tag defines an individual frame as follows:

- *locationOrURL* specifies the URL of the document to be displayed in the frame. The URL cannot include an anchor (hash).

- *name* specifies the frame object's name, which can be used as a target of hyperlink jumps.

Be aware that terminology relating to frames can be confusing. You will sometimes see the term "frame" used to refer to the entire frameset, and the individual frames within it are then called child frames. At other times, the term "frame" is used to refer to the individual frames, and the term parent frame refers to the containing frameset.

The **frames** array contains an entry for each child frame in a frameset.

PROPERTIES

- **frames** is an array reflecting all the frames in a window.

- **name** reflects the NAME attribute of an individual child frame.

- **length** reflects the number of child frames within a frameset.

- **parent** is a synonym for the window containing the current frameset.

- **self** is a synonym for the current frameset.

- **window** is a synonym for the current frameset.

The frames array has the following property:

- **length** returns the number of child frames within the frameset.

METHODS

The **clearTimeout()** and **setTimeout()** methods are used to manipulate the timer. See the individual entries in the Methods section for more information.

EXAMPLE

This example consists of four separate HTML files, FRAMES1.HTML through FRAMES4.HTML, which are shown in Listings 5.2 through 5.5. You run it by loading FRAMES1.HTML into a frames-capable browser. It will

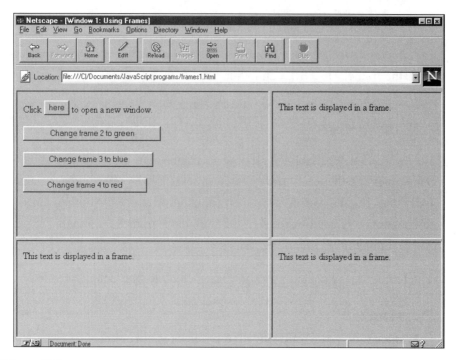

Figure 5.1
The frames demonstration program.

display a page with four frames, as shown in Figure 5.1. One frame displays several buttons which allow you to change the background color of the other frames, and one button which opens a new browser window which will also display a group of frames.

Listing 5.2 FRAMES1.HTML, the main file in the frames demonstration.

```
<HTML>
<HEAD>
<TITLE>Window 1: Using Frames</TITLE>
</HEAD>
<FRAMESET ROWS="60%,40%" COLS="60%,40%">
<FRAME SRC=frames2.html NAME="frame1">
<FRAME SRC=frametxt.html NAME="frame2">
<FRAME SRC=frametxt.html NAME="frame3">
<FRAME SRC=frametxt.html NAME="frame4">
</FRAMESET>
</HTML>
```

Listing 5.3   FRAMES2.HTML.

```
<HTML>
<HEAD>
</HEAD>
<BODY>
<FORM>
Click
<INPUT TYPE="button" VALUE="here"
 onClick="window.open('frames3.html','Window 2')">
to open a new window.
<P>
<INPUT TYPE="button" VALUE="Change frame 2 to green"
   onClick="parent.frames[1] .document.bgColor='green'">
<P>
<INPUT TYPE="button" VALUE="Change frame 3 to blue"
   onClick="parent.frames[2].document.bgColor='blue'">
<P>
<INPUT TYPE="button" VALUE="Change frame 4 to red"
   onClick="top.frames[3].document.bgColor='red'">
</FORM>
</BODY>
</HTML>
```

Listing 5.4   FRAMES3.HTML.

```
<HTML>
<HEAD>
<TITLE>Window 1: Using Frames</TITLE>
</HEAD>
<FRAMESET ROWS="70%,30%" COLS="30%,70%">
<FRAME SRC=frames4.html NAME="frame1">
<FRAME SRC=frames4.html NAME="frame2">
<FRAME SRC=frames4.html NAME="frame3">
</FRAMESET>
</HTML>
```

Listing 5.5   FRAMES4.HTML.

```
<HTML>
<BODY>
<P>This is text in a frame in the second window.
</BODY>
</HTML>
```

Window

This term represents a browser window. The Window object is the "parent" object for each **document**, **location**, and **history** object group. The Window object is the top-level object in the JavaScript hierarchy. Note that a **Frame** object is also a Window.

To define a window, use the open method:

```
newWindow = window.open("URL", "name" [,"features"])
```

- newWindow is the name of the new window. You use this variable when referring to the window's properties, methods, etc.

- URL indicates the document to load into the new window. If URL is an empty string, a blank window is created.

- *name* is the window name. Use the *name* in the TARGET attribute of a <FORM> or <A> tag.

- *features* specifies which of the available window components are to be displayed, as described below.

A Window object supports two events, **Load** and **Unload**. You define event handlers for a Window object in the <BODY> or <FRAMESET> tag of the Window's document:

```
<BODY
   ...
   [onLoad="loadHandler"]
   [onUnload="unloadHandler"]>
</BODY>

<FRAMESET
   ...
   [onLoad="loadHandler"]
   [onUnload="unloadHandler"]>
   ...
</FRAMESET>
```

You specify the features of the new window by including a comma-delimited list of one or more of the following items.

- toolbar

- location

- directories

- status

- menubar

- scrollbars

- resizable

- width=*pixels*

- height=*pixels*

A feature is turned on if its keyword is included in the *features* argument alone, or set to 1 or true. It is turned off by setting it to false or 0.

The existence of the current window is guaranteed, so you do not have to explicitly reference the window in order to access its methods and properties. For example, the property assignment

```
status="Waiting for Godot"
```

will automatically access the current Window object's status property. Likewise,

```
close()
```

calls the Window object's **close**() method. Note, however, that when you open or close a window within an event handler, you must specify **window.open**() or **window.close**() instead of simply using **open**() or **close**(). This is due to the scoping of static objects in JavaScript, which results in a call to **close**() without an object specifier accessing the **document** object's **close**() method.

To reference a Window's **frame** objects in your code, use the **frames** array. This array exists for every Window whose document includes a <FRAMESET> tag.

PROPERTIES

The **self** and **window** properties are synonyms for the current window, and can be used to refer to the current window. For example, you can close the current window by calling either **window.close**() or **self.close**(). You can use these properties to make your code more readable. The **top** and **parent** properties are also synonyms that can be used in place of the window name. The property **top** refers to the top-most Navigator window, and **parent** refers to a window containing a frameset. Other properties are:

- **defaultStatus** returns the default status bar message.

- **frames** is an array reflecting all the frames in a window.

- **length** returns the number of frames in a parent window.

- **name** reflects the *name* argument to the **open()** method.

- **parent** is a synonym for the *name* argument for a window containing a frameset.

- **self** is a synonym for the *name* argument and refers to the current window.

- **status** is used to create a temporary message in the window's status bar.

- **top** is a synonym for the *name* argument and refers to the top-most Navigator window.

- **window** is a synonym for the *name* argument and refers to the current window.

METHODS

- **alert**: Displays an Alert dialog box with a message and an OK button.

- **close**: Closes the Window.

- **confirm**: Displays a Confirm dialog box with the specified message and OK and Cancel buttons. This method returns true if the user selects OK, false for Cancel.

- **open**: Creates a new window.

- **Prompt**: Displays a Prompt dialog box with a message and an input field.

- *clearTimeout* and *setTimeout*: Used to manipulate the timer.

EXAMPLE

The example in Listings 5.6 and 5.7 includes two HTML files. When you load Windows1.html into your browser, it creates a second window and loads Windows2.html into it. It also displays a series of buttons that let you create an entry message window, write a message to it, then close the two new windows.

Listing 5.6   Windows1.HTML.

```
<HTML>
<HEAD>
<TITLE>Window 1</TITLE>
</HEAD>
<BODY>
<SCRIPT>
window2=open("windows2.html","window2","width=300,height=100")
</SCRIPT>
<FORM NAME="form1">
<P><INPUT TYPE="button" VALUE="Open a message window"
onClick="window3=window.open('','messageWindow','width=175,height=50')">
<P><INPUT TYPE="button" VALUE="Display a message"
   onClick="window3.document.writeln('Hi! I am a
 message.');window3.document.close()">
<P><INPUT TYPE="button" VALUE="Close the message window"
   onClick="window3.close()">
<P><INPUT TYPE="button" VALUE="Close the second window"
   onClick="window2.close()">
</FORM>
</BODY>
</HTML>
```

Listing 5.7   Windows2.HTML.

```
<HEAD>
<TITLE>Window 2</TITLE>
</HEAD>
<BODY>
<H2>This is the second window.</H2>
</BODY>
</HTML>
```

Other Stuff

The objects covered in this section don't fall into any particular category, but you'll find some very valuable tools here!

Math

The **Math** object is a built-in JavaScript object that permits you to perform mathematical operations and evaluate selected mathematical constants. Constants are retrieved as properties of the **Math** object and mathematical operations are object methods. The general syntax is:

```
var = Math.property
var = Math.method(argument)
```

PROPERTIES

All of the **Math** object's properties are read-only.

E Euler's constant (e), the base of the natural logarithms.

LN2	The natural logarithm of 2.
LN10	The natural logarithm of 10.
LOG2E	The base 2 logarithm of e.
LOG10E	The base 10 logarithm of e.
PI	The ratio of a circles circumference to its diameter.
SQRT1_2	The square root of 0.5.
SQRT2	The square root of 2.

METHODS

Please refer to the individual methods in the Methods section for further details.

abs()	The absolute value of a number.
acos()	The arc cosine of a number.
asin()	The arc sine of a number.
atan()	The arc tangent of a number.
ceil()	The smallest integer equal to or greater than a number.
cos()	The cosine of a number.
exp()	The constant e raised to a power.
floor()	The largest number equal to or less than a number.
log()	The base 10 logarithm of a number.
max()	Requires two arguments. Returns the larger one.
min()	Requires two arguments. Returns the smaller one.

pow()	Requires two arguments. Returns the first argument raised to the power of the second.
random()	Returns a pseudo random number between 0 and 1. This method is available on Unix platforms only.
round()	The value of a number rounded to the nearest integer.
sin()	The sine of a number.
sqrt()	The square root of a number.
tan()	The tangent of a number.

Date

The **Date** object is used to work with dates and times. To create a Date object, use one of the following syntax forms:

```
dateName = new Date()
dateName = new Date("month day, year hours:minutes:seconds")
dateName = new Date(year, month, day)
dateName = new Date(year, month, day, hours, minutes, seconds)
```

- dateName is the name of the new Date object.

- For the second syntax example, *month*, *day*, *year*, *hours*, *minutes*, and *seconds* are string values. For the third and fourth examples, they are integer values.

The first syntax example creates a **Date** object containing the current date and time. The other examples create a **Date** object set to the specified parameters. If you omit hours, minutes, or seconds from form 2 or 4 of the syntax, the value will be set to zero. JavaScript stores dates internally as the number of milliseconds since January 1, 1970 00:00:00. Dates prior to 1970 are not allowed.

Exceptions: The **Date** object's parse and UTC methods are static methods that you use as follows:

```
Date.UTC(parameters)
Date.parse(parameters)
```

PROPERTIES

None.

METHODS

getDate	Returns an integer between 1 and 31 representing the day of the month.
getDay	Returns an integer between 0 (Sunday) and 6 (Saturday), representing the day of the week.
getHours	Returns an integer between 0 and 23, representing the hour.
getMinutes	Returns an integer between 0 and 59, representing the minute.
getMonth	Returns an integer between 0 (January) and 11 (December), representing the month.
getSeconds	Returns an integer between 0 and 59, representing the second.
getTime	Returns a value indicating the number of milliseconds since January 1, 1970 00:00:00.
getTimeZoneoffset	Returns the number of minutes the current time zone is offset from Greenwich Mean Time (GMT). Reflects daylight savings time also.
getYear	Returns an integer specifying the number of years since 1900. Thus 1996 is returned as 96.
parse	Converts a date string such as "Jan 1, 1996" to a JavaScript date number (milliseconds since January 1, 1970).
setDate	Sets the day of the month of a Date object to the specified date (1-31). The month, year, and time portions of the Date object are not changed.

setHours	Sets the hour of a Date object to the specified value (0-23). The month, year, day, minute, and second portions of the Date object are not changed.
setMinutes	Sets the minutes of a Date object to the specified value (0-59). The month, year, day, hour, and second portions of the Date object are not changed.
setMonth	Sets the month of a Date object to the specified value (0-11). The year, day, and time portions of the Date object are not changed.
setSeconds	Sets the seconds of a Date object to the specified value (0-59). The month, year, day, hour, and minute portions of the Date object are not changed.
setTime	Sets a Date object to the specified value, expressed as milliseconds since January 1, 1970 00:00:00.
setYear	Sets the year of a Date object to the specified value (actual year minus 1900). The month, day, and time portions of the Date object are not changed.
toGMTString	Returns the date as an Internet standard GMT string. The exact format of this string depends on the platform in use.
toLocaleString	Returns the date as a string according to the locale conventions.
UTC	Pass a comma-delimited date string to this method and it returns the Universal Coordinated Time as the number of milliseconds since January 1, 1970 00:00:00.

Note: T he **parse()** and **UTC()** methods are static methods. Use them with the generic Date object rather that with a Date object you have created. For example:

```
var gmt = Date.UTC(96, 11, 1, 0, 0, 0)
```

and not

```
myDate = new Date()
var gmt = myDate.UTC(96, 11, 1, 0, 0, 0)
```

Document

The **Document** object represents the current document. It contains information about the document and provides methods for displaying HTML. To define a document object, use standard HTML syntax:

```
<BODY
    BACKGROUND="backgroundImage"
    BGCOLOR="backgroundColor"
    TEXT="foregroundColor"
    LINK="unfollowedLinkColor"
    ALINK="activatedLinkColor"
    VLINK="followedLinkColor"
    [onLoad="loadHandler"]
    [onUnload="unloadHandler"]>
</BODY>
```

- *backgroundImage* is a filename or URL specifying a GIF or JPG file to tile as the document's background.

- The various *...Color* arguments specify the color to be used to display the associated element in the document. They can be expressed as a hexadecimal RGB triplet (in the format "rrggbb" or "#rrggbb") or as one of the string literals listed in Color Values later in the chapter.

- *loadHandler* and *unloadHandler* are JavaScript code to execute when the associated event occurs.

An HTML document consists of a header inside <HEAD> ... </HEAD> tags, and a body within <BODY> ... </BODY> tags. The header includes information on the document's title and base, the absolute URL base to be used for relative URL links in the document. The body is defined by the current URL, and includes all other HTML elements of the document. The document object includes anchors, forms, and links arrays that permit you to access the associated document elements. These arrays contain an entry for each anchor, form, or link in a document. Note that while the **onLoad** and **onUnload** event handlers are specified in the <BODY> tag, they are actually event handlers for the **Window** object.

PROPERTIES

- **alinkColor** reflects the activated link color (ALINK attribute).

- **anchors** is an array reflecting all the anchors in the document.

- **bgColor** reflects the background color (BGCOLOR attribute).

- **cookie** specifies a cookie.

- **fgColor** reflects the text color (TEXT attribute).

- **forms** is an array reflecting all the forms in a document.

- **lastModified** reflects the date the document was last modified.

- **linkColor** reflects the non-activated link color (LINK attribute).

- **links** is an array reflecting all the links in the document.

- **location** reflects the complete URL of the document.

- **referrer** reflects the URL of the calling document.

- **title** reflects the contents of the <TITLE> tag.

- **vlinkColor** reflects the followed link color (VLINK attribute).

METHODS

clear   Erases the contents of the document window.

close   Closes the document output stream, forcing display of all elements.

open	Opens a stream to collect the output of write or writeln methods. See the Open method for more details.
write	Writes one or more HTML expressions to the document.
writeln	As write(), but adds a newline character at the end of output.

COOKIE MONSTER

What's this "cookie" property? JavaScript has the ability to store small pieces of textual information, called *cookies*, on the local disk. Doesn't this violate the safety provision of JavaScript that it cannot modify the local hard disk? Not really. The cookies are always stored in a file named COOKIES.TXT, which is limited to plain text so it cannot cause any mischief.

Cookies were originally developed in response to a childish and unethical practice of some Web page developers. The impact of some Web pages is evaluated by the number of "hits," or people visiting the site. This is part of the rationale behind the "hit counters" you see on some pages. Firms buying advertising on the site may pay more for a high-impact site. Developers would therefore write "robot" programs that would repeatedly log onto their site and artificially inflate the hit count and the perceived impact of the site. By storing an identifying token in a local cookie, a JavaScript program can identify repeat visitors and refuse to count them more than once.

Hidden

A text object that is not displayed on a form is a hidden object and is used for passing name/value pairs when a form is submitted. To define a hidden object, use the following syntax:

```
<INPUT
   TYPE="hidden"
   NAME="name"
   [VALUE="text"]>
```

- *name* specifies the name of the hidden object.

- *text* specifies the initial value of the hidden object.

A **hidden** object cannot be seen or modified by a user, but you can programmatically change the value of the object by changing its **value** property. You can use hidden objects for client/server communication.

PROPERTIES
The **name** and **value** properties reflect the corresponding attributes of the object.

METHODS
None.

History

The **History** object contains information on the URLs that the user has visited within a particular window. The URLs are stored in the *history list*, and are typically accessible through the browser's Go command. The History object is a built-in property of the **Document** object.

PROPERTIES
The **length** property returns the number of entries in the history list.

METHODS

back	Loads the previous URL in the history list.
forward	Loads the next URL in the history list.
go	Loads the URL at the specified position in the history list, indexed relative to the current location.

EXAMPLES
This code loads the URL that the user visited two steps back in the current window:

```
history.go(-2)
```

This code causes windowNew to go back one item in its history list:

```
windowNew.history.back()
```

This example causes the second frame in a frameset to go back two items:

```
parent.frames[1].history.go(-2)
```

This code causes the frame named indexFrame to go back one item:

```
parent.indexFrame.history.back()
```

The following example causes the frame named indexFrame in indexWindow to go back two items:

```
indexWindow.indexFrame2.history.go(-2)
```

Navigator

The object contains information about the version of Navigator in use. When other browsers that support JavaScript become available, they will probably use this object in a similar fashion. You can, for example, use the Navigator object to determine which version of the Navigator your users have.

PROPERTIES

All of the Navigator object's properties are read-only.

appCodeName   returns the code name of the browser. For Netscape Navigator this is "mozilla."

appName   returns the name of the browser. For Netscape Navigator this is "Netscape."

appVersion   specifies version information for the Navigator in the format releaseNumber (platform; country). releaseNumber is the version number of Navigator; platform is the platform upon which the Navigator is running (e.g., "Win32"); and country is either "I" for the international release, or "U" for the domestic U.S. release (the domestic release has a stronger encryption feature).

userAgent   specifies the user-agent header, information sent from the client to servers for identification purposes. It is usually a combination of the appCodeName and appVersion properties.

METHODS

None.

String

Any series of characters. The **String** object is a built-in JavaScript object. Wherever a series of characters exists, it is a **String** object. A string can be represented as a literal enclosed by single or double quotes. For example, the code

```
var S = "JavaScript"
```

creates a **String** object named S.

PROPERTIES

length returns the length of the string.

METHODS

See the individual method entries for more details.

anchor	Creates an HTML anchor that can be used as a hypertext target.
big	Displays the string in a larger font.
blink	Displays the string blinking.
bold	Displays the string in boldface.
charAt	Returns the character in the string at the specified position.
fixed	Displays the string in a fixed pitch font.
fontcolor	Displays the string in the specified color.
fontsize	Displays the string at the specified font size.
indexOf	Returns the position of a substring in the string.
italics	Displays the string in italics.

lastIndexOf	Returns the position of the last occurrence of substring in the string..
link	Creates a hypertext link to a specified URL.
small	Displays the string in a small font.
strike	Displays the string as struck-out text.
sub	Displays the string as a subscript.
substring	Returns a substring from the string, with the specified starting and ending positions.
sup	Displays the string as a superscript.
toLowerCase	Displays the string in all lowercase letters.
toUpperCase	Displays the string in all uppercase letters.

EXAMPLE

The following code displays the line "JavaScript is great" in the document, with "JavaScript" in large text and "great" in italics.

```
<SCRIPT>
var js = "JavaScript"
var g = "great"
document.write(js.big())
document.write(" is ")
document.write(g.italics())
document.close()
</SCRIPT>
```

Color Values

JavaScript provides a large selection of predefined color names that you can use wherever an RGB triplet is required. These string literals can be used, for example, to specify colors in the **alinkColor**, **bgColor**, **fgColor**, **linkColor**, and **vlinkColor** properties and the fontcolor method. You can also use these color names to set the color in HTML reflections tags, such as the BGCOLOR attribute in the <BODY...> tag. These color names and their RGB values are listed below.

Color	Red	Green	Blue
aliceblue	F0	F8	FF
antiquewhite	FA	EB	D7
aqua	00	FF	FF
aquamarine	7F	FF	D4
azure	F0	FF	FF
beige	F5	F5	DC
bisque	FF	E4	C4
black	00	00	00
blanchedalmond	FF	EB	CD
blue	00	00	FF
blueviolet	8A	2B	E2
brown	A5	2A	2A
burlywood	DE	B8	87
cadetblue	5F	9E	A0
chartreuse	7F	FF	00
chocolate	D2	69	1E
coral	FF	7F	50
cornflowerblue	64	95	ED
cornsilk	FF	F8	DC
crimson	DC	14	3C
cyan	00	FF	FF
darkblue	00	00	8B
darkcyan	00	8B	8B
darkgoldenrod	B8	86	0B
darkgray	A9	A9	A9
darkgreen	00	64	00
darkkhaki	BD	B7	6B
darkmagenta	8B	00	8B
darkolivegreen	55	6B	2F
darkorange	FF	8C	00
darkorchid	99	32	CC
darkred	8B	00	00
darksalmon	E9	96	7A
darkseagreen	8F	BC	8F

Color	Red	Green	Blue
darkslateblue	48	3D	8B
darkslategray	2F	4F	4F
darkturquoise	00	CE	D1
darkviolet	94	00	D3
deeppink	FF	14	93
deepskyblue	00	BF	FF
dimgray	69	69	69
dodgerblue	1E	90	FF
firebrick	B2	22	22
floralwhite	FF	FA	F0
forestgreen	22	8B	22
fuchsia	FF	00	FF
gainsboro	DC	DC	DC
ghostwhite	F8	F8	FF
gold	FF	D7	00
goldenrod	DA	A5	20
gray	80	80	80
green	00	80	00
greenyellow	AD	FF	2F
honeydew	F0	FF	F0
hotpink	FF	69	B4
indianred	CD	5C	5C
indigo	4B	00	82
ivory	FF	FF	F0
khaki	F0	E6	8C
lavender	E6	E6	FA
lavenderblush	FF	F0	F5
lawngreen	7C	FC	00
lemonchiffon	FF	FA	CD
lightblue	AD	D8	E6
lightcoral	F0	80	80
lightcyan	E0	FF	FF
lightgoldenrodyellow	FA	FA	D2

Color	Red	Green	Blue
lightgreen	90	EE	90
lightgrey	D3	D3	D3
lightpink	FF	B6	C1
lightsalmon	FF	A0	7A
lightseagreen	20	B2	AA
lightskyblue	87	CE	FA
lightslategray	77	88	99
lightsteelblue	B0	C4	DE
lightyellow	FF	FF	E0
lime	00	FF	00
limegreen	32	CD	32
linen	FA	F0	E6
magenta	FF	00	FF
maroon	80	00	00
mediumaquamarine	66	CD	AA
mediumblue	00	00	CD
mediumorchid	BA	55	D3
mediumpurple	93	70	DB
mediumseagreen	3C	B3	71
mediumslateblue	7B	68	EE
mediumspringgreen	00	FA	9A
mediumturquoise	48	D1	CC
mediumvioletred	C7	15	85
midnightblue	19	19	70
mintcream	F5	FF	FA
mistyrose	FF	E4	E1
moccasin	FF	E4	B5
navajowhite	FF	DE	AD
navy	00	00	80
oldlace	FD	F5	E6
olive	80	80	00
olivedrab	6B	8E	23
orange	FF	A5	00

Color	Red	Green	Blue
orangered	FF	45	00
orchid	DA	70	D6
palegoldenrod	EE	E8	AA
palegreen	98	FB	98
paleturquoise	AF	EE	EE
palevioletred	DB	70	93
papayawhip	FF	EF	D5
peachpuff	FF	DA	B9
peru	CD	85	3F
pink	FF	C0	CB
plum	DD	A0	DD
powderblue	B0	E0	E6
purple	80	00	80
red	FF	00	00
rosybrown	BC	8F	8F
royalblue	41	69	E1
saddlebrown	8B	45	13
salmon	FA	80	72
sandybrown	F4	A4	60
seagreen	2E	8B	57
seashell	FF	F5	EE
sienna	A0	52	2D
silver	C0	C0	C0
skyblue	87	CE	EB
slateblue	6A	5A	CD
slategray	70	80	90
snow	FF	FA	FA
springgreen	00	FF	7F
steelblue	46	82	B4
tan	D2	B4	8C
teal	00	80	80
thistle	D8	BF	D8
tomato	FF	63	47

Color	Red	Green	Blue
turquoise	40	E0	D0
violet	EE	82	EE
wheat	F5	DE	B3
white	FF	FF	FF
whitesmoke	F5	F5	F5
yellow	FF	FF	00
yellowgreen	9A	CD	32

Methods are the gears that make JavaScript objects come alive.

Chapter 6

Key Topics:

- **Methods listed by functional category.**

- **Working with text.**

- **Managing links, targets, and navigation.**

- **Mathematics and lots more.**

JavaScript Methods and Functions

This chapter presents a complete description of the methods and functions in JavaScript. As you know, methods are associated with objects. In the reference section, on objects, in Chapter 5, I have provided some information about each object's methods. In this section the arrangement is reversed—I describe the use of each method and also give the objects to which it applies. Code examples are given where they might be useful.

This chapter is intended as a reference. I don't really expect you to read it from start to finish! I open with a listing of methods separated into functional categories, which will make it easier for you to find the one you want. The remainder of the chapter is an alphabetical reference to all of JavaScript's methods.

Methods by Category

Displaying Text

- big

- blink

- bold

- fixed

- fontcolor

- fontsize

- italics

- small

- strike

- sub

- sup

- toLowerCase

- toUpperCase

- write

- writeln

Working with Strings

- charAt

- substring

- indexOf

- lastIndexOf

Links and Targets

- anchor

- link

Browser Navigation

- back

- forward

- go

Mathematics

- Abs

- acos

- asin

- atan

- ceil

- cos

- eval

- exp

- floor

- isNaN

- log

- max

- min

- parseFloat

- parseInt

- pow

- random

- round

- sin

- sqrt

- tan

Communicating with the User

- alert

- confirm

- prompt

Dates and Times

- getDate

- getDay

- getHours

- getMinutes

- getMonth

- getSeconds

- getTime

- getTimezoneOffset

- getYear

- parse

- setDate

- setHours

- setMinutes

- setMonth

- setSeconds

- setTime

- setYear

- toGMTString

- toLocaleString

- UTC

The Timer

- clearTimeout

- setTimeout

Miscellaneous

- blur

- clear

- click

- close (document)

- close (window)

- escape

- focus

- open (document)

- open (window)

- select

- submit

- unescape

Alphabetical Listing of Methods and Functions

abs method

Returns the absolute value of a number. The absolute value is simply a number with the minus sign removed. The absolute value of -5 is 5, while the absolute value of 10 is 10.

SYNTAX

```
math.abs(x)
```

where x is any numerical expression.

OBJECTS

```
math
```

EXAMPLE

Both of the following expressions return the value positive 4:

```
math.abs(-4)
math.abs(4)
```

acos

Returns the arc cosine of a number. The return value is expressed in radians.

SYNTAX

```
math.acos(x)
```

where x is a numeric expression in the range -1 to 1. If x is outside this range, no error occurs, but the return value is always 0. If x is within this range, the return value is between 0 and pi radians.

OBJECTS

```
math
```

alert

Displays a dialog box with a user-defined message and an OK button.

SYNTAX

```
alert(message)
```

where *message* is a string or object property.

OBJECTS

```
window
```

EXAMPLE

The following code displays the indicated message in an alert box:

```
alert("Don't do that!")
```

anchor

Creates an HTML anchor that can be used as a hypertext target. Use the *anchor* method in conjunction with the *write()* or *writeln()* method to first create an anchor, then display it.

SYNTAX

```
text.anchor(name)
```

text represents the text that you want the user to see. It can be any string or the property of an existing object. *name* is the <A> tag's NAME attribute, and can also be any string or a property of an existing object.

OBJECTS

```
string
```

EXAMPLE

The following code opens a window, then creates and displays an HTML tag that will display as "Index" and have the NAME attribute "link_index":

```
var AnchorText = "Index"
newWindow = window.open("","theWindow")
```

```
newWindow.document.writeln(AnchorText.anchor("link_index"))
newWindow.document.close
```

asin

Returns the arc sine of a number, in radians.

SYNTAX

```
Math.asin(number)
```

number represents a numeric expression with a value between -1 and 1. If *number* is outside this range, the return value is always zero. Otherwise the return is a value between -pi/2 and pi/2.

OBJECTS

```
Math
```

atan

Returns the arc tangent of a number, in radians. Expressed another way, it returns the angle whose tangent is a given number.

SYNTAX

```
Math.atan(number)
```

number is a numeric expression that represents the tangent of an angle. The value returned is between -pi/2 and pi/2.

OBJECTS

```
Math
```

back

Loads the previous URL from the history list.

SYNTAX

```
history.back()
```

Objects

```
history
```

Example

The following code displays a button that, when clicked, takes the user to the previous URL:

```
<INPUT TYPE="button" VALUE="Go back" onClick="history.back()">
```

big

Dispays a string in a larger font by enclosing it in the HTML tags <BIG> and </BIG>.

Syntax

```
theString.big()
```

theString is any string or the property of an existing object.

Objects

```
string
```

Example

The following code displays the text "JavaScript" in a larger font.

```
theString = "JavaScript"
document.write(theString.big())
```

blink

Displays a blinking string by enclosing it in the HTML tags <BLINK> and </BLINK>.

Syntax

```
theString.big()
```

theString is any string or the property of an existing object.

```
string
```

EXAMPLE

The following code displays a blinking string in the document.

```
theString = "I'm blinking!"
document.write(theString.blink())
```

blur

Removes the focus from an object.

SYNTAX

```
object.blur()
```

object is one of the applicable objects.

OBJECTS

```
password
text
textarea
```

bold

Displays a string in boldface by enclosing it in the HTML tags <B> and </B>.

SYNTAX

```
theString.bold()
```

OBJECTS

```
string
```

ceil

Returns the smallest integer that is equal to or larger than a number.

```
Math.ceil(number)
```

```
Math
```

The following code assigns the value 6 to x and -5 to y:

```
var x = Math.ceil(5.5)
var y = Math.ceil(-5.5)
```

charAt

Returns the single character at a specified position in the string. The first character has position 0.

```
theString.charAt(index)
```

theString is any string or a property of an existing object. *index* is a value between 0 and the string length minus 1.

```
string
```

The following code displays "defg" in the document.

```
theString="abcdefghijklmnop"
document.write(theString.charAt(3))
document.write(theString.charAt(4))
document.write(theString.charAt(5))
document.write(theString.charAt(6))
```

clear

Erases all contents of a window.

```
document.clear()
```

```
document
```

clearTimeout

Cancels a timeout that was set with the **setTimeout** method.

SYNTAX

```
clearTimeout(id)
```

id is the value returned by the timer you are canceling when it was first started.

OBJECTS

```
window
```

EXAMPLE

The following code sets a timeout to execute the function **foo**() after 10 seconds, then cancels it. See the **setTimeout**() method for more information.

```
var timer=setTimeout("foo()", 10000)
...
clearTimeout(timer)
```

click

Simulates a mouse click on the associated object.

SYNTAX

```
object.click()
```

OBJECTS

```
button
checkbox
radio
```

```
reset
submit
```

close (document object)

Closes an open document object and forces its contents to be displayed.

SYNTAX

```
document.close()
```

OBJECTS

```
document
```

EXAMPLE

The following code opens a document, displays some text in it, then closes it.

```
var theString = "This is a short document."
myWindow.document.open()
myWindow.document,write(theString)
myWindow.document.close()
```

close (window object)

Closes a window.

SYNTAX

```
window.close()
```

OBJECTS

```
window
```

EXAMPLE

You can close the current window with any of the following lines of code. **Self** is a synonym for the current window, and the current window is assumed if no object is specified.

```
close()
self.close()
window.close()
```

confirm

Displays a dialog box with a user-specified message and OK and Cancel buttons. Returns true if the user clicks OK, false if he/she clicks Cancel.

SYNTAX

```
confirm(message)
```

message is any string or a property of an existing object.

OBJECTS

```
window
```

EXAMPLE

The following code prompts the user, then calls the function **exit**() only if OK is clicked.

```
if (confirm("Exit - Are you sure?")) {    exit() }
```

cos

Returns the cosine of a number.

SYNTAX

```
Math.cos(number)
```

number is a numeric expression specifying an angle in radians. The cos method returns a value between -1 and 1.

OBJECTS

```
Math
```

escape

Returns the ASCII code of a character in the ISO Latin-1 character set. The return value is in the form "%xx." If you pass an alphanumeric character to **escape**, it returns the same character.

SYNTAX

```
escape(char)
```

OBJECTS

None. The escape function is a built-in JavaScript function.

eval

Forces evaluation of a numeric expression and returns a number.

SYNTAX

eval(*expr*)

expr is any expression or sequence of statements.

OBJECTS

None. The **eval** function is a built-in JavaScript function.

EXAMPLE

If text1 and text2 are text boxes containing the strings "111" and "222" respectively, then the use of **eval**() as shown below forces the data to be treated as numbers rather than as strings. This results in variable X being assigned the value 333 rather than the string "111222."

```
X = eval(text1.value) + eval(text2.value)
```

exp

Returns the value of the constant *e* (Euler's constant) raised to a specified power.

SYNTAX

```
Math.exp(x)
```

x is any numeric expression.

OBJECTS

```
Math
```

fixed

Displays a string in a fixed pitch font by enclosing it in the HTML tags <TT> and </TT>.

SYNTAX

```
theString.fixed()
```

theString is any string or a property of an existing object.

OBJECTS

```
string
```

floor

Returns the largest integer that is smaller than or equal to a specified number.

SYNTAX

```
Math.floor(x)
```

OBJECTS

```
Math
```

EXAMPLE

The following code assigns the value 5 to x and -6 to y.

```
var x = Math.floor(5.5)
var y = Math.floor(-5.5)
```

focus

Sets the focus to a specified object.

SYNTAX

```
object.focus()
```

OBJECTS

```
password
```

```
text
textarea
```

fontcolor

Displays a string in the specified color by enclosing it in the HTML tags <FONT COLOR=xxxx> and </FONT>. You can also use one of JavaScript's color mnemonics as described at the end of Chapter 5.

SYNTAX

```
theString.fontcolor(color)
```

theString is any string or a property of an existing object. *color* is a hexadecimal color RGB triplet or a color mnemonic.

OBJECTS

```
string
```

EXAMPLE

The following code shows two ways to display the string "JavaScript" in salmon color in a document.

```
var s = "JavaScript"
document.write("<P>" + worldString.fontcolor("FA8072"))
document.write("<P>" + worldString.fontcolor("salmon"))
```

fontsize

Displays a string at a specified font size by enclosing it in the HTML tags <FONTSIZE=*size*> and </FONTSIZE>

SYNTAX

```
theString.fontsize(size)
```

theString is any string or a property of an existing object. *size* is an integer between 1 and 7, or a string representing an integer in the same range.

OBJECTS

```
string
```

forward

Loads and displays the next URL in the history list (the one from which you returned.

SYNTAX

```
history.forward()
```

OBJECTS

```
history
```

EXAMPLE

The following code implements forward and back buttons in a document. These will perform the same function as the browser's own forward and back buttons.

```
<INPUT TYPE="button" VALUE="Go Back" onClick="history.back()"><p>
<INPUT TYPE="button" VALUE="Go Forward"
 onClick="history.forward()"><p>
```

getDate

Returns a number giving the day of the month for a given date.

SYNTAX

```
theDate.getDate()
```

theDate is any **Date** object.

OBJECTS

```
Date
```

EXAMPLE

The following code sets the variable day equal to the day of the month for today's date.

```
today = new Date()
day = today.getDate()
```

getDay

Returns a number representing the day of the week for a given date. Sunday is 0, Monday is 1, etc.

Syntax

```
theDate.getDay()
```

theDate is any **Date** object.

Objects

```
Date
```

Example

The following code sets the variable day equal to the day of the week for today's date.

```
today = new Date()
day = today.getDay()
```

getHours

Returns the hour of the day for a given date, in 24–hour format.

Syntax

```
theDate.getHours()
```

theDate is any **Date** object.

Objects

```
Date
```

getMinutes

Returns the minutes in the range 0-59, for a given date.

Syntax

```
theDate.getMinutes()
```

theDate is any **Date** object.

OBJECTS

Date

getMonth

Returns a number representing the month of a given date, with January = 0 and December = 11.

SYNTAX

```
theDate.getMonth()
```

theDate is any **Date** object.

OBJECTS

Date

getSeconds

Returns the seconds in the range 0-59 for a given date.

SYNTAX

```
theDate.getSeconds()
```

theDate is any **Date** object.

OBJECTS

Date

getTime

Returns the time for a given date, expressed as the number of milliseconds since 12:00 A.M., January 1, 1970.

SYNTAX

```
theDate.getTime()
```

theDate is any **Date** object.

OBJECTS

```
Date
```

EXAMPLE

The following code creates two Date objects, both containing the same date.

```
myBirthday = new Date("December 9, 1955")
theParty = new Date()
theParty.setTime(myBirthday.getTime())
```

getTimezoneOffset

Returns the time zone offset, in minutes, for the current locale.

Syntax

```
theDate.getTimezoneOffset()
```

theDate is any **Date** object.

OBJECTS

```
Date
```

getYear

Returns the year of a specified date, expressed as the number of years since 1900.

SYNTAX

```
theDate.getYear()
```

theDate is any **Date** object.

OBJECTS

```
Date
```

go

Loads a URL from the History list.

SYNTAX

```
history.go(position)
history.go("location")
```

position is a position in the History list, relative to the current position. *location* is a string containing all or part of the URL. If you use the second syntax, the *location* argument is compared with URL's in the History list, starting with those nearest to the current location. The first URL that contains a matching substring (case-insensitive) is loaded.

OBJECTS

```
history
```

EXAMPLE

The following code loads the most recently visited URL that contains the string "netscape."

```
history.go("netscape")
```

indexOf

Returns the position in a string of the first occurrence of a given search string.

SYNTAX

```
theString.indexOf(template [, [startAt])
```

template is any string—the string for which you are searching. The optional *startAt* is the position in the string where the search is to start. JavaScript strings are indexed starting at 0. If *startAt* is omitted, the search begins at the first character (index 0).

OBJECTS

```
string
```

The following code sets the variable pos to the value 2.

```
var searchString = "javascript"
pos = searchString.indexOf("v")
```

is NaN

Evaluates an argument to determine whether it is NaN (not a number). Applicable to UNIX platforms only.

SYNTAX

```
isNaN(value)
```

value is the value to be evaluated. Returns **true** or **false**.

OBJECTS

None. isNan() is a built-in JavaScript function. It is most commonly used to determine if the value returned by the **parseFloat()** or **parseInt()** functions is a number.

italics

Displays a string in italics by enclosing it in the HTML tags <I> and </I>.

Syntax

```
theString.italics()
```

theString is any string.

OBJECTS

```
string
```

EXAMPLE

The following code displays the string "JavaScript" in italics in the document.

```
var x = "JavaScript"
document.write(x.italics())
```

lastIndexOf

Returns the position in a string of the last occurrence of a given search string.

SYNTAX

```
theString.lastIndexOf(template [, [startAt])
```

template is any string - the string for which you are searching. The optional *startAt* is the position in the string where the search is to begin. JavaScript strings are indexed starting at 0. If *startAt* is omitted, the search begins at the last character. Otherwise, it starts at the specified index and works toward the beginning of the string.

OBJECTS

```
string
```

EXAMPLE

The following code sets the variable pos to the value 3.

```
var searchString = "javascript"
pos = searchString.lastIndexOf("a")
```

link

Creates an HTML hypertext link.

SYNTAX

```
linkName.link(attrib)
```

linkName is any string; this will be displayed in the document. *attrib* is a string representing the URL of the link target.

OBJECTS

```
string
```

EXAMPLE

This code displays a link that takes the user to the Coriolis Group's home page.

```
var x = "Coriolis"
document.open()
document.write("Go to the " + x.link("http://www.coriolis.com")
document.close()
```

log

Returns the natural logarith of a number.

Syntax

```
Math.log(x)
```

x is any numeric expression that evaluates to a positive value. If you pass an illegal argument, the log method returns -1.797 e+308.

OBJECTS

```
Math
```

max

Returns the larger of two numbers.

SYNTAX

```
Math.max(num1, num2)
```

num1 and *num2* are any numeric expressions.

OBJECTS

```
Math
```

Min

Returns the smaller of two numbers.

SYNTAX

```
Math.min(num1, num2)
```

num1 and *num2* are any numeric expressions.

OBJECTS

```
Math
```

open (document object)

Opens a document for output with the write() and writeln() methods.

SYNTAX

```
document.open(["mimeType"])
```

mimeType specifies one of the following document types:

- text/html (the default)
- text/plain
- image/gif
- image/jpeg
- image/x-bitmap
- plugIn (any supported two-part plug-in MIME type)

The method returns **null** if for some reason the document cannot be opened. If the *mimeType* is text or image, the stream is opened to the browser screen; otherwise, the stream is opened to a plug-in. If a document already exists in the target window, the **open()** method clears it. You must terminate output by using the **document.close()** method, which causes text or images that were sent to layout to actually display. After using **document.close()**, execute **document.open()** again to begin another output stream.

mimeType is an optional argument that specifies the type of document to which you are writing. If you do not specify a mimeType, the **open()** method assumes text/html shown in Table 6.1.

Table 6.1 The supported mimeType arguments.

text/html	A document containing ASCII text with HTML formatting.
text/plain	A document containing plain ASCII text with end-of-line characters.
image/gif	A document with encoded bytes constituting a GIF header and pixel data.
image/jpeg	A document with encoded bytes constituting a jpeg header and pixel data.
image/x-bitmap	A document with encoded bytes constituting a bitmap header and pixel data.
plugIn	Loads the specified plug-in and uses it as the destination for the write() and writeln() methods. For example, "x-world/vrml" loads the VR Scout VRML plug-in from Chaco Communications, and "application/x-director" loads the Macromedia Shockwave plug-in.

OBJECTS

```
document
```

EXAMPLE

The first example opens a new stream, clearing any existing material in the current window, then writes some text to it and calls the **close**() method to force display of the text.

```
document.open()
document.write("Some text")
document.close()
```

The next example sets the variable hasShockWave to **true** or **false** depending on whether the user has the ShockWave plug-in installed. It works by creating a very small temporary window, attempting to open a document of the specified plug-in type, then closing the window.

```
hasShockWave = false
var temp = window.open("", "temp", "width=1,height=1")
if (temp != null)
    {
```

```
if (temp.document.open("application/x-director") != null)
    hasShockWave = true
temp.close()
}
```

open (window object)

Opens a new browser window.

SYNTAX

`[winName = ][window].open("URL", "name", ["features"])`

winName is the new window's name, and will be used to refer to the window's properties and methods.

URL specifies the location to open in the window; if *URL* is a blank string, then an empty window is opened.

name is the window name to use in the TARGET attribute of a <FORM> or <A> tag.

features is a list of features specifying window options. You specify the features of the new window by including a comma-delimited list of one or more of the following items:

- toolbar

- location

- directories

- status

- menubar

- scrollbars

- resizable

- width=*pixels*

- height=*pixels*

A feature is turned on if its keyword is included in the features argument—either alone or set to 1 or true. It is turned off by setting it to false or 0. See the entry for the Window object in Chapter 7 for more information.

OBJECTS

```
window
```

EXAMPLE

The following code opens a new browser window and loads the Coriolis Group's home page.

```
cgWindow = window.open("http://www.coriolis.com",
          "CoriolisWindow","menubar,status,scrollbars")
```

parse

Given a date string as its argument, returns the number of milliseconds since January 1, 1970 00:00:00, local time.

SYNTAX

```
Date.parse(dateString)
```

dateString is a string representing a date, such as "Jan 1, 1996." It can be used in conjunction with the **setTime**() method to set a **Date** object's value based on a string representation of a date. This method accepts the IETF standard date syntax: "Mon, 25 Dec 1995 13:30:00 GMT." It also understands the continental U.S. time zone abbreviations, but for general use you should use a time zone offset; for example, "Mon, 25 Dec 1995 13:30:00 GMT+0430" (4 hours, 30 minutes west of the Greenwich meridian). If you do not specify a time zone, the local time zone is assumed. GMT and UTC are considered equivalent. **parse**() is a static method of **Date**, so you must always use it with the format **Date.parse**() and not as a method of a date object that you created.

OBJECTS

```
Date
```

If **theDate** is an existing **date** object, then the following code sets **theDate** to July 4, 1996:

```
theDate.setTime(Date.parse("Jul 4, 1996"))
```

parseFloat

Parses a string argument and returns a floating point number.

SYNTAX

```
parseFloat(text)
```

text is the string that represents the value you want to parse. If the first character in *text* is not a numeric character, then **parse**() returns 0 (or NaN on UNIX platforms). The first non-numeric character in the string and everything after it is ignored.

OBJECTS

None. parse() is a built-in JavaScript function and is not associated with any object.

EXAMPLE

The following statements all return the floating point value 1.234:

```
parseFloat("1.234QQQ")
parseFloat("1234e-3")
```

The following statement returns 0 or NaN:

```
parseFloat("p1.234")
```

parseInt

Parses a string and returns an integer in the specified radix.

SYNTAX

```
parseInt(text [, base])
```

text is the string to be parsed, and *base* indicates the desired radix. If the first character in *text* cannot be converted, **parseInt**() returns 0 on Windows platforms and NaN on other platforms. Specify *base* as an integer; 16 for hexadecimal (base 16), 8 for octal, and so on. If *base* is omitted or 0, the desired radix is determined by the first character(s) of *text*:

- If text starts with 0X, radix 16 is used.

- If text starts with 0, radix 8 is used.

- If text starts any other numeric character, radix 10 is used.

OBJECTS

None. **parseInt**() is a built-in function and is not associated with a particular object.

EXAMPLE

The following statements all return the integer value 12:

```
parseInt("C", 16)
parseInt("14", 8)
parseInt("1100", 2)
parseInt("12 Oak Street")
```

pow

Raises a number to a specified power.

SYNTAX

```
Math.pow(a, b)
```

a and *b* are numeric expressions. Returns the value of *a* to the *b* power (a^b).

OBJECTS

```
Math
```

prompt

Displays a dialog box permitting the user to enter data.

SYNTAX

```
prompt(msg, [default])
```

msg is any string; it is the text that will be displayed in the dialog box. *default* is a string, integer, or property of an existing object that represents the default value of the input field.

OBJECTS

```
window
```

EXAMPLE

The following code prompts the user and assigns the value entered to the variable country.

```
var country = prompt("What country do you live in?", "USA")
```

random

Returns a pseudo-random number between zero and one. This method is available only on Unix platforms.

SYNTAX

```
Math.random()
```

OBJECTS

```
Math
```

round

Returns the value of a number rounded to the nearest integer.

SYNTAX

```
Math.round.(x)
```

x is any numeric expression. If the fraction part of *x* is .5 or greater, the next larger integer is returned.

OBJECTS

```
Math
```

EXAMPLE

Both of these statements assign the value 6.

```
x = Math.round(5.51)
y = Math.round(6.49)
```

select

Selects the input area of the specified **password**, **text**, or **textarea** object. Any text in the object is highlighted and will be replaced by what the user types.

SYNTAX

```
object.select()
```

object is the name of an instance of one of the applicable objects.

OBJECTS

```
text
textArea
password
```

setDate

Sets a **Date** object's day of the month.

SYNTAX

```
date.setDate(day)
```

date is any *Date* object. *day* is a numeric expression evaluating to an integer between 1 and 31.

OBJECTS

```
Date
```

The following code creates a Date object containing Jan 1, 1996, and then changes it to Jan 15.

```
theDate = new date("Jan 1, 1996")
theDate.setDate(15)
```

setHours

Sets a **Date** object's hours value.

SYNTAX

```
date.setHours(hour)
```

date is any Date object. *hours* is a numeric expression evaluating to an integer between 0 and 23.

OBJECTS

```
Date
```

EXAMPLE

The following code sets a **Date** object to 6:30 and then changes it to 7:30.

```
theDate = new date("Jan 1, 1996 06:30:00")
theDate.setHours(7)
```

setMinutes

Sets a **Date** object's minutes value.

SYNTAX

```
date.setMinutes(mins)
```

date is any Date object. *mins* is a numeric expression evaluating to an integer between 0 and 59.

OBJECTS

```
Date
```

EXAMPLE

The following code sets a **Date** object to 6:30 and then changes it to 6:45.

```
theDate = new date("Jan 1, 1996 06:30:00")
theDate.setMinutes(45)
```

setMonth

Sets a **Date** object's month value.

SYNTAX

```
date.setHours(month)
```

date is any Date object. *month* is a numeric expression evaluating to an integer between 0 and 11 (Jan - Dec).

OBJECTS

```
Date
```

EXAMPLE

The following code sets a **Date** object to January 1 and then changes it to February 1.

```
theDate = new date("Jan 1, 1996")
theDate.setMonth(1)
```

setSeconds

Sets a **Date** object's seconds value.

SYNTAX

```
date.setSeconds(secs)
```

date is any Date object. *secs* is a numeric expression evaluating to an integer between 0 and 59.

OBJECTS

```
Date
```

The following code sets a **Date** object to 6:30:00 and then changes it to 6:30:32.

```
theDate = new date("Jan 1, 1996 06:30:00")
theDate.setSeconds(32)
```

setTime

Sets the value of a **Date** object.

SYNTAX

```
date.setTime(timeVal)
```

date is any **Date** object. *timeVal* is a numeric expression specifying the new date in terms of milliseconds since January 1, 1970 00:00:00. Note that you can obtain this value from a **Date** object with the **getTime()** method.

OBJECTS

```
Date
```

EXAMPLE

The following code creates two **Date** objects both set to Jan 1, 1996 12:00:00.

```
firstDate = new Date("Jan 1, 1996 12:00:00")
secondDate = new Date()
secondDate.setTime(firstDate.getTime())
```

setTimeout

Causes a section of JavaScript code to be evaluated after a specified time has passed.

SYNTAX

```
timeoutID=setTimeout(code, msec)
```

timeoutID is the return value that is used to cancel the timeout with **clearTimeout()**.

code is the JavaScript code to be executed.

msec is the delay, in millisconds, that is to elapse before the code is executed.

The **setTimeout** method causes the code to be executed only once, not repeatedly. To cancel a timeout, execute the **clearTimeout**() method, passing the *timeoutID* value that was returned when the timeout was initially set.

OBJECTS

```
frame
window
```

EXAMPLE

The program in Listing 6.1 implements a simple clock in JavaScript. The trick is to recursively use **setTimeout**() with a 1000 millisecond delay. The program starts by calling a function that sets the timer so that the same function is called again after 1000 milliseconds. Each time the function is called, it (1) displays the current time, and (2) sets another timeout.

Listing 7.1   A JavaScript clock.

```
<html>
<head>
   <title>Clock</title>
<script><!--

function DisplayTime ()
    {
    var now = new Date()
    var hours = now.getHours()
    var mins = now.getMinutes()
    var secs = now.getSeconds()
    var TheTime = "" + ((hours >12) ? hours -12 :hours)
    TheTime += ((mins < 10) ? ":0" : ":") + mins
    TheTime += ((secs < 10) ? ":0" : ":") + secs
    TheTime += (hours < 12) ? " AM" : " PM"
    document.clock.display.value = TheTime
    var theTimer = setTimeout("DisplayTime()",1000)
    }
// end hiding. -->
</script>
</head>
<body>
<br>
<script>
```

```
var today = new Date()
var hour = today.getHours()

document.writeln("<FORM NAME='clock' onSubmit='0'>")

//A text box for the time display.
document.writeln("<INPUT TYPE='text' NAME='display' SIZE=12
  VALUE='">")

//Start the timer running.
DisplayTime()

<!- end hiding  -></script>
</body>
</html>
```

setYear

Sets a **Date** object's year value.

SYNTAX

```
date.setYear(year)
```

date is any Date object. *year* is a numeric expression that evaluates to the desired year, expressed as the year minus 1900.

OBJECTS

```
Date
```

EXAMPLE

The following code creates a **Date** object set to Jan 1, 1995, and then changes the year to 1996.

```
theDate = new Date("Jan 1, 1995")
theDate.setYear(96)
```

sin

Returns the sine of an angle.

SYNTAX

```
Math.sin(x)
```

x is a numeric expression representing the size of an angle in radians. The returned value is between -1 and 1.

OBJECTS

```
Math
```

small

Causes a string to be displayed in a small font by enclosing it in <SMALL>...</SMALL> tags.

SYNTAX

```
string.small()
```

string is any string object.

OBJECTS

```
string
```

EXAMPLE

The following code displays "JavaScript" in the document in small font.

```
var js = "JavaScript"
document.write(js.small())
```

sqrt

Returns the square root of a number.

SYNTAX

```
Math.sqrt(x)
```

x is an expression that evaluates to a non-negative value. The return value is 0 for negative values of *x*.

OBJECTS

```
Math
```

strike

Displays a string in struck-out text by enclosing it in <STRIKE>...</STRIKE> tags.

SYNTAX

```
string.strike()
```

string is any string object.

OBJECTS

```
string
```

sub

Displays a string as a subscript by enclosing it in _{...} tags.

SYNTAX

```
string.sub()
```

string is any string object.

OBJECTS

```
string
```

submit

Submits a form.

SYNTAX

```
name.submit()
```

name is the name of a form or an element in the forms array. Executing the **submit**() method for a form has the same effect as clicking a Submit button.

OBJECTS

```
form
```

substring

Returns a portion of a string.

SYNTAX

```
string.substring(start, stop)
```

- *string* is any string object.

- *start* and *stop* are numeric expressions that evaluate to values between 0 and the length of the string minus 1.

The method returns the subset of the string starting at the character position indicated by the index *start* or *stop* (whichever is smaller) and ending just before the position indicated by the larger index. If either of the index arguments is greater than the string length, the method returns all characters from the other index position to the end of the string. If both indexes are greater than the string length, or if they are equal, an empty string is returned.

OBJECTS

```
string
```

EXAMPLE

The following code displays "cd" in the document.

```
var x = "abcdefg"
document.write(x.substring(2,4))
```

sup

Displays a string as a superscript by enclosing it in ^{...} tags.

SYNTAX

```
string.sup()
```

string is any string object.

OBJECTS

```
string
```

tan

Returns the tangent of an angle.

SYNTAX

```
Math.tan(x)
```

x is a numeric expression that represents the size of an angle in radians.

OBJECTS

```
Math
```

toGMTString

Converts a date to a string, using the Internet GMT conventions.

SYNTAX

```
date.toGMTString()
```

date is any **Date** object. The precise format of the string returned by this function is platform-dependent.

OBJECTS

```
Date
```

toLocaleString

Converts a date to a string, using the current locale's conventions.

SYNTAX

```
date.toLocaleString()
```

date is any **Date** object. Because different locales arrange the components of the date in different ways, you will get more portable results using **getHours**() and similar methods.

OBJECTS

```
Date
```

EXAMPLE

When executed at my locale, the following code:

```
x = new Date()
document.write(x.toLocaleString())
```

created this output in the document:

```
04/16/96 14:52:06
```

toLowerCase

Returns a string with all letters converted to lower case.

SYNTAX

```
string.toLowerCase()
```

string is any string object.

OBJECTS

```
string
```

toUpperCase

Returns a string with all letters converted to upper case.

SYNTAX

```
string.toUpperCase()
```

string is any string object.

OBJECTS

```
string
```

unescape

Returns the ASCII string for the specified value.

SYNTAX

```
unescape("string")
```

string is a string containing charaters in one of the following forms:

- %i where i is an integer in the range 0-255.

- A hexadecimal value in the range 0x00 - 0xFF.

- The returned string is a sequence of characters in the ISO Latin-1 character set.

OBJECTS

None. unescape is a built-in function.

EXAMPLE

The following statement returns "&!#"

```
unescape("%26%21%23")
```

UTC

Returns a value representing a date as the number of milliseconds since Jan 1, 1970 00:00:00 Universal Coordinated Time (GMT).

SYNTAX

```
date.UTC(year, month, day [, hrs] [, min] [, sec])
```

- *year* is a year after 1900.

- *month* is a month between 0 and 11.

- *day* is a day of the month between 1 and 31.

- *hrs* is hours between 0 and 23.

- *min* is minutes between 0 and 59.

- *sec* is seconds between 0 and 59.

UTC is a static method and is always used with the generic Date object and not with a user-created instance of Date.

OBJECTS

```
Date
```

EXAMPLE

The following code creates and initializes a **date** object using GMT instead of local time:

```
gmtDate = new Date(Date.UTC(96, 1, 1, 0, 0, 0))
```

write, writeln

Writes one or more HTML expressions to the document in a window. **writeln**() appends a newline character, whereas **write**() does not. Use **document.close**() to force output created with **write**() and **writeln**() to be displayed.

SYNTAX

```
write(exp_1, ... exp_n)
writeln(exp_1, ... exp_n)
```

exp_1 through *exp_n* are Javascript expressions.

OBJECTS

```
document
```

JavaScript can detect and respond to a variety of user actions. This chapter shows you how it's done.

Key Topics:

- **Event-driven programming.**

- **Responding to mouse actions.**

- **Basics of data verification.**

Responding to User Actions

Driven by Events

Event-driven programming was introduced by Visual Basic and has become an important part of many development languages. The term refers to the ability of the language to automatically detect certain user actions without the need to write any code. Event detection makes it easy for you, the programmer, to create an application that is responsive to the user, allowing it to perform the appropriate actions in response to the user's actions.

JavaScript has a moderate degree of automatic event detection. Given that it is a scripting language and not a full-blown application development tool, its event detection is more than adequate and is an important tool in creation of dynamic, interactive Web pages.

Events do not happen in isolation. An event, such as a mouse click, happens *to* something—in this case, a JavaScript object. The ability to detect events, therefore, is associated with particular JavaScript objects. The events that can be automatically detected differ from one type of object to the next. This makes perfect sense, because the types of events that are meaningful are different for different objects. The objects that can detect events are standard HTML objects such as Text, Form, and Submit that are extended by JavaScript.

CHOOSE YOUR OWN EVENTS

It's up to you. Rather than saying that JavaScript automatically detects certain events, it's more accurate to say that it has the capability to detect certain events. A script will respond only to those events for which you have written event handlers—all other events will be ignored. The choice is yours, therefore, to determine which events it will respond to and which ones it will not.

The code that is executed when a particular event is detected is called an *event handler*. The event handler code is included in the object's definition (its HTML tag) with an identifier that indicates the event to which the code is linked. The general form is like this:

```
onEvent = "code goes here"
```

Here's a complete example. The following tag defines a Button object and defines an event handler for the Click event. When the user clicks the button, the function **compute**() will be executed.

```
<INPUT TYPE="button" VALUE="OK" onClick="compute(this.form)">
```

As is the case here, event handers are often function calls. This keeps the object definition tag from getting too long. If the event handler code is short, you can include it directly in the tag, separating multiple statements with a semicolon.

What Events Can Be Detected?

Nine distinct events can be detected in JavaScript. I'll describe them briefly here, and list the objects by which they can be detected. The remainder of the chapter will show you how to use events for a variety of scripting needs.

- onBlur: Occurs when an object looses the focus. Can be detected by Text, TextArea, and Select objects.

- onChange: Occurs when an object looses the focus after its contents have been modified. Can be detected by Text, TextArea, and Select objects.

- onClick: Occurs when the user clicks the object with the mouse. Can be detected by Button, Checkbox, Radio, Link, Reset, and Submit objects.

- onFocus: Occurs when an object receives input focus by tabbing with the keyboard or clicking with the mouse. Can be detected by Text, TextArea, and Select objects.

- onLoad: Occurs when the browser finishes loading a window or all frames within a <FRAMESET> tag. Detected by the Window object.

- onMouseOver: Occurs once each time the mouse pointer moves over an object from outside that object. Detected by the Link object.

- onSelect: Occurs when a user selects some of the text within a Text or Textarea object. Detected by these two object types.

- onSubmit: Occurs when the user submits a form. Detected by the Form object.

- onUnload: Occurs when the user exits a document. Detected by the Window object.

In the remainder of this chapter, I'll show you some of the useful things you can do with JavaScript event handlers.

Providing Link Information with onMouseOver

When the user moves the mouse pointer over a link in the document, the default behavior of Navigator and most other browsers is used to display the link's destination URL in the status bar. You can use the onMouseOver event to provide more useful information to the user. In the simplest use, you can utilize the Window object's Status property to display your own message in the status bar. Here's an example.

```
<A HREF="http://www.coriolis.com/"
   onMouseOver = "window.status='Go to Coriolis home page';
   return true">
Click here
</A>
```

When the user moves the mouse pointer over this link, the message "Go to Coriolis home page" is displayed in the status bar rather than the default, which would be "http://www.coriolis.com/" in this case.

With the use of frames, you can get a bit more sophisticated in using onMouseOver. With a modest amount of programming, you can devote a frame to the display of information about the link to which the user is pointing. The basics steps are:

1. Use the <FRAMESET> and <FRAME> tags to define the desired frames, including one (usually a fairly small one) for display of the link information.

2. Use the SRC= argument in the <FRAME> tag to load a blank HTML document into the frame. This document should contain only the <HTML> and </HTML> tags. This is necessary—without a loaded document, the frame will display only as a blank area and you won't be able to write information to it.

3. In the main document(s), add an onMouseOver handler to each <A> tag with JavaScript code to display the desired information in the "information" frame.

Listings 7.1 and 7.2 demonstrate this technique. SHOWLINK.HTML is the parent HTML file. Load this file into your browser to run the demonstration.

It defines two frames: one taking up 90 percent of the screen to display the main document, the other with 10 percent of the screen to display link information.

Most of the action goes on in LINKS1.HTML in Listing 7.2. This is the main document, the one containing the links about which you want to display information in the small frame. For each link—and there are only two in this document—I have created a function that clears the information frame and displays the relevant text there. Each function is called in the onMouseOver event handler for the corresponding <A> tag. A more efficient approach would be to keep the messages in an array and have a single display function that is passed the appropriate message, but the principle is the same.

I've made use of the JavaScript timer to add a simple but convenient enhancement to the code. Without this enhancement, the descriptive message that appears in the small window will remain displayed until the user passes the mouse pointer over another link. To prevent confusion, it seemed wise to have the message display only briefly for a few seconds after the link is touched. Each display function sets up a timer that will time out after three seconds and clear the frame.

The demonstration program is shown operating in Figure 7.1. Given the flexibility of HTML, the information about a link that is displayed in the smaller frame is not limited to plain text, but could include almost anything—graphics, fancy backgrounds, and so on.

Listing 7.1 SHOWLINK.HTML, the "parent" HTML file that defines the frames.

```
<HTML>
<TITLE>Display link info in frame</TITLE>

<FRAMESET ROWS="90%,10%">
    <FRAME SRC="links1.htm" NAME="maindoc" MARGINHEIGHT=2>
    <FRAME SRC="blank.htm" NAME="linkinfo" MARGINHEIGHT=2>
</FRAMESET>

<NOFRAME>
This demo requires Netscape 2.x.
</NOFRAME>

</HTML>
```

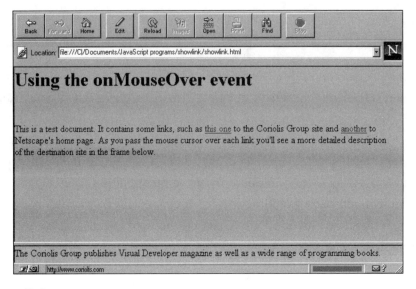

Figure 7.1

SHOWLINK.HTML demonstrates using onMouseOver and frames to display descriptive information about each link in a document.

Listing 7.2   LINKS1.HTML, the main document containing the links.

```
<HTML>
<HEAD>
<SCRIPT>

var theTimer

function Coriolis()
    {
    var msg = "The Coriolis Group publishes Visual
                Developer magazine "
    msg += "as well as a wide range of programming books. "
    clearTimeout(theTimer)
     ClearLinkInfoWindow()
parent.linkinfo.document.open()
    parent.linkinfo.document.write(msg)
     parent.linkinfo.document.close()
     theTimer = setTimeout("ClearLinkInfoWindow()",3000)
    return true
    }

function Netscape()
    {
    var msg = "Netscape Communications are the folks who
                developed the "
```

```
        msg += "Navigator browser as well as a variety of other
                Web-related products."
        clearTimeout(theTimer)
         ClearLinkInfoWindow()
        parent.linkinfo.document.open()
        parent.linkinfo.document.write(msg)
         parent.linkinfo.document.close()
         theTimer = setTimeout("ClearLinkInfoWindow()",3000)
         return true
        }

    function ClearLinkInfoWindow()
        {
        parent.linkinfo.document.clear()
        parent.linkinfo.document.write("")
        parent.linkinfo.document.close()
        }
</SCRIPT>
</HEAD>
<BODY>
<H1>Using the onMouseOver event</H1><BR>
This is a test document. It contains some links, such as
<A HREF="http://www.coriolis.com" onMouseOver="Coriolis()">this one
 </A> to the Coriolis Group site and
<A href="http://www.netscape.com" onMouseOver="Netscape()">another
 </A> to Netscape's home page. As you pass the mouse cursor
over each link you'll see a more detailed description of the
 destination site in the frame below.
</BODY>
</HTML>
```

Web Watch

Sean McGuire has used JavaScript to devise a neat HTML editor that lets you edit HTML in the top half of the screen and see the results in the bottom half. You'll find his page at http://www.math.macalstr.edu/~smcguire/HIE/.

Verifying Data Input with onBlur and onChange

Many Web applications involve data input with forms. As with any situation where you are asking the user for input, things run much more smoothly if you make sure that the data input is what you expect. A later chapter will deal with data verification in detail, but I'll provide an introduction now.

The onBlur and onChange events are ideal for data verification since they are applicable to the three objects that are most commonly used for user input: Text, Textarea, and Select. The onBlur event is triggered when the user moves the focus off the object, which is an ideal time to look at the data that was entered. The onChange event is also triggered when the object loses the focus, but only if the object's value has been changed.

Which event should you use? You might think that onChange would be preferred, since it avoids the unnecessary overhead of checking the data if the user simply moves the focus to the object, then moves it off without changing the data. This poses potential problems, however. What if the object should not be left blank, but starts out blank when the form is first displayed? If the user moves the focus to the object and then off without entering any data, the object's value will not have changed, and onChange will not be triggered.

Another use for the onBlur and onChange events is when the data entered into an object must be assigned to a JavaScript variable for further program processing. The following demonstration includes both data verification and value assignment. The document, which is shown in Figure 7.2, includes a Text object, a Textarea object, and a Select object. The onBlur event is used to make sure that the user does not leave the Text or Textarea fields blank. If the focus leaves one of these objects while it is still blank, an alert is displayed and the focus is returned to the object. The onChange event is used to assign the value selected in the Select list to a variable. There is a button to click to display the value of this variable.

Listing 7.3 DATA_VER.HTML demonstrates using the onBlur and onChange events.

```
<HTML>
<TITLE>Data verification with onBlur and onChange</TITLE>
<HEAD>
<SCRIPT>
function NotBlank(obj)
    {
    // Verifies that the value property of obj is not
    //blank. If it is blank displays an alert and sets
    //focus back to the object.
    if (obj.value == "")
        {
```

```
                alert("This field cannot be left blank.")
                obj.focus()
                }
        }
</SCRIPT>
</HEAD>
<BODY>
<SCRIPT>
var MusicPref = ""
</SCRIPT>
<FORM>
Please enter your name:
<INPUT type="text" name="mytext" size="20" onBlur=
        "NotBlank(this)"><p>
Tell us about yourself:
<TEXTAREA NAME="mytextarea" ROWS="4" COLS="50" onBlur=
        "NotBlank(this)"></TEXTAREA><P>
What is your favorite type of music?
<SELECT SIZE="3" NAME="myselect" onChange=
        "MusicPref=this.options[this.selectedIndex].text">
<OPTION>Early jazz
<OPTION>Modern jazz
<OPTION>Baroque
<OPTION>Classical
<OPTION>Romantic
<OPTION>Blues
<OPTION>Rock and roll
</SELECT>
<P><P>
<INPUT TYPE="button" VALUE="Display Music preference"
        onClick="alert(MusicPref)">
</FORM>
</BODY>
</HTML>
```

Using onFocus to Display Instructions

The onFocus event can be seen as the complement to the onBlur and onChange events—it occurs when an object receives the focus. It's clearly not much use for data verification, since it is triggered before any data is entered, but it does have other uses. One that I have found particularly handy is providing the user with information about what they are supposed to enter in a given field.

Why not just display the instructions as part of the form? This approach is often perfectly suitable, but if you have a complex form with many data fields that need to be filled in, you may find yourself running short of screen real

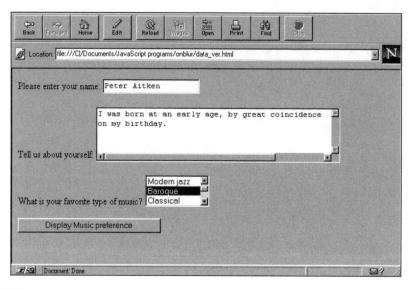

Figure 7.2

The DATA_VER.HTML demonstration program.

estate. Screen space can become even more critical if you need to provide lengthy instructions. You may find yourself compromising the completeness of the information displayed to accommodate your form design.

My method uses frames, with a large frame devoted to displaying the data entry form and a small frame for display of information. Only the instructions for the current data entry field—the one with the focus—are displayed in this frame at any one time. And the onFocus event (you're way ahead of me, aren't you?) is the ideal way to get the proper message displayed at the proper time.

The basic technique is not very different from what we used with the onMouseOver event handler earlier in the chapter to display information about links. Rather than having a separate function for each message, this demonstration places the various messages in an array, and then in the event–handler code, passes the proper message to a single display function.

The demonstration program is shown in action in Figure 7.3. The two documents, FOCUS1.HTML and FOCUS2.HTML, are given in Listings 7.4 and 7.5. FOCUS1 is the "parent" document, setting up the frames and loading the other documents. FOCUS2 is the main document, the one containing the

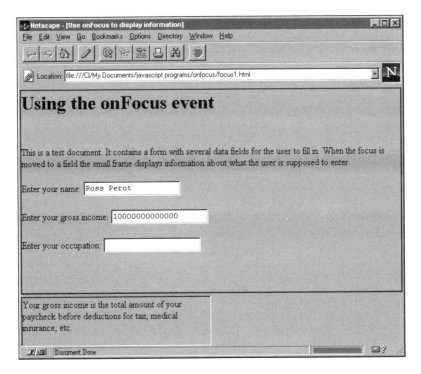

Figure 7.3

Using onFocus to display instructions to the user.

form to be filled in and the event–handler code. In a real application, this document would also require a means of submitting it to the server, but I have omitted it here. The third document, BLANK.HTML, is again an empty HTML document containing only the <HTML> and </HTML> tags.

Listing 7.4 FOCUS1.HTML defines the frames and loads the "child" documents.

```
<HTML>

<TITLE>Use onFocus to display information</TITLE>

<FRAMESET ROWS="80%,20%">
    <FRAME SRC="focus2.htm" NAME="maindoc" MARGINHEIGHT=2>
    <FRAMESET COLS="50%,50%">
    <FRAME SRC="blank.htm" NAME="infowindow" MARGINHEIGHT=2>
    </FRAMESET>
</FRAMESET>

<NOFRAME>
This demo requires Netscape 2.x.
```

```
</NOFRAME>

</HTML>
```

Listing 7.5   FOCUS2.HTM.

```
<HTML>
<HEAD>
<SCRIPT>

function initArray(ArrayLength)
    {
    this.length = ArrayLength
    for (var i = 0; i < this.length; i++)
        this[i+1] = 0
    }

function info(msg)
        {
        ClearInfoWindow()
        parent.infowindow.document.write(msg)
        parent.infowindow.document.close()
        }

function ClearInfoWindow()
    {
    parent.infowindow.document.clear()
     parent.infowindow.document.write("")
    parent.infowindow.document.close()
    }
</SCRIPT>
</HEAD>
<BODY>
<SCRIPT>
// Initialize an array to hold message strings.
var msg = new initArray(4)
msg[1] = "If you don't know what to enter I can't help you!"
msg[2] = "Your gross income is the total amount of your "
msg[2] += "paycheck before deductions for tax, medical "
msg[2] += "insurance, etc."
msg[3] = "Your occupation is what you do to support yourself"
msg[3] += "now, not what you hope to become someday. If you"
msg[3] += "hope to be a writer but are currently working as "
msg[3] += "a waiter, then you should enter waiter here."
</SCRIPT>
<H1>Using the onFocus event</H1><BR>
This is a test document. It contains a form with several
data fields for the user to fill in. When the focus is
moved to a field the small frame displays information about
what the user is supposed to enter.
<p><p>
```

```
<FORM>
Enter your name:
<INPUT TYPE="text" NAME="name" VALUE=""
     onFocus="info(msg[1])">
<p>
Enter your gross income:
<INPUT TYPE="text" NAME="income" VALUE=""
     onFocus="info(msg[2])">
<p>
Enter your occupation:
<INPUT TYPE="text" NAME="occupation" VALUE=""
     onFocus="info(msg[3])">
<p>
</FORM>
</BODY>
</HTML>
```

HOW DUMB IS THAT USER?

A wise programmer always assumes that the users of the program are all as dumb as fence posts. This way you are always planning for the worst and making your program as idiot-proof as possible. If you use the techniques presented in this section to provide instructions to the users, you'll probably want to make those instructions as complete and detailed as possible. But what about those occasional users who are familiar with the program, or whose IQ's squeak into triple digits? They may be bored or put off by such instructions. You can solve this dilemma by letting users indicate on the form, by means of Radio buttons perhaps, whether they are beginning, intermediate, or advanced users. The program would then display appropriately tailored instructions.

Controlling Form Submission with onSubmit

The onSubmit event is triggered when a form is submitted to the server. Submission can be initiated either by the user clicking a Submit button on the form or by executing the Form object's Submit method. You specify an onSubmit handler in the <FORM> tag, as follows:

```
<FORM … onSubmit="handler">
```

The power of the onSubmit handler lies in the fact that its return value controls whether the form is actually submitted. If the event handler returns true, the form is submitted. If false is returned, the form is not submitted. This feature is used for data verification when you want to be sure the form data is okay before submitting it. Generally, you will write a function to perform the data verification; the function should return true or false depending upon whether the data is acceptable. You would then specify the event handler as follows:

```
<FORM … onSubmit = "return checkData(this)>
```

Using onSubmit is only one possible approach to data verification. Chapter 10 covers the important topic of data verification in more detail.

The onLoad and onUnload Event Handlers

The onLoad event is triggered when the browser finishes loading a document in a window or finishes loading all frames specified within a FRAMESET. You specify the event handler either in the <BODY> or in the <FRAMESET> tag, as shown here:

```
<BODY onLoad = "handler">
<FRAMESET … onLoad = "handler">
```

The onUnload event occurs when the user exits a document. This, too, is specified in either the <BODY> or the <FRAMESET> tag, with the same syntax as for onLoad. Note that you can have both onLoad and onUnload handlers defined for a document.

Why use onLoad? You might think that placing JavaScript code in the body of the document would have the same effect. With a document that uses frames, however, it appears that using an event handler is required. I have not found a way to include JavaScript in the body of a document that uses a frameset; so in order to execute code when the document loads, it seems that defining an onLoad handler is the only way to go. Remember that JavaScript is still evolving as I write this, so the final language may include additional capabilities, but for now, at least we know that an onLoad event handler works.

Listing 7.6 shows a simple example of using onLoad. The document defines two frames and loads a blank document into each. When the loading is complete, the onLoad handler is called; code in the handler writes a brief message to each of the frames.

Listing 7.6 Using an onLoad handler to display text in two child frames.

```
<HTML>
<HEAD>
<TITLE>Using onLoad</TITLE>
<SCRIPT>
function writeText()
    {
    parent.doc1.document.write("This is Document 1")
    parent.doc2.document.write("This is Document 2")
    parent.doc1.document.close()
    parent.doc2.document.close()
    }
</SCRIPT>
</HEAD>

<FRAMESET ROWS="50%,50%" onLoad="writeText()" >
    <FRAME SRC="blank1.htm" NAME="doc1">
    <FRAME SRC="blank2.htm" NAME="doc2">
</FRAMESET>

<NOFRAME>
This demo requires Netscape 2.x.
</NOFRAME>

</HTML>
```

Uses for onUnload seem even more limited. If onUnload functioned like onSubmit, in that code could prevent the action from completing – in other words, cancel the unload event—it would be more useful, but this is not the case. If you have experience programming in more traditional languages like C++, you may think of using the onUnload handler to perform various "clean-up" tasks such as freeing memory and closing disk files, but of course these things are not applicable to JavaScript.

The only use I have found for onUnload applies to documents that include a form. If the user tries to exit the document without submitting the form (as indicated by a flag variable that the script maintains), then code in the onUnload event handler can prompt the user and then submit the form, if needed.

MAKING A LINK RESPOND TO EVENTS

A link normally responds to clicking by going to the URL specified in the <A> tag. You can execute JavaScript code instead by specifying an href consisting of the keyword *Javascript* followed by a colon and the code to execute. For example, the link

<A href="Javascript:foo()> click me </A>

will display as a normal link in the document, but when the user clicks it, the JavaScript function foo() will be executed.

With a little help, JavaScript can automatically generate a hypertext outline of your HTML documents.

Chapter

Key Topics:

- **Creating an outline manually.**

- **Collapsing and expanding your outline for greater ease of use.**

- **Generating outlines automatically.**

Outlining Your Documents

An Automatic Outliner

Have you ever visited a Web page that provides an outline or table of contents? You view the outline in one frame and the actual document in another. When you click on a heading in the outline, the document automatically jumps to the corresponding section. The use of an outline can make it a lot easier to navigate through a document, particularly a large one that contains a great deal of information. The user always has the outline in view, and by utilizing the outline for some navigation tasks, the number of links required in the main document is decreased.

An automatically expanding/collapsing outline is even better. Initially, such an outline displays only the top level headings. Click a heading and the subheadings under it are displayed. Click a heading again and its subheadings are again hidden. Clicking any heading in the index displays the relevant section of the document. With an expanding/ collapsing outline, the user has control over the degree of detail that the outline shows. For relatively short and simple documents, this may not seem like such a big deal, but for more complex data—for example, your company's employee manual—a greater degree of control is desirable.

If you poke around the Web, you'll find a few outliners, and some of them work pretty well. They all—or at least all of the ones I've found—suffer from two limitations. The first and most serious drawback is that they are not really automatic. Creating the outline is a separate manual process from creating the main document. If you want to put 10 documents with outlines on your page, you have to manually create 10 outlines. Furthermore, if the document headings or structure changes, you must go and edit the outline information to reflect the changes. This is not what I call "automatic!" Why not let the computer do all the grunt work? Which is exactly what I'll do here.

The second drawback is the way these outliners—at least the ones I have examined closely—are implemented. The authors apparently never heard that JavaScript is an object-based language! The code is a twisted mass of spaghetti that would drive even the most seasoned Italian chef screaming from the room. While such programs may work properly as they are, any attempts to modify or extend them are likely to be very frustrating.

Automation

The basic approach to automating this task is simple. We want to be able to write the main document with little or no concern for the fact that it will eventually be outlined. The process of generating the outline should be performed by a program that searches the text in the data document, looks for the headings that will become entries in the outline and then generates the outline file. Of course, this must include the JavaScript code required to control the interactions between the index and data files.

There's one little problem. JavaScript can neither read nor write disk files, so there's no way it can read the data file or write the index file. But then again, no one ever claimed that JavaScript was a general–purpose programming language that could solve all your problems. Sometimes you'll have to turn to a full–featured programming language such as C++ or Basic to perform the needed task. Sorry, but there's no getting around this fact. I used Microsoft Visual Basic to write the outline generator. Don't worry if you're not a Basic programmer—you'll find a fully functional copy of the program on the companion CD-ROM that you can use to generate outlines without having the foggiest idea of how it works. If you know Basic, however, you'll be able to modify the program to suit your own specific needs.

Doing It by Hand

Before getting to the "automation" part of this project, it will be a good idea to write a JavaScript outliner manually—that is, with the index data coded by hand into the index HTML file. Once we have this outliner code working properly, we'll recognize our target when the time comes to create the automatic outline generator. Listing 8.1 shows the dummy data HTML file that I used for this project. It contains three level 1 HTML headings; two of these have a couple of level 2 HTML headings beneath them. This is the way that headings in the data file will relate to entries in the index file: each level 1 HTML heading (within <H1>...</H1> tags) becomes a top level heading in the index, and each level 2 HTML heading becomes a subheading in the index. The top level index headings are the ones that are always visible, and the subheadings are the ones that expand and collapse.

Listing 8.1   DATA1.HTML, the dummy data file for the outliner.

```
<HTML>
<HEAD>
<TITLE>
Data file for automatic outliner.</TITLE>
</HEAD>
<BODY>
<A Name "H1A"><H1>Heading 1A</H1></A>
This is Heading 1A text. This is more Heading 1A text.
This is Heading 1A text. This is more Heading 1A text.
<A Name "H2A"><H2>Heading 2A</H2></A>
This is Heading 2A text. This is more Heading 2A text.
This is Heading 2A text. This is more Heading 2A text.
<A Name="H2B"><H2>Heading 2B</H2></A>
This is Heading 2B text. This is more Heading 2B text.
This is Heading 2B text. This is more Heading 2B text.
<A Name="H1B"><H1>Heading 1B</H1></A>
```

```
This is Heading 1B text. This is more Heading 1B text.
This is Heading 1B text. This is more Heading 1B text.
<A Name="H1C"><H1>Heading 1C</H1></A>
This is Heading 1C text. This is more Heading 1C text.
This is Heading 1C text. This is more Heading 1C text.
<A Name="H2C"><H2>Heading 2C</H2></A>
This is Heading 2C text. This is more Heading 2C text.
This is Heading 2C text. This is more Heading 2C text.
<A Name="H2D"><H2>Heading 2D</H2></A>
This is Heading 2D text. This is more Heading 2D text.
This is Heading 2D text. This is more Heading 2D text.
</BODY>
</HTML>
```

The organization of the HTML files will be managed by a "parent" file whose job it is to set up the frames for display of the index and the data. This file, MAIN1.HTML, is presented in Listing 8.2. We will have three files to manage: the data file, the index file, and the code file. The code file contains only JavaScript code, with no elements that need to be displayed. We'll hide it by loading it into a frame with a width of zero. Look at Listing 8.2 to see how this is done. By assigning 100 percent of the frameset width to the index data and the main data file, we can load the code file INDEX1.HTML and have access to its functionality without displaying it on screen. Note that the index frame is initially loaded with a blank HTML file, a technique that we have used in several of our projects.

Listing 8.2   The parent HTML file for the automatic indexer, MAIN1.HTML.

```
<HTML>
<HEAD>
<TITLE>Parent document for outliner</TITLE>
<script>
</script>
</HEAD>
<FRAMESET COLS="20%,80%, *">
<FRAME SRC="BLANK.HTML" NAME="theIndex">
<FRAME SRC="DATA1.HTML" NAME="Main">
<FRAME SRC="INDEX1.HTML" NAME="Hidden">
</FRAMESET>
</HTML>
```

All the good stuff is located in INDEX1.HTML. You can learn a good deal about JavaScript programming from this code, so I will take the time to explain how it works in detail. The complete listing for this file is given later in Listing 8.3.

I started this project by deciding how the information for a single index entry would be maintained. Remember, I also want to use JavaScript's object-based capabilities, so the obvious approach is to define an object for the task. An index entry object needs to keep track of the following information:

- The text to be displayed in the index.

- The reference to the corresponding location in the data document. This is the location that the data window "goes to" when the user clicks an index entry.

- A flag indicating whether this entry has any sublevels beneath it.

- Another flag indicating whether the sublevels under this entry (if any) are currently displayed (expanded) or hidden (contracted).

- The level, 1 or 2, of this index entry.

- The reference to the entry's location within the index file.

The need for the last item may not be obvious. If each entry in the index file is itself tagged as a location with <A name=...> ... </A> tags, then we can "goto" it at will. When the user clicks an entry in the index window, code will link to that entry's own location. This may seem redundant—if the user can click an entry, it is already visible on the screen by definition. Why would we need to go to it? Because on some clicks, the index is regenerated to either show or hide subheadings. When the index is regenerated, the display is initialized to the top of the file, which may result in the clicked entry being off the screen. By setting the location object's hash property after regenerating the index, we can ensure that the just-clicked entry is displayed at the top if the index frame.

The following code shows the function that defines the object to hold the index entries:

```
function index_entry(dest, loc, sublevels, value, level, open)
    {
    //Define the object for index entries. There are
    //the following 6 properties:

    //Location in the data document that this
    //index entry points to.
    this.dest = dest
    //Location of this entry in index file.
```

```
this.loc = loc
//True if this heading has sublevels under it.
this.sublevels = sublevels
//Text to display for this level.
this.value = value
//Level (1 or 2 in current implementation) of this index entry.
this.level = level
//True if the subheads under this level are
//currently displayed.
this.open = open
}
```

Once we have defined the object, we need to instantiate one instance for each index element. The number of index elements is hard-coded into the program and passed to the function **make_array**(), which creates an array of type index_entry objects, initializing each property to the default initial values. This function is shown here:

```
function make_array(size)
    {
    //Creates and initializes an array of size elements
    // of index_entry objects.
    this.length = size + 1
    for (var i = 0; i < this.length ; i++)
        this[i + 1] = new index_entry("", false, "", 1, false)
    }
```

Once we have the array of index_entry objects, we need to initialize the objects so that each one is loaded with the real data for an individual index entry. This data is simply hard-coded into the function *init_array*(). It is generating this initialization code that will be the main task of the automatic index generator that we'll develop later in the chapter. Note that the initialization code needs only to set the value, dest, and level properties of each index_entry object—the others are left at their default values and will be changed later, when and if needed. The initialization function is shown here:

```
function init_array()
    {
    //Loads the array with index information for the specific data
    //file that this index is associated with.
    index[1].value ="Heading 1A"
    index[1].dest = "H1A"
    index[1].level = 1
    index[2].value ="Heading 2A"
    index[2].dest = "H2A"
```

```
index[2].level = 2
index[3].value ="Heading 2B"
index[3].dest = "H2B"
index[3].level = 2
index[4].value = "Heading 1B"
index[4].dest = "H1B"
index[4].level = 1
index[5].value ="Heading 1C"
index[5].dest = "H1C"
index[5].level = 1
index[6].value ="Heading 2C"
index[6].dest = "H2C"
index[6].level = 2
index[7].value ="Heading 2D"
index[7].dest = "H2D"
index[7].level = 2

//Once the array has been loaded we go thru the array and set
//the sublevels flag. For a given index entry it should be true
//only if the next index entry has a level of 2.
for (var i = 1; i < num; i++)
if (index[i].level == 1 && index[i+1].level == 2)
index[i].sublevels = true

//Now set the loc property. This is used only to identify
//the location of the index entry within the index document.
//We use a simple string consisting of "loc" followed by the
//element's array position.
for (i = 1; i <= num; i++)
index[i].loc = "loc" + i
}
```

The next task is to display the index, which is done by **display_index**(). This is a deceptively simple matter of writing a string for each index element to the blank document in the smaller of the two frames. I say "deceptively" because most of the work is done by another function named **make_entry**(). The function **display_entry**() is shown here. It works by creating a long string containing all of the index entries, clearing the index frame, then writing the string to the now-blank document. The only thing about this function that is remotely tricky is determining whether to display the subheadings under a particular top level heading. As mentioned earlier, this is controlled by the setting of the top level heading object's **showSubs** property. A couple of if statements is all we need to be in business, as shown here:

```
function display_index()
  {
```

```
//Displays the index in its frame.
var buf = ""
var showSubs
for (var i = 1; i <= num; i++)
    {
    if (index[i].level == 1)
        {
        showSubs = index[i].open
        buf += makeEntry(i)
        }
    if (index[i].level == 2 && showSubs)
        buf += makeEntry(i)
    }
clearIndex()
parent.theIndex.document.open()
parent.theIndex.document.write(buf)
parent.theIndex.document.close()
}
```

The function **makeEntry**() is a bit more complex. It has to take the information from a single index entry and generate the required HTML code and data to be written to the index document. Let's consider what this HTML code needs to accomplish:

1. To make the index more visually appealing, it would be nice to display an image next to each text entry. For the sake of simplicity and speed, I have used two of Netscape's internally defined images: internal-gopher-menu which displays a file folder icon, and internal-gopher-text which displays a page icon. I used the file folder for top level index items and the page icon for the subheadings. The HTML code will therefore need to include an <IMG> tag specifying the icon image.

2. Each element will need to be part of an anchor tag. This permits us to identify the element as a link destination by using the Name= parameter, and also to specify a JavaScript function to execute when the link is clicked with the Href=Javascript: parameter.

3. Finally, each element must include the index element's descriptive text.

We'll identify each element by assigning the string loc*n* to the Name= parameter, where n is the elements position in the array. The JavaScript code to be executed is a function called **clicked**(), which required the array index of the clicked element as its one argument. The complete HTML code for a single index element will look like this, for a top level index element with position 2 in the array:

```
<A name='loc2' href='Javascript:parent.Hidden.clicked(2)'>
<IMG SRC=internal-gopher-menu border=0>
Using JavaScript</A>
```

Here's the function that generates the HTML. It creates the entry appropriately for a top level of sublevel index entry and returns it to the caller:

```
function makeEntry(n)
    {
    //Creates the index document entry for the index object
    //with subscript n.
    var buf = ""

    //For level 1 entries.
    if (index[n].level == 1)
        {
        buf += "<A name = 'loc" + n +""
        buf += " href = 'JavaScript:parent.Hidden.clicked("
                + n + ")'>"
        buf += "<IMG SRC=internal-gopher-menu border=0>"
        buf += "" + index[n].value + "</A>"
        }

    //For level 2 entries
    if (index[n].level == 2)
        {
    buf += "<A name = 'loc" + n +"'"
        buf += " href = 'JavaScript:parent.Hidden.clicked("
                + n + ")'>"
        buf += "<IMG SRC=internal-gopher-text border=0>"
        buf += "" + index[n].value + "</A>"
        }
    buf += "<p>"
    return (buf)
    }
```

The final function is the **clicked**(), which is executed whenever the user clicks on an index entry. This function is passed to the array position of the clicked element, and the object-based planning we did earlier pays off in the simplicity of this function. It's main task is to scroll the data document to the location corresponding to the clicked index element. This is accomplished by setting the data document window's location.hash property to the index element object's dest property. The same method is used to move the index file to the proper location. The only other tasks required of this function are to toggle the element's open flag, and re-display the index if necessary. The code for **clicked**() is shown here:

```
function clicked(n)
    {
    //Called when the user clicks an on-screen index entry.

    //Toggle the clicked item's open property. This is relevant
    //only for level 1 entries but there's no harm in doing it
    //for level 2 entries as well.
    index[n].open = !index[n].open

    //We need to re-display the index only if the user
    //clicked a top-level item that has subheadings.
    if (index[n].level == 1 && index[n].sublevels)
        display_index()

    //Go to the clicked item in the index file.
    parent.theIndex.location.hash = index[n].loc

    //Go to the destination in the data document.
    parent.Main.location.hash = index[n].dest
}
```

LOCATION VS. LOCATION

Don't confuse the Document object's Location property with the Location object associated with each Window object. The former is a read-only property that contains a document's URL. The Location object also contains the URL, but it has properties that permit access to the individual URL components, such as hostname and hash. You can change the Location object's properties, causing the window to load the new URL.

The complete contents of INDEX1.HTML are presented in Listing 8.3. In addition to the functions that were covered above, there is a small amount of JavaScript code in the body of the file. This code specifies the number of index elements, calls the required initialization functions, then displays the index for the first time. Figures 8.1 and 8.2 show the indexer in operation. Figure 8.1 shows it just after loading, and 8.2 shows it after the user clicked on Heading 1A and then clicked on Heading 1C. You can see how both the index and the main document have changed their displays.

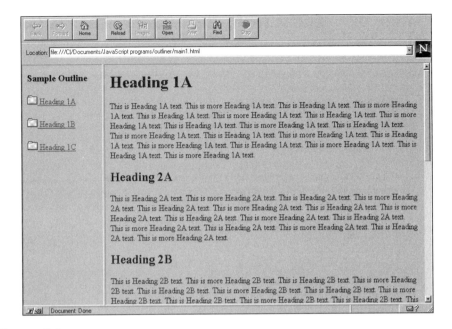

Figure 8.1

The indexer upon first loading...

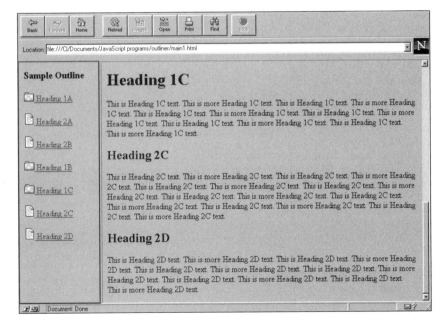

Figure 8.2

...And after clicking on Heading 1A then on Heading 1C.

Listing 8.3   INDEX1.HTML, the indexing code file for the automatic indexer.

```
<HTML>
<HEAD>
<TITLE>Index code file</TITLE>
<script>

function index_entry(dest, loc, sublevels, value, level, open)
    {
    //Define the object for index entries. There are
    //the following 6 properties.

    //Location in the data document that this
    //index entry points to.
    this.dest = dest
    //Location of this entry in index file.
    this.loc = loc
    //True if this heading has sublevels under it.
    this.sublevels = sublevels
    //Text to display for this level.
    this.value = value
    //Level (1 or 2 in current implementation) of this index entry.
    this.level = level
    //True if the subheads under this level are
    //currently displayed.
    this.open = open
    }

function make_array(size)
    {
    //Creates and initializes an array of size elements
    // of index_entry objects.
    this.length = size + 1
    for (var i = 0; i < this.length ; i++)
        this[i + 1] = new index_entry("", false, "", 1, false)
    }

function init_array()
    {
    //Loads the array with index information for the specific data
    //file that this index is associated with.
    index[1].value ="Heading 1A"
    index[1].dest = "H1A"
    index[1].level = 1
    index[2].value = "Heading 2A"
    index[2].dest = "H2A"
    index[2].level = 2
    index[3].value ="Heading 2B"
    index[3].dest = "H2B"
    index[3].level = 2
```

```
        index[4].value ="Heading 1B"
        index[4].dest = "H1B"
        index[4].level = 1
        index[5].value ="Heading 1C"
        index[5].dest = "H1C"
        index[5].level = 1
        index[6].value ="Heading 2C"
        index[6].dest = "H2C"
        index[6].level = 2
        index[7].value ="Heading 2D"
        index[7].dest = "H2D"
        index[7].level = 2

        //Once the array has been loaded we go thru the array and set
        //the sublevels flag. For a given index entry it should be true
        //only if the next index entry has a level of 2.
        for (var i = 1; i < num; i++)
            if (index[i].level == 1 && index[i+1].level == 2)
                index[i].sublevels = true

        //Now set the loc property. This is used only to identify
        //the location of the index entry within the index document.
        //We use a simple string consisting of "loc" followed by the
        //element's array position.
         for (i = 1; i <= num; i++)
            index[i].loc = "loc" + i
        }

function display_index()
    {
    //Displays the index in its frame.
    var buf = "<H3>" + theTitle + "</H3>"
    var showSubs
    for (var i = 1; i <= num; i++)
        {
        if (index[i].level == 1)
            {
            showSubs = index[i].open
            buf += makeEntry(i)
            }
        if (index[i].level == 2 && showSubs)
            buf += makeEntry(i)
        }
    clearIndex()
    parent.theIndex.document.open()
    parent.theIndex.document.write(buf)
    parent.theIndex.document.close()
    }

function clearIndex()
    {
```

```
        //Erases the contents of the Index window. The following line
        //should do the trick:

        parent.theIndex.document.clear()

        //but because of bugs in the current version of JavaScript
        //you sometimes have to use the following:

        //parent.theIndex.document.clear()
        //parent.theIndex.document.write("")
        //parent.theIndex.document.close()

        }

function makeEntry(n)
    {
    //Creates the index document entry for the index object
    //with subscript n.
    var buf = ""

    //For level 1 entries.
    if (index[n].level == 1)
        {
        buf += "<A name = 'loc" + n +"'"
        buf += " href = 'JavaScript:parent.Hidden.clicked("
                + n + ")'>"
        buf += "<IMG SRC=internal-gopher-menu border=0>"
        buf += "" + index[n].value + "</A>"
        }

     //For level 2 entries
     if (index[n].level == 2)
        {
     buf += "<A name = 'loc" + n +"'"
        buf += " href = 'JavaScript:parent.Hidden.clicked("
                + n + ")'>"
        buf += "<IMG SRC=internal-gopher-text border=0>"
        buf += "" + index[n].value + "</A>"
        }
     buf += "<p>"
     return (buf)
     }

function clicked(n)
    {
    //Called when the user clicks an on-screen index entry.

    //Toggle the clicked item's open property. This is relevant
    //only for level 1 entries but there's no harm in doing it
    //for level 2 entries as well.
    index[n].open = !index[n].open
```

```
    //We need to re-display the index only if the user
//clicked a top-level item that has subheadings.
    if (index[n].level == 1 && index[n].sublevels)
        display_index()

    //Go to the clicked item in the index file.
    parent.theIndex.location.hash = index[n].loc

    //Go to the destination in the data document.
    parent.Main.location.hash = index[n].dest
}

</script>
</HEAD>
<BODY>
<script>

//global variables specifying number of index elements and the
//document title.
var num = 7
var theTitle = "Sample Outline"

//Create the array of index objects.
index = new make_array(num)

//Load the array with the index information.
init_array()

//Display the index.
display_index()

</script>
</BODY>
</HTML>
```

Making It Automatic

Our manual outliner works fine, but remember that our primary goal was automation. With the manual version in hand, we can get a better idea of the task faced by the outline generator. It needs to generate the file—which in the above example is named INDEX1.HTML—that contains the index entry definitions and the JavaScript code. There are only two sections of this file that need to be different for each data file:

1. The section of script in the body of the document that defines the number of index elements and the title of the outline.

2. The code in the **init_array**() function that defines the individual outline entries.

Given that most of the index code file will remain unchanged, my approach is to create a copy of this file, a template, that contains all the elements that do not change plus special markers to identify the locations where the document-specific code must be inserted. The markers I used are "[[one]]" to mark the location in the init_array() function where the array of index element objects is initialized, and "[[two]]" for the location in the document body where the variables num and docTitle are initialized. (An explanation of docTitle is just around the corner.) The Visual Basic processing program that we will develop next will read in both the template file and the document. After processing the document to extract the required information, it will combine the HTML and JavaScript from the template file with the properly formatted document information and output the final copy of the index file. The "blank" HTML file and the parent document (the one that defines the frames and loads the data and index documents) are your responsibility. Once this is finished, you'll be able to load the files onto your Web site without further work.

Processing the Data File

We have already decided that level 1 and level 2 headings in the document will become top level and second level headings in the outline. Is it enough, then, to write a processing program that looks for the <H1>...</H1> and <H2>...</H2> tags in the document and extracts everything in between them? Unfortunately, no. Remember that each heading in the document must also be identified by an anchor tag so we can go to it when the user clicks the corresponding entry in the outline. There are two ways we can handle this requirement. One is to write the Visual Basic outline generation program so that it inserts the required <A...> </A> tags around each level 1 and level 2 heading in the data document. This method poses two problems. In any HTML document, level 1 and level 2 headings are already likely to be marked with anchor tags, so any tags we add will be superfluous. More importantly, we would prefer to leave the data document unchanged. Few HTML authors would want to submit their long, complex HTML documents to a process that might screw them up!

For our project, therefore, we will impose certain requirements on the data document. First, each level 1 or 2 heading that will be placed in the outline must be enclosed in anchor tags with a NAME= parameter. Headings that are not so enclosed are permitted in the data document, but they will not be placed in the outline. Secondly, each anchor/heading unit must start on a new line. In other words, the <A ...> tag must be the first thing on a line. This will simplify our coding because we can read in each line of the data file, and if the first two characters are not "<A"—we can ignore it.

Therefore, each heading in the document that you want to be placed in the outline must look like this:

```
<A Name="name"><H1>text</H1></A>
```

where *name* is the name for this anchor and *text* is the heading text that will be displayed in the document and in the outline. Of course, *name* must be unique for each heading. The <A> tag can include other parameters, such as href = if you want the heading to link to another location. As long as there is a name = parameter and everything is on one line, it will work. There's no rule against having headings that do not meet these specifications in the data document. They simply will not be placed in the outline.

One last thing—it might be nice to display a title at the top of the outline. The obvious title to display is the document title—that is, any text enclosed in <Title> ... </Title> tags in the data document. I've added the necessary code to the demonstration files, and included code in the processing program to extract the title text (if present) from the data document.

Figure 8.3 shows OUTLINER in action. To use it, click the Select data File button, then use the dialog box to select the HTML file for which you want to generate an outline. Next, click the Generate Outline button. You will be prompted to enter a name for the outline file, which will be placed in the same folder as the data file. A copy of the template file, TEMPLATE.HTML, must be present in the same folder. Once the index generation is complete, a message to that effect is displayed. You can then exit the program or generate an index for additional data files.

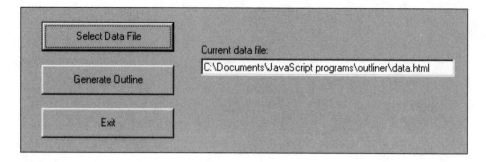

Figure 8.3

The automatic outline generator.

The code for OUTLINER is presented in Listing 8.4. Because this is a JavaScript book and not a Visual Basic book, I will not make any effort to explain how the code works, although I have tried to comment the code completely. From my perspective, if you know Visual Basic, you can figure it out for yourself. In the final analysis, you probably don't even care as long as it works!

You'll find this project's HTML files in the OUTLINER folder on the CD-ROM. The subfolder VB_PROG contains the source and executable for the Visual Basic OUTLINER project. If you do not have Visual Basic 4.0 installed on your system, you'll need to go to the INSTALL subfolder and run the SETUP program to install OUTLINER on your computer.

Listing 8.4   Source code for the Visual Basic OUTLINER program.

```
Option Explicit

Private Sub Command1_Click(Index As Integer)

Dim reply As Integer

Select Case Index
    Case 0
    ' Display File Open dialog with HTML file filter.
        CD1.InitDir = App.Path
        CD1.Filter = "HTML files (*.HTM, *.HTML)|*.HTML;*.HTM"
        CD1.ShowOpen
        DataFileName = CD1.filename
        If DataFileName = "" Then
            Command1(1).Enabled = False
```

```
                Text1.text = "<none>"
        Else
            Command1(1).Enabled = True
            Text1.text = DataFileName
        End If
    Case 1
        ProcessFile
    Case 2
        reply = MsgBox("Exit - are you sure?", vbYesNo + _
                vbQuestion)
        If reply = vbYes Then End
End Select

End Sub


Public Sub ProcessFile()

Dim FN As Integer, buf As String
Dim Template(3) As String, data(2) As String
Dim Path As String, OutFileName As String
Dim TFile As String

' Prompt the user to enter an name for the output
' file then combines it with the path where the data file
' is located and add the HTML extension. If no name entered,
' exit the sub.


OutFileName = InputBox _
        ("Enter output file name (no extension):", _
        "Output File Name")
If OutFileName = "" Then Exit Sub

' Get path from input file name.
Path = Left$(CD1.filename, Len(CD1.filename) - _
        Len(CD1.FileTitle))
OutFileName = Path & OutFileName & ".HTML"

' Get the template sections
TFile = Path & TEMPLATEFILE

If Dir$(TFile) = "" Then
    Dim Msg As String
    Msg = "The index template file " & TFile
    Msg = Msg & " cannot be found."
    MsgBox (Msg)
    Exit Sub
End If

FN = FreeFile
```

```
Open TFile For Input As #FN

' Get the first block of template code up to MARK1.
buf = ""
Template(1) = ""
Dim found As Boolean
found = False

Do
    Template(1) = Template(1) & buf & vbCrLf
    Line Input #FN, buf
    If buf = MARK1 Then
        found = True
        Exit Do
    End If
Loop While Not EOF(FN)

If (Not found) Then
    MsgBox ("This is not a proper template file.")
    Close FN
    Exit Sub
End If

' Now get the second block of the template file.

buf = ""
Template(2) = ""
found = False

Do
    Template(2) = Template(2) & buf & vbCrLf
    Line Input #FN, buf
    If buf = MARK2 Then
        found = True
        Exit Do
    End If
Loop While Not EOF(FN)

If (Not found) Then
    MsgBox ("This is not a proper template file.")
    Close FN
    Exit Sub
End If

' Finally the third block.

buf = ""
Template(3) = ""

Do
```

```
        Template(3) = Template(3) & buf & vbCrLf
        Line Input #FN, buf
Loop While Not EOF(FN)
Close #FN


'**********
' processing of data file will go here
data(1) = GetDataBlock()
data(2) = "var num =" & Str$(numIndexEntries) & vbCrLf
data(2) = data(2) & "var theTitle = " & Chr$(34) & _
            docTitle & Chr$(34) & vbCrLf
'**********

' Now we can output the index file.

FN = FreeFile

Open OutFileName For Output As #FN

Print #FN, Template(1)
Print #FN, data(1)
Print #FN, Template(2)
Print #FN, data(2)
Print #FN, Template(3)

Close #FN

MsgBox ("Outline file generated successfully.")

End Sub


Public Function GetDataBlock() As String

'Processes the data HTML document and extracts the 'information
 required for the outline.

Dim buf As String, temp As String
Dim count As Integer, FN As Integer
Dim level As Integer, quoteType As Integer
Dim p1 As Integer, p2 As Integer, p1sq As Integer
Dim p1dq As Integer
Dim data(500) As indexEntry

count = 1

'Open the data file.
FN = FreeFile
Open DataFileName For Input As #FN
```

```vbscript
'Look for the title.
docTitle = ""

Do
    Line Input #FN, temp
    buf = UCase$(temp)
    If Left$(buf, 7) = "<TITLE>" Then
        p1 = InStr(7, buf, "</T")
        docTitle = Mid$(temp, 8, p1 - 8)
        Exit Do
    End If
Loop While Not EOF(FN)

' Rewind the file
Seek #FN, 1

'Loop once for each line in the data file.
Do
    Line Input #FN, temp

    'If the line doesn't start with <A we're not interested.
    If UCase$(Left$(temp, 2)) <> "<A" Then GoTo NotHead

    'Look for an <H1> tag.
    p1 = InStr(1, temp, "<H1", 1)
    If p1 <> 0 Then
        level = 1
        GoTo A:
    End If


'Otherwise look for an <H2> tag.
    p1 = InStr(1, temp, "<H2", 1)
    If p1 <> 0 Then level = 2 Else GoTo NotHead
A:
    data(count).level = level

    'Look for the first ' or " after "name"
    p1 = InStr(1, temp, "name", 1)
    p1 = p1 + 5
    p1sq = InStr(p1, temp, Chr$(39))
    p1dq = InStr(p1, temp, Chr$(34))
    If (p1sq = 0 And p1dq = 0) Then GoTo NotHead
    If (p1sq > 0 And p1sq < p1dq) Then      ' Single quote
        quoteType = 39
        p1 = p1sq
    Else                        ' Double quote
        quoteType = 34
        p1 = p1dq
    End If
```

```
        ' Find the next occurence of the type of quotation mark.
        p2 = InStr(p1 + 1, temp, Chr$(quoteType))

        ' The name attribute of this heading is located between
        ' position p1 and p2.
        data(count).name = Mid$(temp, p1 + 1, p2 - p1 - 1)

        ' Now find the heading text.
        p1 = InStr(1, temp, "<H", 1)
        p2 = InStr(1, temp, "</H", 1)
        p1 = p1 + 4

        ' The heading text of this heading is located between
        ' position p1 and p2.
        data(count).text = Mid$(temp, p1, p2 - p1)
        count = count + 1

NotHead:
Loop While Not EOF(FN)

Close #FN

count = count - 1

'Now that we have the required information stored in data()
'we can generate the HTML code.
Dim i As Integer
buf = ""

For i = 1 To count
    buf = buf & "index[" & Str(i) & "].value = " & _
        Chr$(34) & data(i).text & Chr$(34) & vbCrLf
    buf = buf & "index[" & Str(i) & "].dest = " & Chr$(34) _
        & data(i).name & Chr$(34) & vbCrLf
    buf = buf & "index[" & Str(i) & "].level = " & _
        Str$(data(i).level) & vbCrLf
Next i

numIndexEntries = count

GetDataBlock = buf
End Function
```

One of the most important uses for JavaScript is data verification. This chapter shows you the ins and outs, presenting a collection of verification functions that you can drop into your own scripts.

Key Topics:

- **Why is data verification so important?**

- **Two approaches to data verification.**

- **Verifying text and number data.**

Using JavaScript for Data Verification

Data Verification— Say What?

Some of you may not be familiar with data verification, and it's important that you understand the term and why it is so important for Web developers. Data verification is relevant only for those Web pages where the user enters information in a form which is then submitted to the server. This sort of page is becoming more and more common as the Web evolves from its function of presenting information to being a more interactive medium. I'm sure you have already seen pages like this. They range from the very simple, such as a page that asks you to register your name and email address, to the complex, such as online ordering and interactive auctions.

If you'll permit me to briefly review, the process works like this. The HTML page is designed with objects, such as **Text** and **Select**, that allow the user to enter information. When all the data has been entered, the page is submitted, which means that the data in the various objects is sent to the server. On the server, a CGI script receives the data and processes it, sending a reply to the client, if necessary.

For the server-side processing to work properly, it is often necessary for the submitted data to follow certain rules. The exact rules will depend on the specific application, but here are a few examples:

- When entering a mailing address, the ZIP field must contain 5 or 9 digits and the STATE field must contain a valid state abbreviation.

- In an online auction, the user's bid must exceed the current high bid.

- When a merchandise order is being placed, both the Quantity and the Item Number fields must be filled in.

There are many more examples, but I'm sure you get the idea. You can avoid a whole array of potential problems if you verify the data to ensure that it meets the requirements of your specific application before the server processes it.

Let the Client Do It

Before JavaScript came along, we only had one way to perform data verification—on the server. The CGI script would contain code to check the submitted data; if problems were found, a response would be sent to the client. All of the work of verification was placed on the server; and while verifying a single data submission is rarely demanding, verifying hundreds or thousands of submissions each day can add up a lot of CPU cycles!

JavaScript moves the verification process to the client computer. The data can be verified before it is submitted, and the work is done by the client computer. In addition to removing some of the processing load from the server, this has the additional advantage of minimizing bandwidth use. This is techie talk meaning that the amount of data that has to be transmitted over the client-server connection is minimized. Not only does this reduce the load on the network, but it improves response time; users don't have to wait for data to be sent to the server and then back again to find out they made a data entry error.

Two Approaches

Data verification depends on JavaScript's event detection capabilities. There are three events of interest to us: **onBlur**, **onChange**, and **onSubmit**. Using these events gives us two general methods of verifying data:

- Use the **onBlur** and **onChange** events to verify each data item as soon as it is entered by the user. I call this the *one-at-a-time* verification method.

- Wait until all data has been entered, then use the **onSubmit** event to verify all the data just before it is submitted. This is the *all-at-once* method.

Generally speaking, I find the one-at-a-time method to be more efficient. One reason for this preference is that the user receives feedback about incorrect data entry as soon as the individual data item has been entered—when they move the focus off the object. A second reason involves shortcomings of the all-at-once verification method when there is more than one data entry error. Without some complex coding, users will find themselves in an annoying cycle where they fix one error, submit, fix the next error, submit again, fix the third error...well, you get the idea!

Despite these stated advantages of the one-at-a-time method, there is one important reason why you usually cannot rely on it alone. If the user never moves the focus to a particular object, they obviously cannot move the focus away from it; which means that the **onBlur** or **onChange** event, where the verification code is located, will not be triggered. For example, a form may contain a **Text** object that is initially blank but that requires some data to be entered. If the user never tabs or clicks to that **Text** object, its verification code will never be executed. If you rely solely on one-at-a-time verification, you may end up with invalid data submitted to the server.

Is there a solution to this apparent dilemma? Yes, and while it involves a bit of additional coding, I think it is well worth the effort. All that is required is to use both methods of validation for each data object—an immediate one that reports errors as soon as they happen, and an **onSubmit** one that will catch any data errors that were missed because of the above problems. You can maintain a flag variable for each data object and set it to true when and if the **onBlur** or **onChange** verification checks the data and finds it to be acceptable. At that point, the code in the **onSubmit** event handler will check only those data objects whose flag has not been set. This avoids the unnecessary process of validating some objects twice; however, to be honest, the overhead is trivial and the few milliseconds required will almost never be noticed.

What Data Objects Can Require Validation?

There are only four JavaScript objects that may require verification. The Text and **Textarea** objects are the most common targets of data verification. Among the verifications required are:

- The object not be left blank.

- The length of the text meets certain criteria. For example, a state abbreviation must be two characters.

- Only acceptable characters have been entered. For example, a ZIP code must be digits only.

- The text meets certain format specification. For example, a phone number must be xxx-xxx-xxxx or (xxx) xxx-xxxx.

- A numeric value falls within a certain range.

The **Select** object sometimes requires verification to ensure that the user has made a selection from the list.

The **Checked** object can require verification—not as a single object, but when several **Checked** objects are on a form and the user is required to check one or more of them. If only one selection is required, of course, you would use a **Radio** object, but if one or more selections is permitted, you must use a group of **Checked** objects.

The only other JavaScript objects that permit user input of data are the **Radio** and **Password** objects. By its very nature, the Radio object ensures that one and only one item is selected, so there is never any need to perform additional verification. As for the **Password** object, there is no point in using it if you aren't going to verify its data, so it does not require any special treatment.

All-At-Once Validation

Performing all-at-once validation does not vary a great deal in principle from doing the job one object at a time. You use the same code techniques to examine the data and compare it with what is acceptable, the same techniques to control the focus, and the same **alert()** function to display messages to the user. The difference is that all this action goes on in the form's **onSubmit** handler. Remember, if the **onSubmit** handler returns **false**, the form submission is cancelled. Thus, your form tag would look something like this:

```
<FORM NAME="myForm" ... onSubmit = "return checkAllData()">
```

The actual data verification would then be performed in the function checkAllData(), shown here in pseudocode:

```
function checkAllData()
    {
    if (all entered data is OK)
        return true
    else
        return false
    }
```

The remainder of this chapter shows you some of the techniques you can use to validate data in JavaScript. I will develop a number of general purpose validation functions that you can use in your own programs.

Validating a Select Object

When your form includes a **Select** object, you may want to require the user to make a selection before submitting the form. How can we do this? My first thought was to use the object's **selectedIndex** property, which returns the zero-base index of the selected item in the list. If no item is slected, however, the behavior of **selectedIndex** is not consistent. Depending upon the version of Navigator that I was using, the **selectedIndex** property of a **Select** object that had no item selected was either -1 or <undefined>. This ambiguity proved difficult to deal with in code, so I was forced to take another approach.

Each **Select** object has an array of elements associated with it that contain all of the individual list items. The **length** property provides the number of elements, and then the **options[]** array provides access to the individual elements. Each element, or option, has a **selected** property that is **true** if the item is selected and false otherwise. Therefore, we can loop through the list with code such as the following:

```
var flag = false
for (var i = 0; i < mySelect.length; i++)
    if (mySelect.options[i].selected)
        flag = true
return flag
```

Putting it all together in a real JavaScript function, we have the code shown in Listing 9.1.

Listing 9.1   A function to ensure that at least one item is selected in a Select object.

```
function checkSelect()
    {
    //Make sure an item is selected. We do this by going
    //thru the options array. If any option has its
    //selected property true, then an item is selected.
    var ok = false
    for (var i = 0; i < document.formName.selName.length; i++)
        {
        if (document.formName.selName.options[i].selected)
            ok = true
        }
    }
```

The code calling this function will take care of the details of displaying a message and returning the focus to the **Select** object.

VERIFICATION IN ACTION

This verification technique and the others that I will develop throughout this chapter will be demonstrated together in a JavaScript program presented at the end of the chapter.

Validating Text and Numbers

Most of the validation, you will perform with JavaScript will involve text and numbers. Since number input on a form is just another form of text, it all boils down to working with text. Unfortunately, JavaScript is not particularly strong when it comes to text manipulation capabilities. If you're used to Basic, for example, you'll find JavaScript sorely lacking. Rather than complaining, however, I decided to look on this shortcoming as a challenge. I found that, with a little creativity, it's possible to do pretty much anything you want to with text in JavaScript.

Text Length

One of the most fundamental text validations is to ensure that the length of text is within certain limits. This includes the basic task of preventing blank text fields—in other words, requiring a length greater than 0. The **length** property of the JavaScript string object makes length validations simple to perform. Listing 9.2 presents a simple function that checks whether the length of a text string is between two specified values.

You can use this function for one-ended validations, too. For example, if the user must enter some text but there is no maximum permitted length, simply call the function with the min argument set to 1 and the max argument set to some huge value.

Listing 9.2   A function to verify text length.

```
function textLength(buf, max, min)
    {
    //Returns true if the length of the text in buf
    //is between max and min. Returns false otherwise.
    if (buf.length <= max && buf.length >= min)
        return true
    else
        return false
    }
```

Phone Numbers

Lots of forms ask for the user's phone number. If you want to be spared the hassle of dialing invalid numbers, it's a good idea to perform some validation on such data. You cannot verify that the number is an actual working number, but you can verify that it is in the proper format for a phone number: xxx-xxx-xxxx where each x represents a digit. Also, you know that the three digits for the area code and for the exchange do not start with 0. Listing 9.3 presents a function that verifies a phone number according to these criteria.

If you examine the code in Listing 9.3, you'll see a couple of "tricks" that would not have been necessary if JavaScript provided a richer set of string manipulation functions. The first three digits should evaluate to a number greater than or equal to 100, since we know the first digit cannot be 0. By using JavaScript's **eval** function, we force a string—in this case, the first three characters of the phone number—to be evaluated as a number. The same technique is used to verify the exchange, the second triplet of digits.

For the separating hyphens, the task is easy: simply extract the character with the **charAt()** method and compare it with "-".

The final four digits presented the most difficulty. We cannot assume any of these digits is not 0, so the trick used earlier for the area code and the exchange cannot be applied. Instead, I created a test template string containing only the digits 0 through 9. Next, I extracted each of the last 4 characters from the phone number in turn and used the **indexOf()** method to verify that the character was found in the test string. Obviously, this test will succeed only if the last four characters are all digits.

Listing 9.3   A function to verify proper phone number format.

```
function isPhonenumber(val)
    {
    //Returns true if val is a phone number in the
    //format xxx-xxx-xxxx. Returns false otherwise.
    if (val.length != 12)
       return false
    //Check first three chars. Since no area codes start with
    // zero the eval of the first three chars must be >= 100.
    if (eval(val.substring(0,3)) < 100)
       return false
    //The 4th character should be a "-"
    if (val.charAt(3) != "-")
       return false
    //The 5th thru 7th characters should evaluate to a
    //number >= 100.
    if (eval(val.substring(4,7)) < 100)
       return false
    //The 8th character should be a "-".
    if (val.charAt(7) != "-")
       return false
    //The last 4 characters are tricky because we cannot assume
```

```
//there is not one or more leading zeros. Instead we see if
//each of the 4 characters is present is a test string
//consisting of the ten digits.
var test = "0123456789"
for (var i = 8; i < 12; i++)
    if (test.indexOf(val.charAt(i)) == -1)
        return false

//All tests passed, so...
return true
}
```

ZIP Codes

The process for verifying ZIP codes is similar to that used above for phone numbers. You require a length of 5 or 10 (for the ZIP + 4 codes). If the length is 5, all characters must be digits. When the length extends to 10, the 6th character must be a hyphen and all other characters must be digits. A function to verify ZIP codes is shown in Listing 9.4. If you read the section on verifying phone numbers, I'm sure you'll be able to figure out how the ZIP code verification works.

Listing 9.4 A function to verify proper ZIP code format.

```
function isZipcode(val)
    {
    //Returns true if val is a 5 digit ZIP code
    //or a 9 digit ZIP code in the format
    // xxxxx-xxxx. Returns false otherwise.
    var len
    if (val.length == 5)
        len = 5
    else if (val.length == 10)
        len = 10
    else
        return false

    var test = "0123456789"

    //First 5 characters must all be digits.
    for (var i = 0; i < 5; i++)
        {
        if (test.indexOf(val.charAt(i)) < 0)
            return false
        }

    //If a 5 digit ZIP we're done.
```

```
    if (len == 5)
        return true

    //The sixth character must be "-".
    if (val.charAt(5) != '-')
        return false

    //The last 4 characters must be digits.
    for (var i = 6; i < 10; i++)
        {
        if (test.indexOf(val.charAt(i)) < 0)
            return false
        }

    return true
    }
```

Numbers

The most basic aspect of verifying number input is making sure that the input is, in fact, a number! This may seem trivial, but your server-side CGI scripts can run into a lot of trouble if, for example, someone enters a lower case "ell" for the digit 1, or an upper case "oh" for a zero.

You might think that verifying numbers could be accomplished using the same techniques as I described above for phone numbers and ZIP codes. It's not that simple, however. A number can contain a decimal point, and in some cases may include a leading plus or minus sign. For currency amounts, a leading dollar symbol may be permissible. For the function presented below, I defined a number as having an optional leading plus or minus sign, at most one decimal point, and otherwise containing only digits. The function in Listing 9.5 does the trick.

It is instructive to look at how this function works. Again, I used the technique of creating a template string that contains the permitted characters and then compared the input text character by character against the template. Since the first character in the string that is being validated can contain + or - as well as a decimal or a digit, we have two test strings—one used for the first character, and the other (lacking the + and - characters) for the remainder of the characters being tested.

There's one more complication. Since only a single decimal point is permitted, we need to maintain a flag indicating whether a decimal point has already been found or not. If this flag is false, then a decimal point will be accepted and the flag set to true; if the flag is true, then another decimal point will not be accepted.

Listing 9.5   A function to verify input of a number.

```
function isNumber(val)
    {
    //Returns true if val is a number defined as
    //    having an optional leading + or -.
    //    having at most 1 decimal point.
    //    otherwise containing only the characters 0-9.
    var test1 = ".+-0123456789'
    var test2 = ".0123456789"
    var c
    var decimal = false
    //The first character can be + - . or a digit.
    c = test1.indexOf(val.charAt(0))
    //Was it a decimal?
    if (c == 0)
        decimal = true
    else if (c < 1)
        return false

    //Remaining characters can be only . or a digit,
// but only one decimal point is allowed.
    for (var i = 1; i < val.length; i++)
        {
        //alert(val.charAt(i))
        c = test2.indexOf(val.charAt(i))
        //alert(c)
        if (c < 0)
            return false
        else
            if (c == 0)
                {
                if (decimal)         // Second decimal.
                    return false
                else
                    decimal = true
                }
        }
    return true
    }
```

Setting Limits

Another common type of validation required with numbers is setting limits—making sure that the value entered is neither too large or too small. If someone visiting your online shoe store orders 5,000 pairs of shoes, you might become suspicious! Verifying that a number falls within a certain range is a simple task, and the function in Listing 9.6 shows how it is done. This function adds a convenient touch by not requiring that you pass the maximum and minimum limits in a set order. Rather, it looks at the two limit arguments and figures out which is the upper limit and which the lower.

Listing 9.6   A function to verify that a number falls within a certain range.

```
function isBetween(val, limit1, limit2)
    {
    //Returns true if val is between limit1 and
    //limit2, or equal to either. Returns false
    //otherwise.
    var max = (limit1 > limit2) ? limit1 : limit2
    var min = (limit1 < limit2) ? limit1 : limit2

    if (val == max || val == min)
        return true
    if (val > min && val < max)
        return true
    return false
    }
```

Trying It Out

I've shown you a variety of techniques for using JavaScript to validate data input. It's time to take a look at these techniques in action. VALIDATE.HTML, in Listing 9.7, demonstrates all of the functions developed in this chapter. If you pay attention to these techniques and take the time to implement data validation in your own HTML forms, your effort will be repaid many times over.

Listing 9.7   VALIDATE.HTML demonstrates the data validation techniques discussed in the chapter.

```
<HTML>
<HEAD>
<script>
```

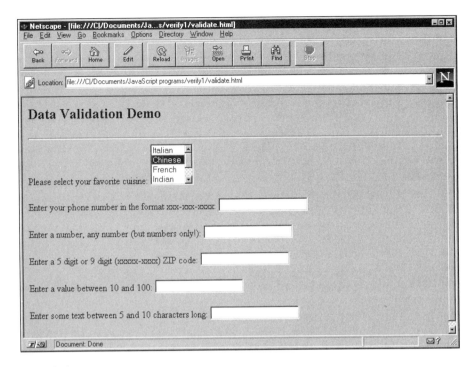

Figure 9.1

Testing the data validation functions with VALIDATE.HTML.

```
function textLength(buf, max, min)

    {
    //Returns true if the length of the text in buf
    //is between max and min. Returns false otherwise
    if (buf.length <= max && buf.length >= min)
        return true
    else
        return false
    }

function isZipcode(val)
    {
    //Returns true if val is a 5 digit ZIP code
    //or a 9 digit ZIP code in the format
    //xxxxx-xxxx. Returns false otherwise.
    var len
    if (val.length == 5)
        len = 5
    else if (val.length == 10)
        len = 10
    else
        return false
```

```
    var test = "0123456789"

    //First 5 characters must all be digits.
    for (var i = 0; i < 5; i++)
        {
        if (test.indexOf(val.charAt(i)) < 0)
            return false
        }

    //If a 5 digit ZIP we're done.
    if (len == 5)
        return true

    //The sixth character must be "-".
    if (val.charAt(5) != '-')
        return false

    //The last 4 characters must be digits.
    for (var i = 6; i < 10; i++)
        {
        if (test.indexOf(val.charAt(i)) < 0)
            return false
        }

    return true
    }

function isPhonenumber(val)
    {
    //Returns true if val is a phone number in the
    //format xxx-xxx-xxxx. Returns false otherwise.
    if (val.length != 12)
        return false
    //Check first three chars. Since no area codes start with zero
    //the eval of the first three chars must be >= 100.
    if (eval(val.substring(0,3)) < 100)
        return false
    //The 4th character should be a "-"
    if (val.charAt(3) != "-")
        return false
    //The 5th thru 7th characters should evaluate to a
    //number >= 100.
    if (eval(val.substring(4,7)) < 100)
        return false
    //The 8th character should be a "-".
    if (val.charAt(7) != "-")
        return false
    //The last 4 characters are tricky because we cannot assume
    //there is not one or more leading zeros. Instead we see if
    //each of the 4 characters is present in a test string
    //consisting of the ten digits.
```

```javascript
    var test = "0123456789"
    for (var i = 8; i < 12; i++)
        if (test.indexOf(val.charAt(i)) == -1)
            return false

    //All tests passed, so...
    return true
    }

function isBetween(val, limit1, limit2)
    {
    //Returns true if val is between limit1 and
    //limit2, or equal to either. Returns false
    //otherwise.
    var max = (limit1 > limit2) ? limit1 : limit2
    var min = (limit1 < limit2) ? limit1 : limit2

    if (val == max || val == min)
        return true
    if (val > min && val < max)
        return true
    return false
    }

function isNumber(val)
    {
    //Returns true if val is a number defined as
    //   having an optional leading + or -.
    //   having at most 1 decimal point.
    //   otherwise containing only the characters 0-9.
    var test1 = ".+-0123456789"
    var test2 = ".0123456789"
    var c
    var decimal = false
    //The first character can be + - . or a digit.
    c = test1.indexOf(val.charAt(0))
    //Was it a decimal?
    if (c == 0)
        decimal = true
    else if (c < 1)
        return false

    //Remaining characters can be only . or a digit, but only
//one decimal point is permitted.
    for (var i = 1; i < val.length; i++)
        {
        //alert(val.charAt(i))
        c = test2.indexOf(val.charAt(i))
        //alert(c)
        if (c < 0)
            return false
        else
```

```
                    if (c == 0)
                        {
                        if (decimal)          // Second decimal.
                            return false
                        else
                            decimal = true
                        }
                }
        return true
        }


//***************************************************

function checkPhone(val)
    {
    if (!isPhonenumber(val))
        {
        var msg = "Please use the xxx-xxx-xxxx format"
          alert(msg)
         document.form1.phone.focus()
         }
    }

function checkNumber(val)
    {
    if (!isNumber(val))
        {
            var msg = "A number, puh-leeese!"
        alert(msg)
            document.form1.number.focus()
            }
    }

function checkZip(val)
    {
    if (!isZipcode(val))
        {
            var msg = "That's not a valid ZIP code, knucklehead!'
        alert(msg)
            document.form1.zip.focus()
        }
}

function checkBetween(val, max, min)
    {
    if (!isBetween(val, max, min))
        {var msg = "Did you flunk math? Try again!"
        alert(msg)
            document.form1.between.focus()
        }
    }
```

```
function checkCuisine()
    {
    //Make sure an item is selected. We do this by going
    //thru the options array. If any option has its
    //selected property true, then an item is selected.
    var ok = false
    for (var i = 0; i < document.form1.cuisine.length; i++)
        {
        if (document.form1.cuisine.options[i].selected)
            ok = true
        }
    if (!ok)
        {
        var msg = "What, not hungry? Please select one!"
        alert(msg)
        document.form1.cuisine.focus()
        }
     return ok
    }

function checkLength(text, max, min)
    {
    if (!textLength(text, max, min))
        {
            var msg = "Forget how to count? Try again, please!"
        alert(msg)
        document.form1.length.focus()
        }
    }
</script>
</HEAD>
<BODY>
<FORM name="form1">
<H2>Data Validation Demo</H2>
<HR>
Please select your favorite cuisine:
<SELECT name="cuisine" size="4" onBlur="checkCuisine()">
<OPTION value="Italian">Italian
<OPTION value="Chinese">Chinese
<OPTION value="French">French
<OPTION value="Indian">Indian
<OPTION value="Mexican">Mexican
<OPTION value="German">German
</SELECT><P>
Enter your phone number in the format xxx-xxx-xxxx:
<INPUT type="text" name="phone" value=""
     onBlur="checkPhone(this.value)"><P>
Enter a number, any number (but numbers only!):
<INPUT type="text" name="number" value=""
     onBlur="checkNumber(this.value)"><P>
Enter a 5 digit or 9 digit (xxxxx-xxxx) ZIP code:
```

```
<INPUT type="text" name="zip" value=""
    onBlur="checkZip(this.value)"><P>
Enter a value between 10 and 100:
<INPUT type="text" name="between" value=""
    onBlur="checkBetween(this.value, 10, 100)"><P>
Enter some text between 5 and 10 characters long:
<INPUT type="text" name="length" value=""
    onBlur="checkLength(this.value, 10, 5)"><P>
</FORM>
<script>
document.form1.cuisine.focus()
</script>
</BODY>
</HTML>
```

Presenting a variety
of JavaScript
techniques and
scripts that you'll
find useful for your
Web documents.

Chapter 10

JavaScript Odds and Ends

Using Java Applets

The term applet means more than simply a small application! Yes, they do tend to be small, but more importantly they are specifically designed for use on the Internet. Being small, an applet is easily downloaded from host to client computer. And that's exactly what is supposed to happen. You, the Web page designer, can write, borrow, or buy applets to perform specific tasks that are beyond the capabilities of JavaScript and HTML. In your Web page's HTML document, you include code to "call" the applet. The applet is downloaded to the client's computer and executed within the browser.

To the user, it all appears perfectly seamless. The applet displays as part of the document being viewed, and all of the behind-the-scenes complexity is hidden. Applets are written in Java, a general purpose programming language that doesn't have much in common with

JavaScript other than the name. Being a general purpose language, Java has many capabilities that are not needed by a scripting language, such as the ability to create graphics and to read and write disk files. Java also has numerous security features built in, and obvious necessity for programs to be delivered online.

WHAT ABOUT ACTIVEX CONTROLS?

The term ActiveX refers to Microsoft's technology for providing essentially the same thing that Java applets do—small, self-contained programs for extending web pages. ActiveX is based on the object linking and embedding (OLE) standard, and while creating an ActiveX object is a bit different from creating a Java applet, using them in your Web page is pretty much the same. ActiveX objects are covered in a later chapter.

This is not a chapter about Java, however. Rather, I will show you how to access Java applets from your HTML documents. There are numerous books available on the Java language, and if you want to explore creating applets then that's where you should turn. Fortunately, using an applet is a lot easier than creating one!

The fundamental HTML tag for incorporating a Java applet in a Web page is as follows:

```
<APPLET code = "className" WIDTH = w HEIGHT = h>
</APPLET>
```

The className argument is the name of the Java class (applet). The WIDTH and HEIGHT parameters specify the size of the area in the browser window where the applet is displayed. These are the minimum components of an <APPLET> tag. Note that this is HTML code, not JavaScript code, and it is placed outside any <SCRIPT> ... </SCRIPT> tags in your document. For example, suppose you want to include the Java applet with the class name "LiveImageDemo.class". Here's the HTML code to do it:

```
<APPLET code="LiveImageDemo.class " WIDTH=200 HEIGHT=150>
</APPLET>
```

When a client loads this HTML file into their browser and this tag is encountered, it verifies that the applet is available on the server, sets the requested rectangular region aside, then downloads the applet and starts executing it.

The <APPLET> tag offers several optional parameters that control various aspects of how the applet and the surrounding document contents are displayed.

- The ALIGN parameter controls how text surrounding the applet is aligned. The possible settings for this parameter are listed in the table below.

- The HSPACE and VSPACE parameters control how much blank space is left between the edges of the applet area and the surrounding material, expressed in pixels.

- The CODEBASE attribute lets you specify a path to the Java applet file if it is not in the same directory on the server as the HTML file.

ALIGN = parameter	Result
TEXTTOP	Top of applet region aligns with the top of the tallest text on the line.
TOP	Top of applet region aligns with the top of the tallest item of any kind on the line.
ABSMIDDLE	Center of applet region aligns with center of tallest item on the line.
MIDDLE	Center of applet region aligns with center of text baseline.
BASELINE or BOTTOM	Bottom of applet region aligns with text baseline.
ABSBOTTOM	Bottom of applet region aligns with bottom of lowest item of any kind on the line.

Here, then, is the <APPLET> tag to incorporate an applet named "test.class" specifying non-default values for ALIGN, HSPACE and VSCPACE, and CODEBASE:

```
<APPLET code="test.class" WIDTH=200 HEIGHT=150 ALIGN="MIDDLE"
 VSPACE=50 HSPACE=50 CODEBASE= "C:/JAVA/APPLETS">
</APPLET>
```

APPLET PARAMETERS

Most applets have parameters, or properties, that control various aspects of their operation. Each individual applet will have its own set of properties, but the procedure for setting them is the same. After the <APPLET> tag, but before the </APPLET> tag, you include a <PARAM> tag for each applet parameter that needs to be set. The basic syntax is:

```
<PARAM NAME="paramName" VALUE="paramValue">
```

The names of the parameters, and the values they can be assigned, will be different for each applet. Refer to the documentation for the applets you are using for further information. You can include as many <PARAM> tags as needed within the <APPLET> ... </APPLET> tags, placing each one on its own line.

Web Watch

If you're interested in Java, you should visit Sun's Java page at http://www.javasoft.com/java.sun.com/products/. You can download their Java Developer's Kit from this site. For lots of information and links related to Java, try http://www.gamelan.com/.

Scrolling a Status Bar Message

You have probably seen Web pages that have a scrolling message display in the browser's status bar. This can be a nice effect that provides a polished and custom appearance to your pages. Have you ever wondered how this is done? You'll find out in this section.

The Window object has a **status** property that you can use to set the text that is displayed in the status bar, like this:

```
window.status = ''My message"
```

So far it seems easy, but the above code will not scroll, of course. In fact, the status bar cannot really scroll at all. We can, however, create the illusion of scrolling by repeatedly displaying a message that changes slightly each time. Let's say the status bar can display 8 characters (it's actually much wider). We start with a message that consists of the actual message with 8 spaces tacked on at the beginning. In this, as well as the following illustrations, the row of X's represents the display positions in the status bar and dashes represent spaces in the message. We start by displaying the following:

```
xxxxxxxx
--------Message
```

The status bar will appear blank because the actual message text is out of sight—past the right edge of the status bar's display area. After a brief delay, we display the following:

```
xxxxxxxx
-------Message
```

Note that we have placed one less space in front of the message. As a result, the first letter of the message text becomes visible at the right side of the status bar. Next, we display this:

```
xxxxxxxx
------Message
```

Now, two letters of the message are visible. Finally, after 9 more cycles, we reach the point where the left end of the message text is "scrolled" out of view:

```
xxxxxxxx
sage----
```

This may seem trivial conceptually, but the programming is a little tricky. We'll use the **Timer** object to control the scrolling—both the delay between "frames" during a scroll and the delay between messages, if we want to scroll the message more than once. I used a variable named offset that keeps track of the number of spaces to be added to the start of the message. If offset becomes negative, it means the message has reached the left edge of the status bar and we must strip characters off the start of the message text.

The function **scrollMessage**() is the heart of the scrolling program. Each time it is called, it uses the value of the offset variable to generate the message, then displays it in the status bar and sets the **Timer** object to call the function again after the specified delay. Once the entire message has been scrolled, the function determines if a repeat scroll has been requested; if so, it starts the whole process again.

If you load the HTML file shown in Listing 10.1 into your browser, you will see a scrolling message in the status bar, as shown in Figure 10.1. It will scroll twice, then quit. You can easily adapt this code to your own HTML files. Several variables that are identified by comments in the code can be utilized to set the scrolling speed, the number of repeats, and other aspects of operation.

Listing 10.1   SCROLLER.HTML demonstrates how to scroll a message in the status bar.

```
<HTML>
<HEAD>
<SCRIPT LANGUAGE="JavaScript">

// SCROLLER
// Scrolls your message in the status bar.
```

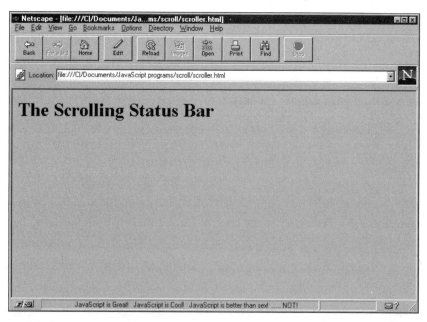

Figure 10.1

Displaying a scrolling status bar message.

```
//
// To start scrolling when your page loads, include the
// statement ONLOAD="startScroll()" in your BODY tag.

// Put you message in the following variables. We split the
// message among multiple variables because there seems to
// be a limit of about 240 characters for a string assignment.
// Use more or fewer strings depending on the length of
// your message.

var s1 = "JavaScript is Great!    "
var s2 = "JavaScript is Cool!    "
var s3 = "JavaScript is better than sex! "
var s4 = " ..... NOT! "
var message = s1 + s2 + s3 + s4

// This blank string determines the initial position of the
// message in the status line. Ideally it should be just a
// bit longer than the width of the status line. Too short
// and your message starts off partially in view; too long
// and there's an annoying delay before the message comes
// into view. Again we use the trick of creating one
// relatively short string and concatenating several of them.
// Change the value of padLength to change the blank string's
// length.

var tenSpaces = "          "
var padLength = 15
var blankString = " "

for (var i = 0; i < padLength; i++)
  blankString += tenSpaces

// Assign higher values for slower scrolling.
var scrollSpeed = 100

// Initial delay before scrolling starts.
var scrollDelay = 500

// Delay before repeating message. Valid only
// if scrollRepeat > 0.
var scrollRepeatDelay = 500

// How many times to repeat the message after the first.
var scrollRepeat = 1

// Number of spaces before the message. If this value
// is negative then we must trim the start of the message.
var offset

// For the Timer object.
var theTimer = null
```

```
function startScroll()
    {
    offset = blankString.length
    theTimer = window.setTimeout("scrollMessage()", scrollDelay)
    }

function scrollMessage()
    {
    if ((offset > 0) && (offset <= blankString.length))
        {
        window.status = blankString.substring(0, offset) + message
        offset—
        theTimer = window.setTimeout("scrollMessage()", scrollSpeed)
        }
    else if (offset <= 0)
        {
        if (-offset < message.length)
        {
          window.status = message.substring(-offset, message.length)
          offset—
          theTimer = window.setTimeout("scrollMessage()",
                    scrollSpeed)
        }
        else
        {
          window.status = ""
          if (scrollRepeat)
            {
                offset = blankString.length
                theTimer = window.setTimeout("scrollMessage()",
                        scrollRepeatDelay)
                if (scrollRepeat > 0)
                    scrollRepeat—
            }
        }
        }
    }
}
//—></SCRIPT>
</HEAD>

<BODY onload="startScroll()">
<H1>
The Scrolling Status Bar
</H1>
</BODY>
</HTML>
```

Web Watch

Many Web applications benefit from the use of custom digit images to display numbers in something other than the standard font. Some digit images look like a digital clock, others like a automobile odometer, and so on. For a collection of digit images that you can use in your own programs (as long as you credit the creator), go to http://www.issi.com/people/russ/digits/digits.html. You'll also find a digit collection on the CD-ROM.

Cookies

No one seems to know where the name cookie came from, and it certainly doesn't seem to make much sense. But it has stuck, so you had better get used to it! A cookie is a small bit of information that can be written to the client computer's disk. Since it is on disk, it is persistent—that is, it will be there in the future. These are technically known as *persistent client state HTTP cookies.*

"Hold on a minute," you are probably saying. "Isn't one of JavaScript's safety features the inability to access the client's disk in any way?" Yes indeed, but cookies are cleverly designed not to compromise that safety. All cookies are kept in a text file named COOKIES.TXT. That's the only choice—the user or programmer has no choice as to the name of the file, its format, or the folder in which it is kept. A single text file is not capable of doing the sort of damage that people fear. At worst, writing a lot of cookies to the file will result in a large COOKIES.TXT file, which is hardly a major problem.

Why do we need cookies at all? As the Web evolved, it became clear to developers that being able to store bits of data on each client that were later retrievable by the server would create significant advantages. Here's an example. Suppose that a retail sales Web page requires each customer to enter a variety of basic information such as name, address, and so on. Without the means to store persistent information on a client, the server would have to query all visitors for this data each time they viewed the page, no matter how many times they had done so before. By storing a cookie, the client is able to identify a visitor and call up that data—either from its own database or from the cookie itself.

Another use for cookies came as a result of an unscrupulous practice of some Web page owners. As I'm sure you have noticed, many Web pages have advertising where the rates that can be charged are dependent upon the number of visitors to your page. Believe me, Yahoo can charge a lot more for advertising than I can! Visits are often tabulated by a counter, which I'm sure you've seen on some of the pages you have visited. Such a counter is implemented with the help of Common Gateway Interface, or CGI, programming. To artificially inflate their "hit" count, some people would write a "robot" program which would repeatedly log on to their page when run on another computer. By storing a cookie on the client computer each time someone visits, repeat visitors could be detected and the count would be maintained honestly.

The Parts of a Cookie

The most important parts of a cookie are its NAME and VALUE components. You can think of these as corresponding to the name of a variable and the value it holds. For example, after I place my first order on the Smith Clothing Company's Web page, their software might write a cookie to my disk with the NAME "SmithClothing" and the Value "Aitken001." When I log on again next week, their software will search my cookie file for a cookie named "SmithClothing." If it did not find one, it would treat me as a new customer. Because it does find one, it will retrieve the VALUE data and use that to identify me.

A cookie can also have an expiration date. After that date passes, the cookie ceases to exist. Actually, all cookies have an expiration date. If an expiration is not specified when a cookie is created, it is automatically set to expire at the end of the user's session.

Each cookie also has domain-name and path attributes, ensuring that a program at one URL does not interfere with or retrieve cookies that do not belong to it.

Finally, a cookie can be marked secure, in which case it will only be transmitted if the communications channel with the host is a secure one—that is, an HTTPS (HTTP over SSL) server. If a cookie is not specified as secure, it is considered safe to send it over unsecured channels.

The Cookie Property

Getting at the cookie is easy and is accomplished by means of the **document** object's cookie property. Remember that the term cookie is used in two ways: both to refer to a specific item identified by a NAME attribute, and also to refer to the entire cookie file. Remember also that access to data in the cookie file is limited by the restrictions of the domain and path attributes.

Working with cookies can be confusing. The cookie property provides access to the entire cookie for the current document, and you must use string methods such as **substring**, **charAt**, **indexOf**, and **lastIndexOf** to obtain the value of specific cookies. The process is made more difficult by the fact that the Netscape cookie specification is still changing, and there's no guarantee that what works today will work in the future. To make your life a bit easier (I hope!), I have created a set of JavaScript functions for working with cookies. Today, these functions work with the current Netscape Navigator, but I will repeat my warning that things may change in the future.

The code for the functions is included in COOKIE.HTML in Listing 10.2, which also includes code to demonstrate the use of the functions. Figure 10.2 shows the demonstration program executing.

In addition to helping you use cookies, this code illustrates another JavaScript capability that we have not covered previously: functions with a variable number of arguments. It's worthwhile to take some time to understand how this works, and that's our next topic.

Listing 10.2   COOKIE.HTML demonstrates how to create and access cookies.

```
<html>
<head>
<title>Functions for Cookies</title>
<script language="javascript">
```

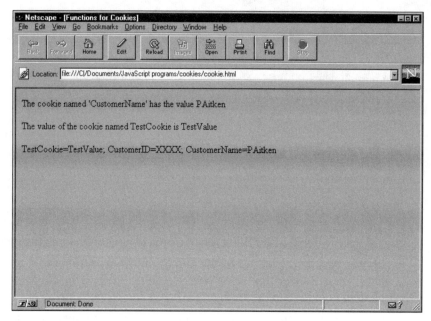

Figure 10.2

COOKIE.HTML demonstrates use of the cookie functions.

```
function getCookieValue (pos)
    {
    // Function to return the decoded value of a cookie. You will
    // not call this in your script; it is used internally.

    var temp = document.cookie.indexOf (";", pos)
    if (temp == -1)
        temp = document.cookie.length
    return unescape(document.cookie.substring(pos, temp))
    }

function getCookie (name)
    {
    //  Returns the value of the cookie specified by "name".
    //  Returns null if the cookie is not found.

    var cName = name + "="
    var len = cName.length
    var cookieLen = document.cookie.length
    var i = 0, j
    while (i < cookieLen)
        {
        j = i + len
        if (document.cookie.substring(i, j) == cName)
            return getCookieValue (j)
        i = document.cookie.indexOf(" ", i) + 1
```

```
            if (i == 0)
                break
        }
    return null
}


// Function to create or update a cookie.
// The function requires two arguments:
//
//        name -   the cookie name.
//            value - the cookie value.
//
// The following arguments are optional:
//    expDate - cookie expiration date in a Date object. If
//     this argument is left out or null, the cookie expires at
//     the end of the current session.
//
//    path - the path for which the cookie is valid. If this
//     argument is left out or null, the calling document's path
//     is used.
//
//    domain - the domain for which the cookie is valid.
//     If this argument is left out or null, the calling document's
//     domain is used.

//     secure - true or false indicating whether cookie is secure.
//
// The optional arguments must be passed in the indicated order.
// Use null for a placeholder as needed.

function makeCookie(name, value)
    {
    var x1 = makeCookie.arguments
    var x2 = makeCookie.arguments.length
    var expDate = (x2 > 2) ? x1[2] : null
    var path = (x2 > 3) ? x1[3] : null
    var domain = (x2 > 4) ? x1[4] : null
    var secure = (x2 > 5) ? x1[5] : false
    var buf = name + "=" + escape (value)
    buf += ((expDate == null) ? "" : ("; expires=" +
            expDate.toGMTString()))
     buf += ((path == null) ? "" : ("; path=" + path))
    buf += ((domain == null) ? "" : ("; domain=" + domain))
    buf += ((secure == true) ? "; secure" : "")
    document.cookie = buf
    }

function deleteCookie (cookieName)
    {
    //  Delete a cookie by setting its expiration date
    //   to the current date and time. The one argument is
    //   the cookie name in a string object.
```

```
        var now = new Date()
        //Set now to one instant ago.
        now.setTime (now.getTime() - 1)
        // Get the cookie's value.
        var cookieValue = getCookie (cookieName)
        document.cookie = cookieName + "=" + cookieValue +
                          "; expires=" + now.toGMTString()
    }

</script>
</head>
<body>
<script language="javascript">
<!- begin script

//Set a basic cookie.

makeCookie("CustomerName", "PAitken")
//Retrieve its value.

document.write("The cookie named 'CustomerName' has the value ")
document.write(getCookie("CustomerName"))
document.write("<P><P>")

//Create a cookie with expiration in 48 hours.

// Create a date object.
var theDate = new Date ()
theDate.setTime (theDate.getTime() + (48 * 60 * 60 * 1000))
makeCookie("TestCookie", "TestValue", theDate)

//Display the value of the cookie named "TestCookie"
var buf
buf = "The value of the cookie named TestCookie is "
buf += getCookie("TestCookie")
buf += "<P><P>"
document.write(buf)

//Display the entire cookie for this document.
document.write(document.cookie)

// end script ->
</script>
</body>
</html>
```

Functions with a Variable Number of Arguments

A function in JavaScript, like almost everything else, is treated as an object. A function object is identified by the function name. The two properties of interest provide access to the number of arguments passed and the arguments themselves. Thus, for a function named **foo**(), **foo.ar guments.length** returns the number of arguments passed and the array **foo.arguments[]** provides access to the actual arguments. This includes arguments that are passed in named parameters that are part of the function header.

An example will make this clearer. Suppose we define a function named **foo**() as follows:

```
function foo(count)
    {
    args = foo.arguments
    numargs = foo.arguments.length
    // Other function code.
    }
```

Then, suppose we call **foo**() like this:

```
x = foo(10)
```

Within **foo**(), the variable numArgs will have the value 1, and args[0] will have the value 10. Note that count will also have the value 10 in this case. Next, let's we call **foo**() like this:

```
x = foo(10, "Smith", "Kansas")
```

In this situation, numArgs will have the value 3, and args[0] through args[2] will have the values 10, "Smith," and "Kansas" respectively. You can see that using named parameters, such as count in the earlier example, is optional. You always have access to the arguments array, which contains all the passed arguments. When a function requires certain arguments and others are optional, the usual practice is to provide named parameters for the required arguments and have any optional arguments listed last.

To demonstrate using this feature of JavaScript, I have written a function that will return the average when passed any number of numeric arguments. The program is presented in Listing 10.3.

Listing 10.3 Demonstrating a function that takes a variable number of arguments.

```
<HTML>
<HEAD>
<TITLE>Demonstrating variable number of function arguments.
</TITLE>
<script language = "javascript">

function average()
    {
    var numArgs = average.arguments.length
    var args = average.arguments
    var total = 0

    for (var i = 0; i < numArgs; i++)
        total += args[i]

    return total/numArgs
    }

</script>
</HEAD>
<BODY>
<script>
var x
x = average(1,4,76,34,65)
document.write("The average of 1, 4, 76, 34, and 65 is ")
document.write(x)
document.write("<P>")
x = average(456,765,12,34,65,98,67,45,34)
document.write("The average of 456, 765, 12, 34, 65, 98, 67,
                45, and 34 is ")
document.write(x)

</script>
</BODY>
</HTML>
```

Web Watch

Ziff-Davis has a pretty neat home page at http://www.zdnet.com/home/
filters/main.html. I suggest you browse through their software library,
which includes a lot of useful shareware and freeware that you can
download. Another good site for downloading programs, with an
emphasis on Windows 95, is http://www.iag.net/mgoetz/win95.html.

Chapter 11

VBScript from Step One

Before presenting the nuts and bolts of VBScript, I want to be sure that you know where I am coming from. Some of you will take the time to read the sections in this book about JavaScript, others will not. Some of you will be experienced Visual Basic programmers, others will know nothing about basic programming at all. To make things more difficult for everyone, VBScript itself is in a preliminary and unfinished state. I'll just do my best to meet the needs of a diverse audience. For those of you that are new to Basic, that means covering the essentials. If you are already familiar with Basic, you'll no doubt find lots of material here that you already know and may even seem a little boring. Regardless, I strongly suggest that you don't skip any parts of these chapters, because there are many ways—some subtle and some not so subtle—in which VBScript differs from traditional Basic.

In addition to those finer distinctions, I will make occasional reference to JavaScript, particularly in those areas where VBScript and JavaScript differ significantly in the way they perform and approach various tasks. I'll make a special effort to point out tasks that VBScript can do, but not JavaScript, or vice versa.

An Overview

Perhaps the most important difference between these two scripting languages is the extent to which they rely on objects. As you have seen, JavaScript is a strongly object-based language that relies on objects and their attendant methods and properties for a great deal of its functionality. In contrast, VBScript—at least in its current incarnation—relies much less upon objects and much more on built-in functions. To illustrate, let's take a quick look at how these two languages deal with strings.

As you learned earlier in the book, JavaScript has the built-in **string** object. Whatever text data exists in a JavaScript program—for example, in a named variable—a **string** object automatically exists. You can then use this object's methods and properties to manipulate and obtain information about the string data. The following JavaScript code creates a variable named buffer and loads it with the text "JavaScript."

```
var buffer = "javascript"
```

Now, you can use the string object's **length** property to determine the length of the text:

```
len = buffer.length
```

Similarly, you can call upon the string object's charAt() method to extract a single character from a specified position in the string:

```
char = buffer.charAt(5)
```

VBScript permits the same types of string operations, but uses built-in functions instead. Here is the VBScript code to create a variable and initialize it to "VBScript":

```
Dim buffer
buffer = "vbscript"
```

To obtain the length of the string, call the **Len()** function:

```
length = Len(buffer)
```

Likewise, to extract a single character from the string, we use the **Mid()** function:

```
char = Mid(buffer, 5, 1)
```

Is one approach better than the other? You will hear a lot of programmers preach the object-oriented gospel, claiming that any programming technique that is object-based is automatically superior to anything else. In certain programming situations, much can be said for this point of view. In the case of scripting languages, however, it does not hold true. Object-oriented programming languages are indeed vastly superior for large, complex, traditional programming tasks. For example, if I were writing a large, sophisticated statistical analysis program, I would certainly choose an object-oriented language such as C++ over a non object-oriented language. For the small and relatively simple programs that are written with JavaScript and VBScript, the advantages of object-oriented programming mostly fade away.

The Structure of a VBScript Program

In many ways a VBScript program is like a JavaScript program, at least in terms of how it fits in an HTML file. Procedures, defined as discreet blocks of code that have been assigned a name, are placed in the file's header, the section between the <HEAD> and </HEAD> tags. Other non-procedure code is placed in the file body. Also, VBScript code must be enclosed in <SCRIPT> tags with a modifier that identifies the script language in use. Finally, VBScript code should be enclosed in HTML comment tags to prevent it from being displayed in browsers that do not support VBScript. The basic (pun intended?) structure of an HTML file with VBScript is as follows:

```
<HTML>
<HEAD>
<script language = "VBS"
<!-
VBScript code goes here
->
</script>
```

```
</HEAD>
<BODY>
<script language = "VBS">
<!-
VBScript code goes here too.
->
</script>
</BODY>
</HTML>
</script>
```

VBScript and Visual Basic

Many programmers who are starting to use VBScript to enhance their Web pages have had previous experience with the "big" Visual Basic. How much of that experience can be transferred to VBScript? The answer is, "Quite a lot." Remember that VBScript is a subset of Visual Basic, so nearly everything in VBScript is part of Visual Basic. The major difference lies in what is lost: a significant number of things included in Visual Basic are not a part of VBScript.

THE VISUAL BASIC FAMILY

The Visual Basic product line actually has three members. At the top is Visual Basic 4.0, a complete applications development tool with powerful client/server capabilities that let you create distributed applications. Next is Visual Basic for Applications, Microsoft's Windows application script language. This is a subset of Visual Basic 4.0, lacking client/server data access, distributed computing, and team source code control. Finally, we have VBScript, a subset of Visual Basic for Applications, designed specifically for Internet use.

For those of you familiar with Visual Basic, it may be useful to look at some of the differences. Table 11.1 is not complete, but describes some of the more important differences between these two versions of Basic. You can see that many of Visual Basic's capabilities have been omitted from VBScript. This is not to imply that VBScript is inferior or crippled in any way. Remember that VBScript was designed for a specific task. Potentially unsafe capabilities such as file access have been purposely omitted, and other features, such as Visual Basic's rich set of data types, have been omitted for the sake of simplicity.

Table 11.1   Differences between VBScript and Visual Basic.

CATEGORY	IN VBSCRIPT	IN VBA BUT NOT VBSCRIPT
Arrays	Dim, Static, ReDim, Erase	Option Base, LBound <> 0
Calling DLL's	No	Yes
Control Flow	Do...Loop For...Next For Each ... Next While...Wend If...Then...Else	DoEvents GoSub...Return GoTo Line numbers and labels On Error
Data Types	Variant	All others (Boolean, Integer, etc.)
Error Trapping	On Error Resume Next Err object	Erl, Error, Error$ On Error ... Resume Resume, Resume Next
File Operations	None	Open, Write #, etc.
Graphics	None	Circle, Line, Pset, etc.
Structures	No	Type ... End Type
Creating Classes	No	Dim x as New ... Set x = New ... With ... End With

ActiveX Controls and Java Applets

You may have heard about Java applets and ActiveX controls, particularly how they are supposed to revolutionize the way we use the Web. What are these things, and how do they relate to VBScript? Both ActiveX and Java were designed for the same purpose—providing additional functionality to Web users—but they go about it in different ways. First, let's take a look at how they are supposed to function, then we'll see how they are different.

People who create Web pages are striving to provide more and more value to their users. It's an extremely competitive business, and if someone else's page offers more features and dazzle than yours, you know where people will go. It's depressing to see your page's hit counter stuck at 3 (especially when one of those visitors was your mother) for weeks on end!

There is a downside to all that dazzle, however. Added functionality—whether it be animated graphics, sophisticated financial analysis capabilities, or whatever—requires both computer processing power and *bandwidth*, or the capability to transfer data between host and client systems. You can program all the fancy stuff you like on your host system, but if more than a few people log on at once, you'll find the system slowing to a crawl and your net connection sorely overtaxed. This is a serious problem, because nothing turns potential users (and customers) away from a site more quickly than having to deal with sluggish response.

The answer is to let the client computer do some of the work—which is one of the rationales behind the development of JavaScript and VBScript. The instructions (script code) become part of the HTML file, and the processing is done by the client computer. With ActiveX and Java applets, this philosophy as been taken to an even higher level. Rather that downloading just a script, an entire program is downloaded to the client computer, and then executed.

Let's look at an example. Suppose a financial-service provider wants to let their customers visit their Web page, obtain historical stock prices for a specific issue, apply a variety of technical-analysis procedures to the data and display the results as graphs. Using the old methods, the analysis program would reside on the host computer. The processing would be done there, and the resulting graphs (and graphics files are usually pretty big!) would be downloaded to the client for display. If the user wanted to make a slight change in the analysis parameters, the commands would have to be uploaded, the analysis repeated, and the new graph downloaded.

A better approach would be to download a copy of the analysis program, created either with Java or ActiveX, to the client computer. You might think that downloading a program would require more bandwidth than sending data back and forth, but that is often not the case. First of all, both Java and ActiveX were designed specifically to create small, executable files, minimizing download time. Also, both techniques were designed to make use of *intelligent caching*, a system by which recently-used downloads are kept on the client system after being downloaded the first time. No download is required for subsequent uses.

While ActiveX and Java have similar goals, their method of implementation is different. Java is a new, object-oriented programming language that was developed at Sun Microsystems. ActiveX is the new name for Microsoft's Object Linking and Embedding (OLE) controls. While different in many respects, the two standards do share similar features that optimize them for small components that are suitable for downloading.

But this is not a book about Java or ActiveX, and we need to return back to our main topic of VBScript. Suffice it to say that both JavaScript and VBScript will eventually allow your Web pages to make use of Java applets and ActiveX controls.

Chapter 12

VBScript Data, Statements, Operators, and Procedures

VBScript and JavaScript have a great number of similarities. In fact, it's probably accurate to say that they are more similar than they are different. After all, both are computer languages designed for essentially the same purpose. It is true that they have different histories. JavaScript is based on the C language, while VBScript is of course Basic. Even so, both languages use + to mean addition, = for assignment, and < for less than. They both have named variables, functions, loops, conditional statements, and so on. If you know

283

JavaScript, you could probably understand a VBScript program, and vice versa. Still, there are plenty of differences to trip you up. In this and the following chapters, I will assume that you are a total newcomer—you know no JavaScript and no Visual Basic. If you happen to be familiar with another language, Visual Basic in particular, these chapters will go quickly for you.

Program Comments

Like any programming language, VBScript allows for comments in code—text that is ignored as far as script execution is concerned, and serves only to document and explain the operation of the code. VBScript provides two ways to identify comments: the Rem statement and the apostrophe. When Rem or an apostrophe is the first thing on a line, the entire line is treated as a comment. You can also place a comment at the and of a line of code by preceding the comment with Rem or an apostrophe. When you use Rem, however, there must be a colon between the end of the code and the Rem keyword. Here are some examples:

```
'This is a comment
Rem this is also a comment
document.write("Hello ") : Rem another comment
document.write("y'all") ' and yet another.
```

I always advise readers to use comments liberally in their code, no matter which programming language they are using. You may think you will remember the details of the code you wrote—but unless your memory is a lot better than mine, you will be in for a nasty surprise when you look at the script several months down the road! Comments are also a great help when you let other programmers use your code, or when you examine some code you downloaded from the Web.

Data and Variables

VBScript has a single data type, called a *Variant*. A Variant is a general purpose data type that can contain any type of information. This is in distinct contrast to many other languages that have many different data types, and is one of the best examples of how VBScript is a simplified version of Visual Basic.

A Variant can contain either a number or text (string data). VBScript is clever enough to treat the data appropriately depending on the context. In other words, a Variant behaves as a number when you're using it in a numeric context and as a string when you use it in a string context. If you need to make a number behave like a string, enclose it in quotation marks.

When dealing with numeric data, a Variant can make further distinctions about the specific nature of the information. For example, you can have numeric information that represents a date or a time. When used with other date or time data, the result is always expressed as a date or a time. Other numeric data can range in size from simple yes/no Boolean values to enormous floating-point values. All these different types of numeric information that a Variant can contain are called *subtypes*. The majority of the time, you can just place your data in a Variant and VBScript will treat it appropriately.

The Variant numeric data subtypes are shown in Table 12.1. Some of these subtypes may not mean much to you at present; they will be explained later.

Table 12.1 Variant numeric subtypes.

Subtype	Meaning
Empty	Variant is uninitialized. Value is either 0 for numeric variables or a zero-length string ("") for string variables.
Null	Variant intentionally contains no valid data.
Boolean	Contains either True or False.
Byte	Contains integer in the range 0 to 255.
Integer	Contains integer in the range -32,768 to 32,767.
Long	Contains integer in the range -2,147,483,648 to 2,147,483,647.
Single	Contains a single-precision, floating-point number in the range -3.402823E38 to -1.401298E-45 for negative values; 1.401298E-45 to 3.402823E38 for positive values.
Double	Contains a double-precision, floating-point number in the range -1.79769313486232E308 to 4.94065645841247E-324 for negative values; 4.94065645841247E-324 to 1.79769313486232E308 for positive values.

continued

Table 12.1   Variant numeric subtypes (continued).

Subtype	Meaning
Date (Time)	Contains a number that represents a date between January 1, 100 to December 31, 9999.
String	Contains a variable-length string that can be up to approximately 2 billion characters in length.
Object	Contains an OLE Automation object.
Error	Contains an error number.

VBScript provides several special data values. The Boolean values true and false are represented by the keywords True and False. False has the numerical value 0, and True is 1. Remember, however, that any non-zero value is considered to be true in a logical evaluation.

The value **Empty** represents the value in a variable that has not been initialized. Thus, immediately after the statement

Dim x

the variable x contains the special value **Empty**. Note that variables, when first created (declared), are initialized to 0 or the empty string (""). It seems to me that the value **Empty** is provided as a way of distinguishing between a variable that has the value 0, because it has never been initialized (that is, nothing has been assigned to it), and a variable that has been explicitly assigned the value 0. However, in the preliminary release of Internet Explorer that I am currently using, a variable that has been assigned the value 0 is also considered to be **Empty**—and I believe this to be a program bug.

The **Null** keyword is used to indicate that a variable contains no valid data. You assign the **Null** designation to a variable using the assignment operator:

```
x = Null
```

Program code can determine if a variable is **Null**, permitting you to distinguish valid data from invalid.

The **Nothing** keyword is used when working with objects, a topic we will cover soon. When a variable contains an object reference, you can assign the value **Nothing** to the variable to dissociate it from its object reference.

Declaring Variables

A VBScript variable should be declared before you use it. To declare a VBScript variable, you use the **Dim** keyword, as shown here:

```
Dim var1 [,var2 , var3...]
```

As the example shows, you can declare more than one variable in a single **Dim** statement by separating the variable names with commas. Your **Dim** statement(s) should be placed at the start of your script code:

```
<SCRIPT LANGUAGE="VBS">
<!—
Dim InterestRate, PrimeRate
—>
</SCRIPT>
```

Note that I said you *should* declare your variables, not that you *must*. VBScript allows implicit variable declaration simply by using the variable name somewhere in your script. This is a bad idea, however, because a misspelled variable name will not be caught as an error, but will instead result in creation of a new variable, with potentially troublesome results. To avoid this possibility, you should include the **Option Explicit** statement as the first line in any <SCRIPT> block:

```
<SCRIPT LANGUAGE="VBS">
OPTION EXPLICIT
Dim X, Y
...
```

The **Option Explicit** statement disables implicit variable declaration, so any variable not explicitly declared in a **Dim** statement will cause an error. Misspelled variable names will not slip through to cause trouble!

Variable Names

The rules for naming variables are the same as the rules for naming anything in VBScript:

- Must start with a letter
- Cannot contain a period
- Must be less than 256 characters in length
- Must be unique within its scope (more on scope later)

Thus, the following are all legal VBScript variable names:

OJSimpson

X56!2-1

chopsuey

However, the following types of names are preferred:

- Total
- AmountOwed
- Sales1996

Why are these preferred? In each case the name describes the data being stored in the variable. It may take a bit more trouble to create such variable names initially, but the program code will be easier to understand later.

Variable Scope

The term *scope* refers to the parts of your VBScript program where a variable is visible. Since the concept of scope doesn't make a whole lot of sense until you've been introduced to procedures, I'll cover that subject later in the chapter.

Arrays

An array is an extremely useful method of data storage. A simple variable, the type discussed earlier in this chapter, can hold only a single piece of data, but an array can hold as many as you need. You declare an array like this:

```
Dim ArrayName(n)
```

where ArrayName is the name of the array, and *n* is the number of data elements you want the array to be able to hold. Thus, the statement

```
Dim data(10), results(100)
```

creates an array named data that can hold 10 data items, and an array named results that can hold 100 data items. Each individual element in an array is like any other VBScript variable and can hold the same types of data. You access an individual element of an array by using a subscript. For example, to store the value 50 in the 13th element of the array data(), you would write

```
data(13) = 50
```

Likewise, to add the 5th and 6th elements of the array data() and assign the sum to the 1st element of results(), you would write the following:

```
results(1) = data(5) + data(6)
```

ZERO-BASED?

VBScript arrays are actually zero-based, meaning that the first array element has index 0. If you declare an array with 100 elements like this:

Dim x(100)

you actually get an array with 101 elements indexed 0 through 100. It's counter-intuitive, however, to write

Dim x(99)

when you want an array with 100 elements! What many people do, and this includes myself, is to forget about the array's first element (index 0) and treat the array as having elements 1 through n. True, you waste a little space. But in most situations it will be trivial and won't make any practical difference.

Multidimensional Arrays

VBScript permits you to define multidimensional arrays. The type of array that we just saw is a one-dimensional array, an array with only a single index subscript. Multidimensional arrays can be very useful for certain data storage needs.

You can think of a one-dimensional array as a column of data items, with the single dimension representing position in the column. Following this analogy, a two-dimensional array would represent a page with both rows and columns, where row position is one dimension and column position is the other. You declare a multidimensional array like this:

```
Dim multi(5, 10)
```

This would create a two-dimensional array with 6 rows, indexed 0 through 5, and 11 columns, indexed 0 through 10. The array as a whole would contain 66 individual elements. You can create arrays with as many as 60 dimensions, although it's rare to need more than 3 or 4 (and even these are not all that common).

Dynamic Arrays

The arrays we have reviewed so far are called *static* arrays, because their dimensions are fixed at the time they are declared and cannot change during script execution. VBScript also supports *dynamic* arrays whose size can change while the script is executing. You create a dynamic array by using **Dim** or **ReDim** to declare the array without specifying the dimensions:

```
Dim myArray()
ReDim anotherArray()
```

Declaring a dynamic array in this way is not enough. Before you can use a dynamic array for the first time, you must use **ReDim** to specify the array size. The following statements specify the sizes for the arrays declared above:

```
ReDim myArray(20)
ReDim anotherArray(5, 5)
```

You can use **ReDim** as many times as you like to change the array size. You can also change the number of dimensions of the array. After creating, sizing, and using the arrays as just explained, you could execute the following:

```
ReDim myArray(5, 4)
ReDim anotherArray (10,10)
```

If you want the data in the existing array to be preserved when you use **ReDim**, simply use the **Preserve** keyword, as shown here:

```
ReDim Preserve myArray(100)
```

When using **Preserve**, you cannot change the number of array dimensions, and in a multidimensional array, you can only change the size of the last dimension. Suppose we again start with these declarations:

```
Dim myArray()
Dim anotherArray()
ReDim myArray(20)
ReDim anotherArray(5, 5)
```

The following is illegal because it changes the number of array dimensions:

```
ReDim Preserve myArray(8, 8)
```

Likewise, the following is illegal because it changes the size of an array dimension other than the last one:

```
ReDim Preserve anotherArray(10, 5)
```

The following two statements would be perfectly legal:

```
ReDim Preserve myArray(100)
ReDim Preserve anotherArray(5, 20)
Erasing Arrays
```

To delete an array, use the **erase** statement. The syntax is as follows:

```
erase arrayname
```

where *arrayname* is the name of the array to be erased. You must be aware that the **erase** statement works differently for dynamic and regular arrays. When you erase a dynamic array, the array ceases to exist and the memory it occupied is now free. When you erase a regular (or *static*) array, the array remains in existence, but all of its elements are initialized. In other words, the array is in the same condition as when it was first declared.

Constants

A constant is a named data item that does not change during program execution. This will be a short section for one simple reason: unlike other versions of Basic, VBScript has no constants. However, you can access all the benefits of named constants by using variables as constants and adopting a naming convention to differentiate "constant" variables from "variable" variables. For example, all constant variables names could start with CN_. You initialize the "constant" near the start of the script:

```
Dim CN_Rate
CN_Rate = 0.06
```

Then, throughout the remainder of the script, you will recognize this variable name as a constant by the CN_ prefix.

CONSTANTS: ANY BENEFITS?

You may be wondering exactly what the benefits of constants might be. Many programs contain items of information that do not change while the program is executing; however, you may want to change them while you are developing the program. For example, let's say you want all the display text in your program to be dark blue. You could enter the literal expression specifying dark blue everywhere you need to set the color. What happens if you change your mind later and decide on pink text? You'll have to go through the code, locating and changing every instance of "dark blue." To avoid that inconvenience, you can define a constant for text color and assign it the desired color value only once, near the start of the program; then you'll have only a single change to make.

VBScript Operators and Expressions

Much of what you'll do in VBScript will involve manipulating data in various ways. VBScript provides a full array of operators that allow you to perform a variety of operations on your data. First, however, I need to introduce the concept of expressions.

An *expression* is any combination of VBScript variables, literals, operators, and functions that evaluates to a single piece of data, either numerical or string. If we have declared a variable named total and assigned it a value, as follows:

```
Dim total
total = 15
```

then total is an expression. Likewise, the sum of total and another variable is also an expression:

```
total + subtotal
```

Another way of defining an expression is to say that anything you can place thumb the right side of an equal sign is an expression.

THE ASSIGNMENT OPERATOR

The assignment operator is represented by the equal sign. In VBScript, assignment means to store a data value in a variable. In other words, you assign the value to the variable. This is different from the use of the equal sign you may remember from algebra class. In algebra, writing x = y means that x has the same value as y. In VBScript, the identical notation means to assign the value of y to x.

The Arithmetic Operators

The arithmetic operators are used to perform arithmetic operations (no kidding!). Table 12.2 lists the arithmetic operators provided in VBScript, giving an example and brief explanation of each. You are most likely already familiar with the majority of these, although the modulus, integer division, and exponentiation operators may be new to some of you.

Table 12.2   VBScript arithmetic operators.

Operator	Operation	Example	Meaning
+	Addition	a + b	add a to b
-	Subtraction	a - b	subtract b from a
*	Multiplication	a * b	Multiply a times b
/	Division	a/b	Divide a by b. If b = 0 an error occurs

continued

Table 12.2 VBScript arithmetic operators (continued).

Operator	Operation	Example	Meaning
\	Integer division	a \ b	Divide a by b and return the nearest integer. For example, 7 \ 3 returns 2
^	Exponentiation	2^4	2 to the 4th power (16)
Mod	Modulo	10 Mod 3	The remainder after an integer division. 10 Mod 3 evaluates to 1
&	Concatenation	"The" & "end"	Combines two strings

Comparison Operators

VBScript's comparison operators are used to perform comparisons between expressions. In other words, asking questions such as "is x larger than y" or "is total equal to 100." When you create an expression using a comparison operator, the expression evaluates to either true or false, as shown in Table 12.3. As we learned earlier, the logical value false is represented by numerical 0, and true by -1. We will learn later in this chapter how the results of comparisons can be used to control program execution.

Table 12.3 VBScript's comparison operators.

Operator	Comparison	Example	Evaluates to True if Ö
=	Equality	x = y	x is equal to y
<>	Inequality	x <> y	x is not equal to y
>	Greater than	x > y	x is greater than y
<	Less than	x < y	x is less than y
>=	Greater than or equal	x >= y	x is greater than or equal to y
<=	Less than or equal	x <= y	x is less than or equal to y
Is	Object equivalence	x Is y	x and y refer to the same object

The use of the comparison operators with numbers is probably crystal clear to you. With strings, however, it is not as simple. Two strings are considered to be equal only if they are identical character for character, including the case of letters. Thus, "Peter" and "PETER" are considered not equal by VBScript. In regard to less than and greater than, letters are treated alphabetically—with the one strange exception that any upper case letter is considered less than any lower case letter. Therefore, "J" is less than "k," as you would expect; but "Z" is less than "a," which is certainly counter-intuitive.

CASELESS COMPARISONS

Since string comparisons should almost always be done without regard for case, you can use VBScript's UCASE() function to convert the letters in the strings being compared to upper case, so that the result of a "greater than" or "less than" comparison will come out properly. Note that this function does not actually change the original string, but only returns a temporary copy with the letters changed to upper case. If the variables str1 and str2 contain strings, we would compare them as follows:

UCASE(str1) < UCASE(str2)

You can also use the Strcomp Function, covered in Chapter 14, for caseless string comparisons.

The "order" of non-letter characters is determined by the ASCII code, the numerical equivalents used by the computer to represent characters internally.

Logical Operators

The logical operators are used to combine and manipulate logical expressions. Remember, logical expressions deal with the values true and false. Many programming situations arise where you need to make decisions based on two or more individual logical values. The logical operators provided by VBScript are listed in Table 12.4. In this table, X and Y are variables containing logical values for true or false:

Table 12.4   VBScript logical operators.

Symbol	Operation	Example	Result (continued)
Symbol	Operation	Example	Result
And	Logical conjunction	X And Y	returns true if both X and Y are true; returns false otherwise
Or	Logical disjunction	X or Y	returns false if both X and Y are false; returns true otherwise
Xor	Logical exclusion	X Xor Y	returns true if X and Y are different, one true and the other false; returns false otherwise
Eqv	Logical equivalence	X Eqv Y	returns true if X and Y are the same, both true or both false; returns false otherwise
Imp	Logical implication	X Imp Y	if X is true, returns true only if Y is true also. If X is false, returns true regardless of the value of Y
Not	Logical negation	Not X	returns the opposite of X: true if X is false, false if X is true

If one or both of the operators in a logical expression is **Null**, the result is **Null** also. The only exceptions are with the logical implication operator. If X is **Null**, the expression evaluates to true if Y is true, and evaluates to **Null** if Y is false or **Null**. If Y is **Null**, the expression evaluates to true if X is false, and to **Null** if X is true.

How are the logical operators used? For the most part, you will use them in conditional statements to control the flow of script execution. We'll see how this is done later in the chapter.

Controlling Program Flow

Many of the statements available in VBScript are used to control program flow. In other words, these statements control which parts of your script are executed, how many times they are executed, and when they are executed. The control of program flow is an important part of programming, since it enables you to write scripts that carry out different actions depending on factors such as user input. As I promised you earlier, we'll see how logical expressions and logical operators are used in conjunction with program flow statements.

LINE CONTINUATION CHARACTER

VBScript lets you split a long program statement over two lines by using the line continuation character, an underscore preceded by a space at the end of a line. Thus, the code

total = subtotal1 + subtotal2 + _

subtotal3

is exactly equivalent to

total = subtotal1 + subtotal2 + subtotal3

The only place the line continuation character is not permitted is within a quoted string literal. The following is not legal:

myName = "Peter _

Aitken"

---

if...then...else

The **if...then...else** construct is used to execute one group of program statements if a specified condition is true, and another group of statements if the condition is false. The syntax of **if...then...else** is as follows:

```
if condition then
    block 1
else
    block 2
end if
```

In this syntax, condition is any logical expression—in other words, an expression that evaluates to true or false. The program statements in block 1 are executed if condition evaluates as true, and the program statements in block 2 are executed if condition is false. The **else** part of this construct is optional, You can write an **if** statement as follows:

```
if condition then
    block 1
end if
```

The result of this syntax is that block 1 is executed if *condition* is true, and no statements are executed if *condition* is false. A more complex syntax is possible, having the effect of nesting several **if** statements. The syntax is as follows:

```
if condition1 then
    block 1
elseif condition2 then
    block 2
...
else
    block-n
end if
```

You can have as many **elseif** statements within the **if...end if** block as you like. Each condition is evaluated, and the block of statements following the first true condition is executed. If none of the condition expressions evaluates as true, then the block following the **else** statement is executed. You will note that, at most, one block of statements will be executed. If two of the condition expressions evaluate as true, only the block of code associated with the first true condition will be executed.

For simple situations where the blocks of code consist of single VBScript statements, you can use the following simplified syntax:

```
if condition then statement1 else statement2
```

As previously shown, the **else** part of this construct is optional. Note that the **end if** component is not required when this single line form of the **if** statement is used.

NULL IS FALSE

If the condition in an if statement evaluates to Null, it is treated the same as false. This is true for other program control statements as well.

Do...Loop

The **do...loop** construct is used to execute a block of VBScript statements zero, one, or more times based on evaluation of a logical expression. Implicit in the **do...loop** construct is that code within the block will modify the program data on which the logical expression depends. The **do...loop** construct has several syntax variations. In its most basic form, the syntax is as follows:

```
do while condition _
  statements
loop
```

When execution reaches the first statement in this construct, condition is evaluated. If it evaluates to true, the statements between the **do** and the **loop** are executed; execution loops back to the **do**, and condition is again evaluated. The block of statements is executed repeatedly as long as condition remains true.

A variation of **do...loop** executes the block of segments repeatedly as long as a condition is false. The syntax is similar to what I presented above:

```
do until condition _
  statements
loop
```

Note that using the **until** keyword is equivalent to using while and the **Not** logical operator. Thus, the **do until** block above is exactly equivalent to the following:

```
do while Not condition _
  statements
loop
```

These two syntax forms where the logical condition is evaluated at the start of the loop may result in the block of statements not being executed at all, if the condition initially evaluates as false (with **while**) or as to (with **until**). An alternate syntax places the evaluation of the condition at the end of the loop, guaranteeing that the block of statements will be executed at least one time. Here is how it looks:

```
do
    statement
loop [until | while] condition
```

When using **do...loop**, you must be aware of the possibility of setting up a so-called infinite loop—a loop that repeats forever. Obviously, you do not want infinite loops in your VBScript programs! An infinite loop occurs when the code in the loop has no effect on the condition that controls loop execution.

You can use the **exit do** statement to terminate execution of a **do...loop** prematurely, before the condition has changed. This ability provides additional flexibility in using **do...loop**. As an example, here is a loop that repeats until condition1 or condition2 is true for:

```
do
    ...
    if condition1 then exit do
loop until condition2
```

Note that the exact same result could be obtained as follows:

```
do
    ...
loop until (condition1 Or condition2)
```

In fact, almost anything you can do with **exit do** could be done without it, but sometimes at the expense of complex conditional expressions.

While...Wend

The **while...wend** construct is a holdover from earlier versions of Basic which did not support the **do...loop** statement. You use **while...wend** to execute a block of statements repeatedly, as long as a condition is true. The syntax is as follows:

```
while condition
    statements
wend
```

Clearly, you can use **do...loop** to accomplish the same thing as **while...wend**. If you are learning Basic for the first time, I suggest that you forget all about **while...wend** and use **do...loop** instead.

For...Next

The **for...next** construct is used to execute a block of statements a specified number of times. Execution of the loop does not depend on a logical condition; rather, the repeat count is set. The syntax of **for...next** is:

```
for counter = start to stop [step st]
    statements
next
```

In this syntax, *counter* is a variable that you should have declared previously. *Start* and *stop* are numeric expressions, as is the optional *st*. When execution first reaches the **for** statement, the variable *counter* is set equal to the value of *start* and the statements in the block are executed. When execution reaches the **next** statement, it loops back to the **for** statement. The value of *counter* is increased by 1 (or by *st*, if the optional **step** is included) and the block of statements are executed again. Execution of the loop terminates following the iteration in which *counter* is equal to *stop*.

The **for...next** loop is not limited to counting up. By specifying a *stop* value less than the *start* value, and a negative **step** value, you can count down. You can also count by fractional steps, by specifying a **step** value that is not an integer. The following loop will count down from 10 to 5 by 0.1 intervals:

```
for counter = 10 to 5 step -0.1
...
next
```

One of the values of **for...next** is that you have access to the counter variable within the loop. This is useful for stepping through the elements of an array. Here is a loop that sets all elements of a 100 element array to the value 2:

```
Dim i, myArray(100)
for i = 1 to 100
    array(i) = 2
next
```

Within a **for...next** you can use the **exit for** statement to terminate loop execution prematurely. When an **exit for** statement is counter, the loop terminates immediately and execution passes to the first statement after the **next** statement. Here is code to determine whether an array contains a value greater than 100. As soon as a value greater than 100 is found, **exit for** is used to terminate the loop and avoid unnecessary processing. In this and most subsequent examples, I will assume that the variables being used have been declared elsewhere.

```
bigger_than_100 = false
for count = 1 to 100
    if myArray(count) > 100 then
    bigger_than_100 = true
    exit for
    end if
next
```

> ## WHAT ABOUT SELECT CASE?
>
> If you are familiar with Visual Basic, you may be wondering about the select case statement. To be honest, it is a bit of a mystery as far as VBScript is concerned. In the preliminary VBScript documentation, it states that select case is not supported—but also provides instructions on using it. If you try to use select case in a real script, however, it does not work. Once VBScript is finalized and released commercially, we may have a working select case to use...and we may not. Stay tuned!

VBScript Procedures

A VBScript procedure is an independent block of code that has been assigned a name. The procedure code can be executed by referring to its name in other code, and data can be passed to the procedure by means of arguments. A procedure in VBScript is essentially identical to a JavaScript function. The major difference is that VBScript has two types of procedures: *functions*, which return a value to the calling program; and *subs*, which do not. Beyond this distinction and minor differences in the way they are called, functions and subs in VBScript are identical. I will cover sub procedures first, then explain how functions differ.

Using a sub procedure requires two parts. You must first define the procedure, which you need do only once in each script. Then you call the procedure as many times as necessary. A sub procedure is defined within **sub...end** sub statements. The syntax is as follows:

```
sub subname(arguments)
...
end sub
```

Within the sub, you can include just about any VBScript code you like with the exception of defining another sub or function. Code in one sub can call other subs or functions. When execution of code in a sub terminates, execution passes back to the script location from where the sub was called.

Here is a sub that uses VBScript's built-in **MsgBox** function to display a message on screen:

```
sub displayMessage()
    MsgBox "Hello, there"
end sub
```

To call a sub procedure, you have several options. You can use the **call** keyword followed by the procedure name, as shown here:

```
Call displayMessage()
```

You can also use the sub name by itself, without the call keyword:

```
displayMessage()
```

For subs that do not take arguments, the empty parentheses following the sub name are optional when calling the sub. They must be included, however, when defining the sub.

In the sub definition, the parentheses following the sub name contain the procedure arguments. Each argument represents a variable that is passed to the procedure when it is called. For example, here is a variation on the above sub that permits the message that is to be displayed to be passed as an argument, rather than being defined in the sub code:

```
sub displayMessage(message)
    MsgBox message
end sub
```

You then call the sub like this:

```
call displayMessage("Hello")
```

You can use any valid expression as an argument. For example, this code does the same thing as the preceding line of code, using a variable rather than a string literal as the sub procedure argument:

```
myMessage = "Hello"
call displayMessage(myMessage)
```

Here is another example, this time using the concatenation operator to combine a variable with a literal:

```
myMessage = "Hello"
call displayMessage(myMessage & " there!")
```

When a sub has more than a single argument, separate individual arguments by commas when calling the sub. Remember that the arguments must be passed in the order expected by the sub. In other words, passed in the same order in which they are listed in the sub definition.

Execution exits a sub when it reaches the **end sub** segment that marks the end of the sub definition, or if it encounters an **exit sub** statement within the sub code.

No Type Checking

If you are accustomed to using other versions of Basic that have a range of different data types, you should be aware that VBScript does not perform type checking on arguments passed to procedures. With only the single, general-purpose Variant data type, the programmer is responsible to ensure that appropriate data is passed to the procedure each time it is called.

Everything I have said about sub procedures applies to function procedures as well, with a few exceptions. A function is defined within *function...end function* statements, as shown here:

```
function myFunction()
...
end function
```

Defining and passing arguments is done in exactly the same manner as for sub procedures. One major difference is that a function returns a value to the calling program. Within the function, you specify the value to be returned by assigning it to the function name. In the following example, the function shown here returns the value true:

```
function myFunction()
...
myFunction = true
end function
```

You can assign as many values as you like to the function name, but only the most recent assignment will determine the value that is returned by the function. Assigning a value to the function name does not, obviously, terminate the function. The function terminates only when execution reaches the **end function** statement, or when an **exit function** statement is encountered within the function. If you exit a function without assigning a value to the function name, the value it returns is **Empty**.

Since a function returns a value, it can be considered a Basic expression. Thus, you can use a function anywhere you would use an expression in VBScript code. For example, to assign the return value of a function to a variable, simply use the function on the right side of an assignment statement:

```
myVar = myFunction()
```

You could also use a function as an argument to another function or to a sub procedure. For example, if you have defined functions named **square**() and **cube**() to calculate respectively the square and the cube of a number, you could square a number, then cube the result as follows:

```
answer = cube(square(10))
```

Where Should Procedures Go?

When a script executes, you cannot call a procedure until its definition as been processed. Therefore, procedure definitions need to be placed ahead of any script code that calls them. The place for this is in the HTML file header section between the <HEAD> and </HEAD> tags. You can define procedures in the body of the HTML file, as long as they proceed any call to the procedure, but it makes more sense to keep all procedure definitions together in the header.

Variable Scope and Procedures

Earlier, I alluded to something called variable scope, saying that it had to do with procedures. Now it's time to explain: If you declare a variable within a procedure, it is a local variable and exists only while program execution is within the procedure. You can create a variable of the same name in another procedure (or in non-procedure code), and it will be a completely independent variable, even though it has the same name.

If you declare a variable at the script level—that is, outside a procedure—its scope is the entire HTML file. In other words, you can access and change the value stored in the variable both in script level and procedure level code. If you declare a variable at the procedure level, its scope is limited to that procedure. If a script level variable of the same name exists, the procedure level variable takes precedence and the script level variable is out of scope within that procedure. A demonstration will help to make the concept of scope clear. The program SCOPE1.HTML, presented in Listing 12.1, declares a script level variable named X and assigns it the value "hello." You will find two procedures, cleverly named proc1 and proc2. In one procedure, a procedure level variable with the same name is declared and assigned the value 20. In the other procedure, no variables are declared. The program uses the **document.write** method to display the value of X at various points in program execution. You can see that, at the script level, X has the value "hello," as we would expect. In the first procedure, the procedure level X has precedence and its value of 20 is displayed. In the second procedure, the script level X is in scope, since no same-name variable was declared in the procedure, and the value "hello" is again displayed.

The separation of script level and procedure level variables makes the programmer's life easier. You can name and use variables within procedures without having to worry if the same variable names have been used elsewhere in the program.

Listing 12.1   SCOPE1.HTML demonstrates the concept of variable scope in a VBScript program.

```
<HTML>
<HEAD>
<title>
Demonstrates variable scope. </title>
<script language="vbs">
sub proc1()
    dim x
    x = 20
    document.write("In proc1, x = " & x)
end sub
sub proc2()
    document.write("In proc2, x = " & x)
end sub
```

```
</script>
</HEAD>
<BODY>
<script language="vbs">
dim x
x = "hello"
document.write("At script level, x = " & x)
document.write("<BR>")
call proc1
document.write("<BR>")
call proc2
</script>
</BODY>
</HTML>
```

Chapter 13

Using Objects and Events

Using Objects

Like JavaScript, VBScript is an object-based language. You cannot create objects, at least not in the sense of a full-blown object-oriented language like C++, but you have a rich palette of objects that you can use in your scripts. The objects you can use fall into two categories. First, there is the standard assortment of HTML objects, such as Document, Button, and Select. Making use of these HTML objects in VBScript is essentially the same as with JavaScript. Some differences, primarily detecting user actions, are covered later in this chapter.

The second category, much more powerful and flexible, is called ActiveX. This is Microsoft's term for a new breed of OLE (object linking and embedding) components that are designed with Web use in mind. An ActiveX object, or control, can be almost anything, ranging in complexity from a simple label to a complete spreadsheet. All of the functionality of an ActiveX control is built into the control itself by the programmer who designed it. All that you need to do to use the control in your Web pages is to insert it in your HTML document. If you have ever used Visual Basic, you are already familiar with this approach.

WHAT ABOUT JAVA APPLETS?

A Java applet is a component created with the Java programming language. In many respects, a Java applet is like an ActiveX control. It is a prepackaged software component that you can easily plug into your Web pages. From the perspective of VBScript, ActiveX and Java objects are treated essentially the same.

Each ActiveX control is inserted into an HTML page using the <OBJECT> tag. Strictly speaking, inserting a control is not part of VBScript, since the tag is not part of a script. However, to make use of many controls requires use of a scripting language. Some controls, it is true, serve a primarily decorative purpose—when they are displayed, there is no script interaction with the control. Other controls require script interaction if you are to make use of their capabilities. As with other objects, controls are accessed by means of their properties and methods. To use a particular control, you must have knowledge about that control's properties and methods. There are many controls available at present, and the number can only grow in the future. I cannot teach you how to use individual controls, so I'll limit myself to a general discussion of how controls are placed in your Web pages and how VBScript code interacts with them. I will use Microsoft's Active Label control in my examples, which is one of the ActiveX controls that you can download from Microsoft's Web site.

Web Watch

To take a peek at the ActiveX controls being developed by Microsoft, and to download samples and obtain information about including them in your Web pages, take a look at http://www.microsoft.com/ie/appdev/controls.

The <OBJECT> tag to insert a control must specify the control's **classid** and also its identification, or **id**. You also specify the height and width of the control, its alignment on the document page, and the amount of vertical and horizontal space to leave around the control. These parts of the <OBJECT> tag generally need to be included for all objects.

The <OBJECT> tag can also include parameter, or property, settings for the object. Each type of object has its own set of properties, of course. These properties control the appearance and behavior of the object. You will have to refer to the documentation for each specific object to determine what properties are available and their settings.

Let's look at an example. The following code defines an Active Label control with an **id** of lblActiveLbl. It is this **id** that you will use in your VBScript code to refer to the object. This code also sets several object properties such as its display angle, text, and font. The location of the control in the document will, of course, depend on where in the HTML file the <OBJECT> tag is placed.

```
<OBJECT
    classid="clsid:99B42120-6EC7-11CF-A6C7-00AA00A47DD2"
    id=lblActiveLbl
    width=150
    height=150
    align=left
    hspace=10
    vspace=10
>
<PARAM NAME="Angle" VALUE="45">
<PARAM NAME="Alignment" VALUE="2">
<PARAM NAME="BackStyle" VALUE="0">
<PARAM NAME="Caption" VALUE="Hi, I'm a label!">
<PARAM NAME="FontName" VALUE="Arial">
<PARAM NAME="FontSize" VALUE="16">
<PARAM NAME="FrColor" VALUE="0">
</OBJECT>
```

What about those intimidating class identifiers? How can you be expected to remember these long and apparently meaningless collections of letters and digits? Each control has its own class identifier, and this information must be entered in the <OBJECT> tag with perfect accuracy. The documentation for each object will include its class id.

\<OBJECT\> Tags the Easy Way

Microsoft has developed a neat utility that takes all of the hassle out of inserting tags for ActiveX controls in your HTML documents. Called the ActiveX Control Lister, this utility searches your system and creates a list of all controls that it finds. Select a control from the list, and the complete \<OBJECT\> tag, including class id, is placed on the clipboard. You can then paste the tag into your HTML file. A copy of this utility is provided on the CD-ROM.

You can see, I hope, that the procedure for inserting and using ActiveX objects is quite simple. Of course, this is the way Microsoft intended it to be. Making things easier for the programmer/Web page developer is perhaps the best way to ensure wide acceptance of your development tools and standards.

The following program in Listing 13.1 is a complete HTML file that demonstrates using the Active Label control and modifying its properties in response to user input. The code creates a document that contains only a single Active Label control and three standard HTML button objects. Each button is linked to a VBScript event procedure that responds when the user clicks the corresponding button. Code in the event procedures modifies the appearance of the label by changing an object property. Figure 13.1 shows what this

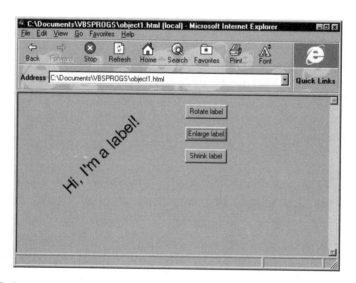

Figure 13.1

Demonstrating an ActiveX control.

program looks like when executing. You must have the Active Label control on your system in order for this program to work. It is supposed to be installed when you install Microsoft Internet Explorer. If necessary, you can download this control as part of the ActiveX gallery on the Microsoft Web site.

Listing 13.1 OBJECT1.HTML demonstrates using an ActiveX control.

```
<HTML>
<HEAD>
<script language="vbs">
sub btnRotate_onClick()
    lblActiveLbl.Angle = lblActiveLbl.Angle + 45
end sub

sub btnGrow_onClick()
    lblActiveLbl.FontSize = lblActiveLbl.FontSize + 2
end sub

sub btnShrink_onClick()
    lblActiveLbl.FontSize = lblActiveLbl.FontSize - 2
end sub

</script>
</HEAD>
<BODY>

<OBJECT
    classid="clsid:99B42120-6EC7-11CF-A6C7-00AA00A47DD2"
    id=lblActiveLbl
    width=250
    height=250
    align=left
    hspace=10
    vspace=10
>
<PARAM NAME="Angle" VALUE="45">
<PARAM NAME="Alignment" VALUE="2">
<PARAM NAME="BackStyle" VALUE="0">
<PARAM NAME="Caption" VALUE="Hi, I'm a label!">
<PARAM NAME="FontName" VALUE="Arial">
<PARAM NAME="FontSize" VALUE="16">
<PARAM NAME="FrColor" VALUE="0">
</OBJECT>
<p>
<INPUT TYPE="button" NAME="btnRotate" VALUE="Rotate label">
<p>
```

```
<INPUT TYPE="button" NAME="btnGrow" VALUE="Enlarge label">
<p>
<INPUT TYPE="button" NAME="btnShrink" VALUE="Shrink label">
</BODY>
</HTML>
```

Responding to User Actions

Very often, you will want your Web page to respond to input from the user beyond the really basic responses that HTML can provide (such as a **Submit** button). In other words, you want to execute VBScript code in response to user actions. If you read the parts of this book dealing with JavaScript, you know that JavaScript can do this. After inventing event-driven programming with Visual Basic, Microsoft provided the same capabilities with VBScript. If you have used Visual Basic at all, the entire procedure will seem very familiar to you. And if you've already worked with JavaScript, it will seem familiar as well, although there are some minor differences in detail.

Events, or user actions, are detected by HTML objects. Thus, a **Button** object can detect when it has been clicked, a **Select** object can detect when it looses the focus, and so on. The detectable events and the objects that can respond to them are listed here:

- onBlur: Occurs when an object looses the focus. Can be detected by Text, TextArea, and Select objects.

- onChange: Occurs when an object looses the focus after its contents have been modified. Can be detected by Text, TextArea, and Select objects.

- onClick: Occurs when the user clicks the object with the mouse. Can be detected by Button, Checkbox, Radio, Link, Reset, and Submit objects.

- onFocus: Occurs when an object receives input focus by tabbing with the keyboard or clicking with the mouse. Can be detected by Text, TextArea, and Select objects.

- onLoad: Occurs when the browser finishes loading a window or all frames within a <FRAMESET> tag. Detected by the Window object.

- onMouseOver: Occurs once each time the mouse pointer moves over an object from outside that object. Detected by the Link object.

- onSelect: Occurs when a user selects some of the text within a Text or Textarea object. Detected by these two object types.

- onSubmit: Occurs when the user submits a form. Detected by the Form object.

- onUnload: Occurs when the user exits a document. Detected by the Window object.

To have your page respond to a user action, you must write an *event handler* for the object/event combination. In JavaScript, as you may recall, the code to be executed was included as part of the object's HTML tag. VBScript is different, as there's no need to modify the HTML tag at all. Rather, you place a sub procedure in the document's header, giving the procedure the name with the form *objName_eventName*. For example, if you had created a Button object with the NAME attribute MyButton and you want to respond when the user clicks the button, you would create a sub as follows:

```
sub MyButton_onClick()
...
end sub
```

> **EVENT DETECTION ANOTHER WAY.**
> While VBScript lets you connect an event procedure with an object simply by means of the procedure name, you can also do it by including the event code in the object tag, as you learned earlier in the book for JavaScript. Thus, to define a Button object with an OnClick event procedure you could write the following
>
> <INPUT TYPE="Button" . . . OnClick="foo()">
>
> where foo() is the functionn to be executed. There's actually an advantage to this method as it permits arguments to be passed to the event procedure.

The name of the sub links the procedure to a specific object and a specific action. You can include any VBScript code in the sub, including calls to other procedures. It's that simple—VBScript and your browser do all the work behind the scenes. Listing 13.2 presents a simple demonstration. You'll see a lot more in Chapter 15.

Listing 13.2   EVENT1.HTML demonstrates event-driven VBScript programming.

```
<HTML>
<HEAD>
<script language="vbs">
sub btn1_onclick()
    msgbox("btn1 has been clicked.")
end sub

sub txt1_onblur()
    msgbox("text1 has lost the focus.")
end sub

sub txt1_onchange()
    msgbox("text1 has been changed.")
end sub

</script>
</HEAD>
<BODY>
<INPUT TYPE="button" NAME="button1" VALUE="Click Me">
<INPUT TYPE="text" NAME="text1" VALUE="Change me">
<script language="vbs">
</script>
</BODY>
</HTML>
```

Qualifying Object References

VBScript provides the capability to qualify object references, a technique that can simplify programming. To declare a VBScript variable, use the **Set** statement to associate it with a particular object, such as a form in your document. Once this has been done, you can use the variable to refer to the object instead of writing out the full object reference.

Suppose your document contains a form named MainForm, and on that form is a **Textarea** object named InputBox and a **Text** object named Text1. You can always use the full reference to the object in order to gain access to its properties, such as here:

```
buf1 = document.MainForm.InputBox.value
buf2 = document.MainForm.Text1.value
```

To use qualified shorthand, first declare a variable, then use **Set** to "point" it at the object of interest. For example, you could create a variable that is associated with the form:

```
Dim theForm
Set theForm = document.MainForm
```

Once this is done, you could access objects on the form like this:

```
buf1 = theForm.InputBox.value
buf2 = theForm.Text1.value
```

As an alternative, you could qualify variables to be associated with the individual objects on the form:

```
Dim ob1, ob2
Set ob1 = document.MainForm.InputBox
Set ob2 = document.MainForm.Text1
```

And then access properties like this:

```
buf1 = ob1.value
buf2 = ob2.value
```

The program in Listing 13.3 demonstrates the use of qualified object references in conjunction with an event procedure. The form displays two Text objects. If you change the contents of either one, a message box pops up displaying the contents of both of them.

This program demonstrates another technique, calling an event procedure in code. Here, the **onChange** event procedure for the Text object Text2 calls the **onChange** procedure that is associated with the other **Text** object.

Listing 13.3   EVENT2.HTML demonstrates using qualified object references in an event procedure.

```
<HTML>
<HEAD>
```

```
<script language="vbs">

sub text1_onchange()
    Dim msg, theObj
    set theObj = document.myForm
    msg = "Your entries now read " & theObj.text1.value _
        & " and " & theObj.text2.value
    msgbox(msg)
end sub

sub text2_onchange()
    call text1_onchange()
end sub

</script>
</HEAD>
<BODY>
<FORM NAME="myForm">
<INPUT TYPE="text" NAME="text1" VALUE="Change me!"><p>
<INPUT TYPE="text" NAME="text2" VALUE="Change me too!">
</FORM>
</BODY>
</HTML>
```

Key Topics:

- **String manipulation functions**

- **Data classification functions**

- **Mathematical functions**

- **Trapping run-time errors**

VBScript Functions and Error Trapping

It's hard to imagine a VBScript script that was written without making use of its rich function library. Likewise, I don't want to even think about a script that does not make use of VBScript's error-trapping capabilities. These may not be the most glamorous parts of VBScript, but they are things that you, as the programmer, most definitely need to know.

Functions

VBScript provides the programmer with a wide range of built-in functions—that is, functions that are part of the scripting language and do not need to be defined by the programmer. As I have mentioned in an earlier chapter, VBScript depends a great deal more on these built-in functions than does JavaScript, and a lot less on

319

properties and methods. If you are going to derive the most out of VBScript, you need to be familiar with the functions that are available. In this section, I'll explain how to use the functions and provide working VBScript examples in some cases. Rather than approach them alphabetically, I have divided them up by category. Table 14.1 provides an alphabetical list of functions, offering a brief description of what each one does, and an indication of the section where it is covered.

Table 14.1   VBScript functions.

Function	What it does	Category
Abs	Returns the absolute value of its argument	Data Conversion
Asc	Returns the ASCII code of the first character of its argument	Data Conversion
Atn	Returns the arc tangent of its argument	Mathematical
CBool	Returns its argument as a Variant of the Boolean subtype	Data conversion
CByte	Returns its argument as a Variant of the Byte subtype	Data conversion
CDate	Returns its argument as a Variant of the Date subtype	Data conversion
CDbl	Returns its argument as a Variant of the Double Precision subtype	Data conversion
Chr	Returns the character corresponding to a specified ASCII code	Data Conversion
CInt	Returns its argument as a Variant of the Integer subtype	Data conversion
CLng	Returns its argument as a Variant of the Long subtype.	Data conversion
Cos	Returns the cosine of its argument	Mathematical
CSng	Returns its argument as a Variant of the Single Precision subtype	Data conversion
CStr	Returns its argument as a Variant of the String subtype	Data conversion

continued

Table 14.1   VBScript functions (continued).

Function	What it does	Category
Date	Returns the current date	Date and time
DateSerial	Returns a specified date converted into a date serial number	Date and time
DateValue	Returns a standard format date converted into a date serial number	Date and time
Day	Returns the day of the month	Date and time
Exp	Returns e raised to the specified power	Mathematical
Fix	Returns the integer part of its argument	Data Conversion
Hex	Returns the hexadecimal representation of a number	Data Conversion
Hour	Returns the hours value for a time	Date and time
InptBox	Obtains input from the user	Input/output
Instr	Finds one string within another	String
Int	Returns the integer part of its argument	Data Conversion
IsArray	Determines if a variable is an array	Data Classification
IsDate	Determines if a variable contains a valid date	Data Classification
IsEmpty	Determines if a has been initialized	Data Classification
IsNull	Determines if a variable contains null	Data Classification
IsNumeric	Determines if a variable contains a numeric value	Data Classification
IsObject	Determines if a variable contains an object	Data Classification
LCase	Converts a string to lowercase	String
Left	Extracts characters from the beginning of a string	String
Len	Returns the length of a string	String
Log	Returns the natural logarithm of its argument	Mathematical

continued

Table 14.1   VBScript functions (continued).

Function	What it does	Category
LTrim	Removes leading spaces	String
Mid	Extracts characters from the middle of a string	String
Minute	Returns the minutes value for a time	Date and time
Month	Returns the month of the year	Date and time
MsgBox	Displays a message	Input/output
Now	Returns the current date and time	Date and time
Oct	Returns the octal representation of a number	Data Conversion
Randomize	Seeds the random number generator from the system clock	Mathematical
Right	Extracts characters from the end of a string	String
Rnd	Returns a pseudorandom number	Mathematical
RTrim	Removes trailing spaces	String
Second	Returns the seconds value for a time	Date and Time
Sgn	Returns the sine of its argument	Data Conversion
Sin	Returns the sine of its argument	Mathematical
Space	Returns a string containing the specified number of spaces	String
Sqr	Returns the square root of its argument	Mathematical
StrComp	Compares two strings	String
String	Returns a string containing the specified number of any single character	String
Tan	Returns the tangent of its argument	Mathematical
Time	Returns the current time	Date and time
TimeSerial	Returns a specified time converted into a time serial number	Date and time

continued

Table 14.1   VBScript functions (continued).

Function	What it does	Category
TimeValue	Returns a standard format time converted into a time serial number	Date and time
Trim	Removes leading and trailing spaces	String
Function	What it does	Category
UCase	Converts a string to uppercase	String
VarType	Determines the type of data contained in a variable	Data Classification
Weekday	Returns the day of the week	Date and time
Year	Returns the year	Date and time

Mathematical Functions

The mathematical functions perform a variety of commonly needed mathematical and trigonometric calculations. With trigonometric calculations, angles are always expressed in radians (1 radian = 57.2957 degrees). The functions are as follows:

- **Atn**—The arc tangent of its argument.

- **Cos**—The cosine of its argument.

- **Sin**—The sine of its argument.

- **Tan**—The tangent of its argument.

- **Exp**—The value *e* raised to the specified power. *e* is the base of the natural logarithms, and has a value of approximately 2.718282.

- **Log**—The natural (base *e*) logarithm of the argument.

- **Sqr**—The square root of its argument.

Remember that the usual mathematical constraints apply to these functions. **Log**, for example, must have an argument greater than 0, or an error occurs. Likewise, **Sqr** requires a non-negative argument. These are not limitations of VBScript—it's just the way math works!

Two of the mathematical functions apply when you need to work with random numbers. The **Rnd** function returns a pseudorandom number, with some options controlled by its argument (as shown in Table 14.2):

```
rn = Rnd(arg)
```

Table 14.2   How the argument controls the Rnd function.

IF *ARG* IS	THE RND FUNCTION RETURNS
Less than zero	The same number every time, using *arg* as the seed
Greater than zero or omitted	The next random number in the sequence
Equal to zero	The most recently generated number

It's important to realize that no computer can generate truly random numbers. Instead, VBScript takes a *seed* number and plugs it into a complex algorithm that generates a series of pseudorandom numbers. For most purposes, these can be treated as if they were truly random. Each different seed value generates a different sequence of numbers, but it's also true that using the same seed repeatedly will generate the same sequence over and over. To avoid this problem, call the **Randomize** sub before using **Rnd**. **Randomize** seeds the random number generator with a value obtained from the system timer, ensuring a different sequence of numbers each time.

Data Conversion Functions

You may wonder why VBScript requires data conversion functions, because it has only the one **Variant** data type. Remember, however, that data can be represented in different forms within a **Variant**. In certain programming situations, you will want to ensure that your data is represented in the proper form. Several functions are available for this purpose, each of which has a name beginning with C. Each of these functions takes a single argument, and returns that argument as a **Variant** of the specified type:

- **CBool**—Boolean

- **CByte**—Byte

- **CDate**—Date

- **CInt**—-Integer

- **CDbl**—Double precision

- **CLng**—Long

- **CSng**—Single precision

- **CStr**—String

Why would you need to perform such conversions? The type of mathematical operations that VBScript performs differs depending on the internal data type of a number stored in a Variant. For example, division and multiplication with subtype **Double** is more accurate than with other types. To illustrate, suppose that variables A and B contain the values 10 and 3, respectively. If you do the division A/B, VBScript automatically treats the result as a subtype **Single**, and the answer is accurate to 6 decimal places. For example, the statement

```
document.write(A/B)
```

displays 3.333333 in your document. If you want more accuracy, use the **CDbl** conversion function to convert to subtype Double first:

```
document.write(cdbl(A)/cdbl(B))
```

Now, the answer is 3.33333333333333, accurate to 14 decimal places. If, instead, you wrote the following statement:

```
document.write(cint(a/b))
```

then the answer would be 3, with all decimals truncated.

The **CStr** function is particularly flexible, because the string it returns is automatically tailored to the data subtype of its argument. Table 14.3 describes the various possibilities.

Table 14.3   How CStr returns a string tailored to its argument.

IF THE ARGUMENT IS	CSTR RETURNS
Boolean	A String containing "True" or "False"
Date	A String containing a date in the short-date format of your system
Null	A run-time error
Empty	A zero-length String ("")
Error	A String containing the word Error followed by the error number
Other numeric	A String containing the number

For example, look at the following statement:

```
document.write(cstr(cbool(6)))
```

The result is "True" displayed in the document. Why is this? Remember, any non-zero value is considered true by VBScript. The **Cbool** function says, in effect, "Treat the value 6 as a true/false value." When this value is passed to the **CStr** function, it returns the string "True", as specified in Table 14.3.

There are a number of other functions that fall into the data conversion category:

- **Abs**—Returns the absolute value of its argument. Negative values are changed to positive, and other values are not changed.

- **Asc**—Returns the ASCII code of the first character in its argument. For example, Asc("Aitken") returns 65—the ASCII code for "A" is 65.

- **Chr**—Returns the character corresponding to the specified ASCII code. Use to include non-keyboard characters in strings, as well as quotes. For example, to display "VBScript" (with quotes) in your document, you would write **document.write(chr(34) & "VBScript" & chr(34))** because 34 is the ASCII code for the double quote character.

- **Hex**—Returns a string containing the hexadecimal (base 16) representation of a number. For example, **Hex(255)** returns FF.

- **Oct**—Returns a string containing the octal (base 8) representation of a number. For example, **Oct(255)** returns 377.

- **Fix**—Returns the integer part of a number. For example, **Fix(8.12)** returns 8.

- **Int**—Returns the integer part of a number. Differs from **Fix** only for negative arguments. **Fix** returns the next integer larger than its argument, while **Int** returns the next smaller integer. Thus, **Fix(-4.5)** returns -4 while **Int(-4.5)** returns -5.

- **Sgn**—Returns 1 if its argument is greater than 0, -1 if its argument is less than 0, and 0 if its argument is equal to 0.

Date and Time Functions

VBScript represents dates and times internally as special serial numbers. The integer portion of the serial number represents the number of days since December 31, 1899, with negative numbers for dates prior to that. The fractional portion of the serial number represents the time as a fraction of the 24-hour day. The permissible range of dates is from January 1, 100 to December 31, 9999. Here are some examples:

- 35065—January 1, 1996

- 0.5—12:00 noon

- 35066.75—6:00 PM on January 2, 1996

Remember that the actual values are the **Variant** subtype **Date**. The special date functions are explained here:

- **DateSerial**—Returns the serial number for a specified date expressed as YY, MM, DD. For example, **DateSerial(1990,6,1)** returns the serial number for June 1, 1990. To calculate the number of days between two dates, you can subtract one date serial number from another: **NumDays = DateSerial(1990,6,1) - DateSerial(1990,12,25)**.

- **DateValue**—Returns the serial number for a date expressed in any one of several standard formats, such as 12/1/95; Dec. 1, 1995; or December 1, 1995.

- **TimeSerial**—Returns the serial number for a time expressed as HH, MM, SS. For example, **TimeSerial(11, 15, 30)** returns the serial number for 11:15:30.

- **TimeValue**—Returns the serial number for a time expressed in any one of several standard formats, including hh:mm:ss and hh:mm PM.

- **Now**—Returns the current date and time, as set on your system clock.

- **Date**—Returns the current date, as set on your system clock.

- **Time**—Returns the current time, as set on your system clock.

- **Day**—Returns a number 1-31 representing the day of the month represented by the specified date serial number.

- **Weekday**—Returns a numbespecified date serial number. Sunday is 1, Saturday is 7.

- **Month**—Returns a number 1-12 representing the month of a specified date serial number.

- **Year**—Returns a number representing the year of the date serial number.

- **Second**—Returns a number 0-59 representing the seconds value of a specified time serial number.

- **Minute**—Returns a number 0-59 representing the minutes value of a specified time serial number.

- **Hour**—Returns a number 0-23 representing the hours value of a specified time serial number.

FORMATTING DATES

Remember that the **CStr** conversion function can be useful when working with dates. When passed a **Date** subtype as its argument, **CStr** returns the date formatted in your system's short date format.

Input/Output Functions

Only one input function, **InputBox**, is used to allow the user to enter data into the program. At its most basic, **InputBox** displays a dialog box with a prompt and a field where the user can enter information. When the user closes the dialog box, the data that was entered is passed to the program as the function's return value. Here's an example; the following code causes the display in the dialog box shown in Figure 14.1.

```
reply = InputBox("Please enter your name.")
```

As used here, the InputBox function requires only one argument, which is the prompt to be displayed. It is a great deal more flexible than this, however. The full syntax is as follows:

```
InputBox(prompt[, title][, default][, xpos][, ypos]
        [, helpfile, context])
```

Figure 14.1

Getting user input with the InputBox function.

- **title**—The dialog box's title. If this argument is omitted, the application name is displayed in the title bar of the dialog box.

- *default*—The string to be returned by the function if the user closes the dialog box without entering anything.

- *xpos*, *ypos*—The screen position of the dialog box, both horizontal (*xpos*) and vertical (*ypos*). Expressed in *twips* from the edge of the screen (1 inch = 1440 twips). The default horizontal position is centered; the default vertical position is about 1/3 of the distance from the top of the screen.

- *helpfile*—The name of the Helpfile to use for context-sensitive Help. If you specify a Helpfile, you must also specify a context.

- *context*—The Help context number assigned to the dialog box's context-sensitive Hlp.

If the user cancels the input dialog box, the return value is an empty string. If you provide *helpfile* and *context* arguments, a Help button is automatically displayed in the dialog box.

To display messages to the user and, optionally, permit the user to make choices, use the **MsgBox** function. The syntax is:

```
MsgBox(prompt[, buttons][, title][, helpfile, context])
```

- *prompt*—The message to display in the dialog box.

- *buttons*—A numeric value specifying which buttons and/or icons are to be displayed. (Explained in detail below).

- *title*—The dialog box's title. If this argument is omitted, the application name is displayed in the title bar of the dialog box.

- *helpfile*—The name of the Helpfile to use for context-sensitive Help. If you specify a Helpfile, you must also specify a context.

- *context*—The Help context number assigned to the dialog box's context-sensitive Hlp.

The *buttons* argument provides much of the **MsgBox** function's flexibility. You have the option of displaying a variety of buttons (e.g., Yes and No) and several different icons in the dialog box. You can also control which button is the default (that is, which button will be selected if the user presses Enter), and whether the dialog box is system modal or application modal. Each element or set of elements has a number associated with it, as listed in the Table 14.4. To create a **MsgBox** with specified elements, you add up the numbers associated with the desired elements and pass the sum as the *buttons* argument.

Table 14.4   Values associated with an element or set of elements.

VALUE	EFFECT
0	Display OK button
1	Display OK and Cancel buttons
2	Display Abort, Retry, and Ignore buttons
3	Display Yes, No, and Cancel buttons
4	Display Yes and No buttons
5	Display Retry and Cancel buttons
16	Display Critical Message icon (a red circle with a white X in it)
32	Display Warning Query icon (a balloon with a question mark in it)
48	Display Warning Message icon (a yellow triangle with an exclamation point in it)
64	Display Information Message icon (a balloon with an "i" in it)
0	First button is default
256	Second button is default
512	Third button is default
768	Fourth button is default
0	Application modal; the user must respond to the message box before continuing work in the current application
4096	System modal; all applications are suspended until the user responds to the message box

Here's an example. Suppose you want a **MsgBox** with Yes and No buttons, and a Warning Query icon with the second (No) button as the default. Add up the values for these options (4 + 32 + 256 = 292) and pass that value as the *buttons* argument to the **MsgBox** function.

The MsgBox function's return value indicates which button the user selected, as shown in Table 14.5. Your script will use this value, in an if statement for example, to take appropriate action, depending on the choice the user selected.

Table 14.5   Return value indicates button selected.

RETURN VALUE	BUTTON SELECTED
1	OK
2	Cancel
3	Abort
4	Retry
5	Ignore
6	Yes
7	No

String Functions

VBScript's string functions are used for working with strings. (Surprise, surprise.) A wide variety of functions are available and,in fact, string handling is one of VBScript's strong points.

INSTR

To determine the position of a substring within another string, use the **Instr** function. In its most basic form, the syntax is as follows:

```
InStr(target, template)
```

Target is the string being searched, and *template* is the string you are trying to find. The function returns a number indicating the position of the first occurrence of *template* in *target* (the first character is position 1), and returns 0 if *template* is not found. The search is case-sensitive. In its full form, **Instr** is a bit more flexible. The syntax is:

```
InStr(start, target, template, compare)
```

The *target* and *template* arguments are as above. *Start* is the character position in *target* where the search is to begin. *Compare* specifies the type of comparison to be performed. A value of 0 (the default) performs a binary comparison that is case-sensitive. A value of 1 performs a case-insensitive comparison, which is usually appropriate when comparing strings. If you pass a *compare* argument, you must specify *start* as well. Table 14.6 lists potential return values for Instr.

Table 14.6 The possible return values for Instr.

IF ...	INSTR RETURNS
template is zero-length	the value of **start**
target is zero-length	0
template or **target** is null	null
start is greater than the length of **target**	0

StrComp

To compare two strings, use the **StrComp** function. Pass two strings to this function, and its return value indicates whether the strings are equal—or if not equal, which string is greater. The syntax is:

```
StrComp(s1, s2, compare)
```

The arguments *s1* and *s2* are the string expressions being compared. The optional *compare* argument determines whether a case-sensitive comparison (*compare* = 0 or omitted) or a case-insensitive comparison (*compare* = 1) is performed.

> ### Use StrComp to Alphabetize
> The **StrComp ()** function, with the compare argument set to 1, is ideal for case-insensitive alphabetizing of text items.

Len

To determine the length of a string (number of characters), use the **Len** function. Its syntax is:

```
Len(string)
```

where *string* is the expression whose length you want to determine. If *string* contains a numeric value, Len returns the length of the corresponding string (as if you had applied the **Cstr** function first).

UCASE AND LCASE

To convert the letters in a string into all uppercase or all lowercase, use the **Lcase** and **Ucase** functions. The syntax is:

```
Lcase(string)
UCase(string)
```

The return value is *string* with all letters converted to the specified case. Non-alphabetic characters are not affected. If *string* is null, the return value is null.

LEFT, RIGHT, AND MID

To extract characters from a string, use the **Left**, **Mid**, and **Right** functions. Left and Right extract the specified number of characters from the start or end of a string, respectively. **Mid** extracts characters from within a string. The syntax is:

```
Left(string,n)
Right(string,n)
Mid(string,start,n)
```

The argument *string* is the string expression from which you want to extract characters. *n* is the number of characters to extract. With **Mid**, *start* is the character position in *string* where the extraction is to begin. When using **Mid**, the *n* argument is optional. If it is omitted, all characters from *start* to the end of *string* are extracted.

The **Space** and **String** functions return a string containing a specified number of a certain character. **Space** creates strings containing spaces, while **String** can create strings containing any character. The syntax is:

```
Space(n)
String(n, char)
```

where *n* is the desired length of the string, and *char* is the desired character.

LTRIM, RTRIM, TRIM

These functions remove leading and/or trailing spaces from a string. **Ltrim** removes leading spaces, **Rtrim** removes trailing spaces, and **Trim** removes both. The syntax is:

```
RTrim(string)
LTrim(string)
Trim(string)
```

where *string* is the string from which you want to remove spaces.

Data Classification Functions

The data classification functions are used to determine whether an item of data falls into certain categories. Six of these functions are passed a variable name as argument, and return a true/false value indicating whether the variable falls into the specified classification. These functions are listed in Table 14.7.

Table 14.7   Six data classification functions.

FUNCTION	CLASSIFICATION
IsArray	Does the variable contain an array?
IsDate	Can the variable be converted to a valid date?
IsEmpty	Is the variable uninitialized?
IsNull	Does the variable contain null?
IsNumeric	Does the variable contain a numeric value?
IsObject	Does the variable contain an object?

The last data classification function, **VarType** , takes a variable name as its argument and returns a numeric value indicating the data subtype of the variable. The possible return values are explained in Table 14.8.

Table 14.8 Data classification return values.

VarType RETURN VALUE	MEANING
0	Empty (uninitialized)
1	Null (no valid data)
2	Integer
3	Long integer
4	Single-precision floating-point number
5	Double-precision floating-point number
6	Currency
7	Date
8	String
9	OLE Automation object
10	Error
11	Boolean
12	Variant (used only with arrays of Variants)
13	Non-OLE Automation object
17	Byte
8192	Array

Note that the return value for Array is never returned alone. Rather, it is added to the return value for the data type of the array, and the sum is returned. For example, if you pass the name of an array of subtype Boolean to **VarType**, the return value is 8203 (8192 + 11).

Dealing with Errors

Like any program, a VBScript program can experience certain errors while it is running. Such errors are called run-time errors. Careful programming can minimize the likelihood that such errors will occur, but it can never eliminate them entirely—at least not in my experience! Fortunately, VBScript provides several tools that help in dealing with errors. The goal is to handle errors gracefully and not let the script crash or leave the user hanging.

At the heart of VBScript's error-handling capability is the **Err** object. When a run-time error occurs, **Err** knows about it, and you can obtain information about the nature and source of the error from **Err**'s properties. This isn't enough, however. You must also use the **On Error Resume Next** statement to specify what VBScript does when an error occurs. Let me explain.

When an untrapped run-time error occurs, VBScript's default is to immediately halt script execution and display a dialog box with a description of the error. For example, Figure 14.2 shows the dialog box that is displayed when you try to use the **Log** function with a negative argument. While such information is useful to the programmer, it isn't much help at all to the end user.

If, however, you execute **On Error Resume Next**, it instructs VBScript to make note of the error and continue executing your script. This does not make the error go away, of course, but permits you to defer handing it until a more convenient time. More importantly, you can handle the error in a graceful way—for example, instructing the user to take corrective action.

How does one "handle" an error? There's no single answer to this question, because there are so many different kinds of errors. You need to be aware of

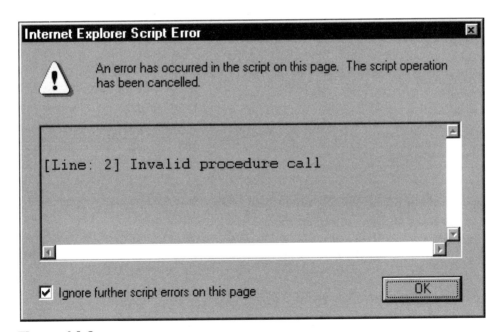

Figure 14.2

An untrapped run-time error is announced by this dialog box.

what's going on in the script, what errors might occur, and what can be done about them. For example, if the user is prompted to enter a value, and then that value is used as the divisor in a calculation, the chance of a divide-by-zero error exists. A proper handling in this situation would be to prompt the user to enter a non-zero value, then loop back and perform the calculation again.

I should point out before we continue that VBScript error handling is designed to be used within procedures. This is not actually a shortcoming, because a well-designed script will have most of its code inside procedures. Within each procedure that requires error handling, here's what you do:

1. Execute **On Error Resume Next** as the first statement in the procedure.

2. Within the procedure, at one or more locations, test the value of the **Err** object's **Number** property. If this value is non-zero, it means that an error has occurred.

3. Use the Err object's properties to obtain information about the error, and take the appropriate handling steps.

THE DEFAULT PROPERTY?

Objects in VBScript can have a default property. When you use the object name by itself as an expression, you automatically access its default property. Because **Number** is the **Err** object's default property, the statement

if Err then

is exactly equivalent to

if Err.Number then

What information can the **Err** object provide? Its three properties are listed here:

- Number—The number of the error.

- Description—A short text description of the error. This is the same text that is displayed by VBScript if the error is not trapped.

- Source—Identification of the source (application) that caused the error.

Unfortunately, the **Number** property is not as useful as it might be, because Microsoft has not yet released information on which error numbers correspond with which errors. When the VBScript documentation is more complete, you'll be able to use the **Number** property to determine the exact nature of the error that occurred. At present, we are limited to the knowledge that a non-zero value indicates an error, and a value of zero indicates that no error has occurred.

It is important to remember that the **Err** object contains information about only one error, the most recent one. This information is cleared when execution exits the procedure or when an **On Error Resume Next** statement is executed. You can clear the **Err** object in code by executing its **Clear** method. In fact, you must do this in certain circumstances to prevent the **Err** object from retaining information about a previous error. You will see an example of this in the demonstration program below.

To demonstrate fundamental VBScript error trapping, the program in Listing 14.1 asks the user to enter two numbers, the dividend and divisor for a division calculation. If a value of 0 is entered for the divisor, the division generates a run-time error. Error trapping code in the procedure catches the error, prompts the user to enter a non-0 value, and repeats the calculation. Once an error-free division has occurred, the answer is displayed on screen.

Listing 14.1   An example of error trapping.

```
<HTML>
<HEAD>
<script language="vbs">
sub calculate()

dim x, y, z, msg
on error resume next
x = InputBox("Enter the dividend:")

do while (true)
    y = InputBox("Enter the divisor:")
    z = x / y

    if err then
        msg = "You must enter a non-zero divisor!"
        msgbox(msg)
        err.clear
    else
            break
```

```
      end if
loop

msg = "The answer is " & z
MsgBox(msg)

end sub
</script>
</HEAD>
<BODY>
<script language="vbs">
call calculate
</script>
</BODY>
</HTML>
```

You've learned the basics of VBScript. Now it's time to see some real-world examples.

Key Topics:

- **Data verification**

- **On-screen calculator**

- **Using the Timer**

VBScript in Action

Data Verification with VBScript

One of the main tasks for which VBScript is used is data verification, making sure that data entered by the user on an HTML form meets certain requirements before being submitted to the server for processing. Chapter 9 covered the general principles of data verification and the advantages of performing verification with a scripting language. If you haven't read that chapter yet, I suggest you go back and review at least the first section before we get started with anything VBScript-specific.

VBScript is an excellent scripting language for data verification tasks. In fact, it is markedly superior to JavaScript in light of its many built-in string manipulation and data classification functions. I suspect that anything you can do with VBScript can also be done with JavaScript, but often at the cost of more involved programming.

> **VERIFYING A SELECT OBJECT**
> Using VBScript to verify that a **Select** object has at least one item selected is essentially identical to using JavaScript. You can look at the example in Chapter 9 to see how it's done.

Validating Text Length

As I have discussed previously, length is used for fundamental text validations, including the basic task of preventing blank input fields. VBScript's **len** function makes for simple length validations. Listing 15.1 presents a function that checks whether the length of a text string is between two specified values. To verify a non-zero length, call the function with the *min* argument set to 1 and the max argument set to some huge value.

Listing 15.1   A function to validate the length of text.

```
function textLength(buf, max, min)

'Returns true if the length of the text in buf
'is between max and min. Returns false otherwise.

if (len(buf) <= max And len(buf) >= min) then
    textLength = true
else
    textLength = false
end if

end function
```

Validating ZIP Codes

Any Web application that requests address information from the user will need to deal with ZIP codes. For reliable delivery, you need a valid ZIP code. If you mail a letter to ZIP code 12GX#, the post office will probably send it to Guam and leave it under a rock somewhere! There's no way to tell if the ZIP code that the user enters is, in fact, his or her correct ZIP, but you can be sure that it is at least in the proper format: either 5 digits alone, or followed by a dash and four more digits (for ZIP + 4).

The function in Listing 15.2 validates ZIP codes. Pass it the text containing the code, and it returns True only if the text is in a valid 5- or 9-digit format. Here's the way it works:

- The code must be either 5 or 10 characters long.

- If it's 5 characters long, it must evaluate to a number tested with the built-in **isNumeric** function.

- If it's 10 characters long, then (1) the first 5 characters must evaluate to a number; (2) the 6th character must be a dash (-); and (3) the last 4 characters must be a number.

Listing 15.2   A function to validate 5 or 9 digit ZIP codes.

```
function isZipcode(x)

'Returns true if x is a 5 digit ZIP code
'or a 9 digit ZIP code in the format
'xxxxx-xxxx. Returns false otherwise.

dim ln
isZipCode = false

if (len(x) = 5) then
    ln = 5
elseif (len(x) = 10) then
    ln = 10
else
    exit function
end if

'First 5 characters must all be digits.
if (NOT isNumeric(left(x,5))) then exit function

'If it"s a 5 digit ZIP we're done.
if (ln = 5) then
    isZipCode = true
    exit function
end if

'The sixth character must be "-".
if (instr(x,"-") <> 6) then exit function

'The last 4 characters must be digits.
if (NOT isNumeric(right(x,4))) then exit function
```

```
'Success!
isZipCode = true

end function
```

Validating Phone Numbers

Telephone numbers are another type of data that often requires validation. The function presented in Listing 15.3 does the job. The techniques used are quite similar to those used in validating ZIP codes, as shown in the previous section. In brief:

- The overall length should be 12 characters.

- The first three characters should evaluate to a number greater than 100 (since no area codes begin with zero).

- The 4th character should be a dash.

- The 5th through 7th characters should evaluate to a number greater than 100 (again, no exchanges begin with zero).

- The 8th character should be a dash.

- The 9th through 12th characters should evaluate to a number.

We make use of several built-in VBScript functions here: **len**, **left**, **right**, **mid**, and **isNumeric**. If you'll compare this function with the JavaScript phone number validation function in Chapter 9, you'll get a good idea of how VBScript's built-in functions make certain programming jobs a lot easier.

Listing 15.3   A function to validate a phone number.

```
function isPhonenumber(x)

'Returns true if x is a phone number in the
'format xxx-xxx-xxxx. Returns false otherwise.

isPhonenumber = False

'It must be 12 characters long.
if (len(x) <> 12) then exit function

'Check first three chars. Since no area codes start with
'zero the value of the first three chars must be >= 100.
if (left(x,3) < 100) then exit function
```

```
'The 4th character should be a "-"
if (mid(x,4,1) <> "-") then exit function

'The 5th thru 7th characters should evaluate to a
'number >= 100.
if (mid(x,5,3) < 100) then exit function

'The 8th character should be a "-".
if (mid(x,8,1) <> "-") then exit function

'The last 4 characters must be numeric.
if (NOT isNumeric(right(x,4))) then exit function

'All tests passed, so...
isPhonenumber = True

end function
```

Validating Numbers

Validation of number data can take may forms, but the most common need is to verify that a number entered by the user falls within a certain range. Listing 15.4 presents a VBScript function that performs this task. You don't have to pass the limits in any particular order, because code in the function will determine which is the upper and which the lower limit.

Listing 15.4   A function to verify that a number is between two values.

```
function isBetween(x, limit1, limit2)

'Returns true if x is between limit1 and
'limit2, or equal to either. Returns false
'otherwise.

dim max, min

if (limit1 > limit2) then
    max = limit1
    min = limit2
else
    max = limit2
    min = limit1
end if

if (cint(x) = min Or cint(x) = max) then
    isBetween = true
elseif (cint(x) > min And Cint(x) < max) then
    isBetween = true
```

```
else
    isBetween = false
end if

end function
```

A Demonstration

The file VALIDATE.HTML, presented in Listing 15.5, demonstrates the VBScript data validation functions we have developed in this section. It is shown in Figure 15.1. There are five Text objects, each requesting the input of a specific type of data. If invalid data is entered, the program displays a message to the user. It is also supposed to return the focus to the Text object that contains invalid data, using the object's **focus**() method. In the current version of Internet Explorer (the first beta), however, this method is not working properly. Perhaps the version you are using will be functioning more smoothly.

Listing 15.5 VALIDATE.HTML, a demonstration of the VBScript data validation functions.

```
<HTML>
<HEAD>
<script language = "vbs">

'***************
' The general data validation functions start here.
'***************

function textLength(buf, max, min)

'Returns true if the length of the text in buf
'is between max and min. Returns false otherwise.

if (len(buf) <= max And len(buf) >= min) then
    textLength = true
else
    textLength = false
end if

end function

'***************
function isZipcode(x)

'Returns true if x is a 5 digit ZIP code
'or a 9 digit ZIP code in the format
'xxxxx-xxxx. Returns false otherwise.
```

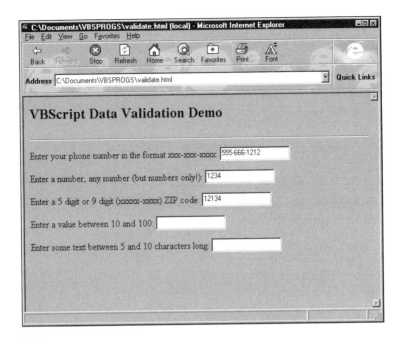

Figure 15.1

The VBScript data validation demonstration.

```
dim ln
isZipCode = false

if (len(x) = 5) then
    ln = 5
elseif (len(x) = 10) then
    ln = 10
else
    exit function
end if

'First 5 characters must all be digits.
if (NOT isNumeric(left(x,5))) then exit function

'If it's a 5 digit ZIP we're done.
if (ln = 5) then
    isZipCode = true
    exit function
end if

'The sixth character must be "-".
if (instr(x,"-") <> 6) then exit function

'The last 4 characters must be digits.
if (NOT isNumeric(right(x,4))) then exit function
```

```vbscript
'Success!
isZipCode = true

end function

'****************
function isPhonenumber(x)

'Returns true if x is a phone number in the
'format xxx-xxx-xxxx. Returns false otherwise.

isPhonenumber = False

'It must be 12 characters long.
if (len(x) <> 12) then exit function

'Check first three chars. Since no area codes start with zero
'the val of the first three chars must be >= 100.
if (left(x,3) < 100) then exit function

'The 4th character should be a "-"
if (mid(x,4,1) <> "-") then exit function

'The 5th thru 7th characters should evaluate to a
'number >= 100.
if (mid(x,5,3) < 100) then exit function

'The 8th character should be a "-".
if (mid(x,8,1) <> "-") then exit function

'The last 4 characters must be numeric.
if (NOT isNumeric(right(x,4))) then exit function

'All tests passed, so...
isPhonenumber = True

end function

'****************
function isBetween(x, limit1, limit2)

'Returns true if x is between limit1 and
'limit2, or equal to either. Returns false
'otherwise.

dim max, min

if (limit1 > limit2) then
    max = limit1
    min = limit2
else
```

```vbscript
        max = limit2
        min = limit1
    end if

    if (cint(x) = min Or cint(x) = max) then
        isBetween = true
    elseif (cint(x) > min And Cint(x) < max) then
        isBetween = true
    else
        isBetween = false
    end if

end function

'***************
' The demonstration-specific event procedures start here.
'***************

sub phone_onchange()

dim msg, x
x = document.form1.phone.value
if (NOT isPhonenumber(x)) then
    msg = "Please enter a phone number in the xxx-xxx-xxxx format"
    msgbox(msg)
    document.form1.phone.focus()
end if

end sub

'***************

sub number_onchange()

dim msg, x, reply
x = document.form1.number.value
if (NOT isNumber(x)) then
    var msg = "A number, puh-leeese!"
    msgbox(msg)
    document.form1.number.focus()
end if

end sub

'***************

sub zip_onchange()

dim msg, x
x = document.form1.zip.value
if (NOT isZipcode(x)) then
```

```
            msg = "That's not a valid ZIP code, knucklehead!"
            msgbox(msg)
            document.form1.zip.focus()
    end if

    end sub

    '***************

    sub between_onchange()

    dim msg, max, min, x
    max = 100
    min = 10
    x = document.form1.between.value
    if (NOT isBetween(x, max, min)) then
            msg = "Did you flunk math? Try again!"
            msgbox(msg)
            document.form1.between.focus()
    end if

    end sub

    '***************

    sub length_onchange()

    dim msg, max, min, text
    max = 10
    min = 5
    text = document.form1.length.value
    if (NOT textLength(text, max, min)) then
            msg = "Forget how to count? Try again, please!"
            msgbox(msg)
            document.form1.length.focus()
    end if

    end sub

    </script>
    </HEAD>
    <BODY>
    <FORM name="form1">
    <H2>VBScript Data Validation Demo</H2>
    <HR>
    Enter your phone number in the format xxx-xxx-xxxx:
    <INPUT type="text" name="phone" value="">
    <P>
    Enter a number, any number (but numbers only!):
    <INPUT type="text" name="number" value=""><P>
    Enter a 5 digit or 9 digit (xxxxx-xxxx) ZIP code:
```

```
<INPUT type="text" name="zip" value=""><P>
Enter a value between 10 and 100:
<INPUT type="text" name="between" value="" ><P>
Enter some text between 5 and 10 characters long:
<INPUT type="text" name="length" value="" ><P>
</FORM>
</BODY>
</HTML>
```

Web Watch

You'll find a few interesting VBScript demonstrations at http://
www.microsoft.com/vbscript/us/vbssamp/vbssamp.htm. You'll also find
some VBScript/ActiveX examples at http://www.nuke.com/vbscript/
vbscript.htm.

A VBScript Calculator

What, another calculator!?! It does seem that calculators are everyone's favorite
example for Web scripting languages, but they are a good learning tool. You're
all familiar with what a calculator is supposed to do; and any implementation
will have to include many of the central elements of Web scripting, such as
event detection, numerical calculations, and so on. The on-screen calculator
is presented in Listing 15.6.

This calculator uses a different approach than the JavaScript calculator that
we saw earlier in the book. Instead of an RPN (Reverse Polish Notation) design,
this calculator uses the more familiar algebraic model. A good project for
aspiring VBScript programmers would be to enhance the calculator with a
memory and perhaps some trigonometric functions. The calculator is shown
operating in Figure 15.2.

Listing 15.6 CALCULATOR.HTML demonstrates how to implement an on-screen calculator in VBScript.

```
<HTML>
<HEAD>
<TITLE>VBScript Calculator</TITLE>

</HEAD>
<BODY>
<SCRIPT LANGUAGE="VBScript">
```

```
<!-
Dim Operand    ' operand waiting for operation
Dim NewNum     ' Flag indicating a new operand is being entered
Dim Oper       ' Pending operation

sub PressKey(Byval Num)
    If NewNum Then
        Document.calc.display.value = Num
        NewNum = False
    Else
        If Document.calc.display.value = "0" Then
            Document.calc.display.value = CStr(Num)
        Else
            Document.calc.display.value = _
    Document.calc.display.value & CStr(Num)
        End If
    End If
end sub

sub Decimal_onClick()
    Dim cv            ' Current value
    cv = Document.calc.display.value
    If NewNum Then
        cv = "0."
        NewNum = False
    Else
```

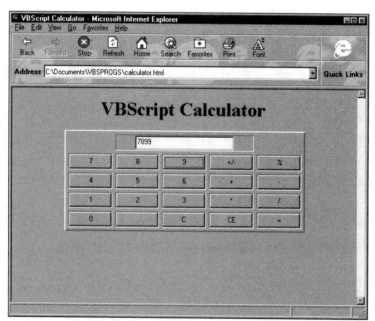

Figure 15.2

The VBScript calculator in action.

```vbscript
            If instr(cv, ".") = 0 Then
                cv = cv & "."
            End If
        End If
        Document.calc.display.value = cv
    end sub

    sub calculate(ByVal Op)
        Dim cd              ' Current display
        cd = Document.calc.display.value
        If NewNum And Op <> "=" Then
        Else
            NewNum = True
            Select Case oper
            Case "+"
                Operand = CDbl(Operand) + CDbl(cd)
            Case "-"
                Operand = CDbl(Operand) - CDbl(cd)
            Case "/"
                Operand = CDbl(Operand) / CDbl(cd)
            Case "*"
                Operand = CDbl(Operand) * CDbl(cd)
            Case Else
                Operand = cd
            End Select
            Document.calc.display.value = Operand
            oper = Op
        End If
    end sub

    sub ClearEntry_onClick()
        Document.calc.display.value = "0"
        NewNum = True
    end sub

    sub Clear_onClick()
        Operand = 0
         oper = ""
        ClearEntry_onClick
    end sub

    sub Neg_onClick()
        Document.calc.display.value = -1 * _
      CDbl(Document.calc.display.value)
    end sub

    sub Percent_onClick()
        Document.calc.display.value = _
      (CDbl(Document.calc.display.value) / 100) * Operand
    end sub
```

```
-->
</SCRIPT>

<CENTER>
<H1>
VBScript Calculator
</H1>
<FORM Name="calc">
<TABLE>
<B>
<TABLE BORDER=2 WIDTH=50 HEIGHT=60 CELLPADDING=1 CELLSPACING=5>
<TR>
<TD></TD>
<TD COLSPAN=3 ALIGN=MIDDLE>
<INPUT NAME="Display" TYPE="Text" SIZE=30 VALUE="0" WIDTH=100%>
</TD>
<TD></TD>
</TR>
<TR>
<TD>
<INPUT NAME="Seven" TYPE="Button" VALUE="  7  "
 OnClick="PressKey(7)">
</TD>
<TD>
<INPUT NAME="Eight" TYPE="Button" VALUE="  8  "
 OnClick="PressKey(8)">
</TD>
<TD>
<INPUT NAME="Nine" TYPE="Button" VALUE="  9  " OnClick="PressKey(9)">
</TD>
<TD>
<INPUT NAME="Neg" TYPE="Button" VALUE=" +/- " >
</TD>
<TD>
<INPUT NAME="Percent" TYPE="Button" VALUE="  %  " >
</TD>
</TR>
<TR>
<TD>
<INPUT NAME="Four" TYPE="Button" VALUE="  4  " OnClick="PressKey(4)">
</TD>
<TD>
<INPUT NAME="Five" TYPE="Button" VALUE="  5  " OnClick="PressKey(5)">
</TD>
<TD>
<INPUT NAME="Six" TYPE="Button" VALUE="  6  " OnClick="PressKey(6)">
</TD>
<TD ALIGN=MIDDLE>
<INPUT NAME="Plus" TYPE="Button" VALUE="  +  "
 OnClick='calculate("+")'>
</TD>
```

```html
<TD ALIGN=MIDDLE>
<INPUT NAME="Minus" TYPE="Button" VALUE="   -   "
 OnClick='calculate("-")'>
</TD>
</TR>
<TR>
<TD>
<INPUT NAME="One" TYPE="Button" VALUE="  1  " OnClick="PressKey(1)">
</TD>
<TD>
<INPUT NAME="Two" TYPE="Button" VALUE="  2  " OnClick="PressKey(2)">
</TD>
<TD>
<INPUT NAME="Three" TYPE="Button" VALUE="  3  "
 OnClick="PressKey(3)">
</TD>
<TD ALIGN=MIDDLE>
<INPUT NAME="Multiply" TYPE="Button" VALUE="  *  "
 OnClick='calculate("*")'>
</TD>
<TD ALIGN=MIDDLE>
<INPUT NAME="Divide" TYPE="Button" VALUE="   /   "
 OnClick='calculate("/")'>
</TD>
</TR>
<TR>
<TD>
<INPUT NAME="Zero" TYPE="Button" VALUE="  0  " OnClick="PressKey(0)">
</TD>
<TD>
<INPUT NAME="Decimal" TYPE="Button" VALUE="   .   " >
</TD>
<TD>
<INPUT NAME="Clear" TYPE="Button" VALUE="  C  " >
</TD>
<TD>
<INPUT NAME="ClearEntry" TYPE="Button" VALUE="  CE " >
</TD>
<TD>
<INPUT NAME="Equals" TYPE="Button" VALUE="  =  "
 OnClick='calculate("=")'>
</TD>
</TR>
</TABLE>
</TABLE>
</B>
</FORM>
</FONT>
</BODY>
</HTML>
```

Using the Timer Control

One of the most useful ActiveX objects is the **Timer** control. A **Timer** control does not display in your browser, but works behind the scenes to permit you to trigger events at a predefined interval. To add a **Timer** to your document, use the following OBJECT tag:

```
<OBJECT
    classid="clsid:59CCB4A0-727D-11CF-AC36-00AA00A47DD2"
    id=timerName >
</OBJECT>
```

The identifier *timerName* is a name you assign via VBScript's variable naming rules. You'll be using this in your code to refer to the **Timer** object. Two of the properties will be used most often:

- TimeOut is the Timer interval, in milliseconds.

- Enabled is set to True to start the Timer running, and to False to turn it off.

The initial values of these properties are, of course, set with <PARAM> tags within the <OBJECT> tag. Here is code that creates a Timer object with an id of "timer1," an interval of 50 milliseconds; it is set to start running immediately:

```
<OBJECT
    classid="clsid:59CCB4A0-727D-11CF-AC36-00AA00A47DD2"
    id=timer1 >
<param name="TimeOut" value="50">
<param name="enable" value="1">
</OBJECT>
```

A **Timer** control has a "time out" event procedure associated with it. You create this procedure by writing a sub with the name in the form **timerName_time**, where timerName is the id attribute assigned to the **Timer** in its OBJECT tag. Each time the **Timer** times out, the procedure is called, and it's in this procedure that you carry out the desired actions. A **Timer** can be used for repetitive actions by simply letting it run continuously. You can also use it for one-shot events by setting its **Enable** property to False in its time-out event procedure.

The program TIMER.HTML demonstrates use of the Timer control, shown in Figure 15.3. It also uses the **Active Label** control that we met earlier. The

Figure 15.3

TIMER.HTML demonstrates the Timer control by rotating a label.

program uses the **Timer** to change the color, size, and orientation of the label text. The effect is somewhat like animation and can be used to great effect on your Web pages. The program is presented in Listing 15.7.

Listing 15.7   Demonstrating the ActiveX Timer control.

```
<HTML>
<HEAD>
<TITLE>ActiveX/VBScript Timer Example</TITLE>

<SCRIPT LANGUAGE="VBS">
<!-
dim step
step = 3

sub timer1_time

if theLabel.Angle = 360 then
    theLabel.Angle = 1
end if
```

```
    theLabel.Angle = theLabel.Angle + 2
    theLabel.FontSize = theLabel.FontSize + step
    theLabel.forecolor = rnd() * 16777216
    if theLabel.FontSize > 100 then
        step = -3
    end if
    if theLabel.FontSize < 10 then
        step = 3
    end if

    end sub

    sub toggle_onClick()
        if (timer1.enable) then
            timer1.enable = 0
        else
            timer1.enable = 1
        end if
    end sub
    ->
    </SCRIPT>
    </HEAD>
    <BODY>
    <H1>VB Script Timer Example</H1>
    You must be running a VBScript enabled browser and
    have the Microsoft ActiveX controls
    installed for this demonstration to work.
    Click this button
    <INPUT TYPE="button" NAME="toggle" VALUE="On/Off" >
    to turn the demo on and off.
    <BR>
    <HR>
    <CENTER>
    <OBJECT
        classid="clsid:99B42120-6EC7-11CF-A6C7-00AA00A47DD2"
        id=theLabel
        width=400
        height=400
        align=center
        hspace=20
        vspace=20 >
    <param name="_extentX" value="50" >
    <param name="_extentY" value="700" >
    <param name="angle" value="0" >
    <param name="alignment" value="2" >
    <param name="BackStyle" value="0" >
    <param name="caption" value="VBSCRIPT">
    <param name="FontName" value="Arial">
    <param name="FontSize" value="10">
    <param name="FontBold" value="0">
    <param name="frcolor" value="6">
```

```
</OBJECT>
</CENTER>
<BR>

<OBJECT
    classid="clsid:59CCB4A0-727D-11CF-AC36-00AA00A47DD2"
    id=timer1 >
<param name="TimeOut" value="50">
<param name="enable" value="1">
</OBJECT>
<BR>
<HR>
</BODY>
</HTML>
```

Some readers may be new to the Internet. Even if you consider yourself a "heavy user," you may still have a few questions about all that it contains and how it works. I'll try to provide some answers here. Just the basics, though! For detailed information on Internet workings, I recommend "The Internet Complete Reference," 2nd edition, by Harvey Hahn.

Appendix A

Internet and Web Basics

What is the Internet?

This is not an easy question! It's difficult, if not impossible, to give a clear and complete definition of the Internet. It's huge, it's complex, and there seems no doubt that it will become increasingly important. Let me try to provide some sort of useful definition, which will consists of three parts. The Internet is: A large number of computers that are connected so that they can exchange data and a set of protocols, or rules, that specifies how information is exchanged between computers.

The main reason behind the explosive growth of the Internet is its openness. From the very beginning, the protocols and tools for using the Internet have been available, usually free, to anyone who wants them. Likewise, connection to the Net is not restricted. While some individuals may be faced with practical obstacles to connecting to the Net, there are no rules that prevent certain people from connecting. This openness attracted more and more people to the Net—and the more people who used it, the more valuable a tool it became. More people were attracted, and…well, you know the rest!

How Did It Start?

The Net was created by people, mostly scientists and other technical people, who needed it for a tool. Their goal was to create a system by which information could quickly and easily be exchanged. They were not concerned with selling software, increasing profits, or getting rich. The resulting cooperation, as opposed to the more common competition, was a key factor in Web growth.

The genesis of the Internet (although it wasn't called that yet) was actually a project called ARPANET sponsored by the Department of Defense. Their goal was to create a network by which information could be exchanged, and that would remain functional under extreme conditions such as a nuclear war. Started in 1968, the project soon expanded to include the more general goal of creating a network to permit researchers to exchange information freely. In 1969, ARPANET was officially started by connecting a grant total of—hold your breath—four computers located in four different cities.

Pretty soon it became clear that a single network would never be able to provide the desired functionality. Instead, developing the means to connect various existing networks to each other was seen as holding a great deal more promise. The goal became "internetwork" communication—in other words, the Internet.

The Physical Internet

Many people, when they first start learning about the Internet, want to know exactly *where* the Internet is located. Asking this question indicates a lack of familiarity with how the Internet works. There is no one place where the Internet "is." You can't point to a big building full of computers somewhere and say, "That is the Internet." The Internet consists of all the computers that are connected to it as well as the connections between them. If your computer is connected to the Internet, then it's part of the Net. When you disconnect your computer, it's no long part of the Net. As you can see, computers are added to and removed from the Net every day.

If there's any heart to the Net, it is within the communication links and routers. The communication links are the means by which information is transmitted from one place to another. All sorts of methods are used to transmit information—fiber optic connections, undersea cables, high-speed telephone lines, satellite links—and these links are designed to be redundant. That is, no single link is essential to operation of the Net. If the main cable between New York and Chicago is cut, Internet traffic will be routed, say, first to Detroit and then to Chicago.

Routers are specialized computers whose jobs are described by their names—to guide, or route, data to its destination. To be honest, I have no idea how many routers the Internet has, or where they are located. I do know, however, that whenever I sit down at my computer and interact with another computer on the Net, it's the routers that see to it that the information I send reaches the desired destination, and the information sent back to me arrives as planned. As with the communication links, the routers are redundant; if a router goes down, its tasks will be taken over by other parts of the Internet. Things may slow down a bit, but the Net will still work!

TCP/IP

Since one of the major goals of the Internet was openness, it couldn't be restricted to one type of computer or one type of operating system. Since different computers and operating systems often have distinctly different ways of communicating, some means had to be created that would permit different systems to talk to each other. The answer was Transmission Control Protocol/ Internet Protocol, or TCP/IP. A *protocol* is a set of rules describing in precise technical detail how a task is to be performed. TCP/IP specifies the various formats that are used for data sent over the Internet. There's a format for mail, another format for HTML hypertext pages, and so on. The general designation TCP/IP actually encompasses many dozens of specialized Internet protocols, and its name is derived from the two most important ones.

Don't worry, I am not going to subject you to an army of technical protocol details! You don't need to know anything about them (that's one of the beauties of the Internet!). I will, however, describe in broad terms how the protocols work together to enable communications over the Internet.

Suppose that your computer is hooked up to the Internet and you are using Internet mail to send a message to your pal at bill_gates@microsoft.com. You compose the message, enter the address, and click the Send button. Here's what happens.

At your end of things, Transmission Control Protocol (the TCP part of TCP/IP) will break the message into a number of small chunks, called *packets*. Each packet contains (in addition to part of the message text) the addresses of the recipient and sender, the packet's sequence number, and some error correction information.

Each packet is sent over the network. Now it is the job of Internet Protocol (the IP part) to get the packets to their destination. Each and every computer on the Net has a unique Internet Protocol address, or IP address, consisting of four three-digit numbers separated by periods, such as 123.321.001.111. As I will describe later in the chapter, this address is used to route the packets to their destination. Each packet is transmitted individually. There's no guarantee, and in fact no need, for the packets to be transmitted in a certain order or even over the same route. What is important is their safe and sound arrival at the destination system.

Once the packets have been received, TCP takes over. Each packet is checked for errors, and if an error is detected, a request is sent for the packet to be re-sent. Once all of the packets are received error-free, TCP puts them back together and your message appears in Bill's mailbox.

The same basic sequence of events occurs whether you are sending mail, browsing the Web, using FTP to transfer files, or whatever. Different protocols may be involved, but the same pattern is followed:

1. Break the data into packets.

2. Send the packets to the destination.

3. Reassemble the packets.

Connecting to the Net

End users like you and I have two basic ways to connect to the Net. The first and preferred method is to have what's called a *direct* connection. This means that the computer you use is part of a local network that is itself connected to the Internet. You will be connected to the network with an Ethernet, Token Ring, or other high–speed network connection. Your computer is actually part of the Net, and with the right software (and access permissions), you can do just about anything Net-related.

The second method is to connect over the telephone lines via a modem. Almost everyone working from their home has this type of connection. It has the disadvantage of being relatively slow. Even the fastest modems are limited to transmitting data at about 28,000 bits per second, while an Ethernet connection is at least 10 million bits per second. That's quite a difference, and explains why people with modem connections are jealous of us lucky folks with direct connections. A complex Web page with lots of graphics may take a minute or two to display over a modem, but will pop up in a few seconds over a direct connection.

If you connect via a modem, your computer is not actually part of the Internet. The host computer to which you are connected is part of the Net, and your computer is acting as a remote terminal to the host. You can send and receive mail, surf the Web, and use FTP, but you would not be able to set up your own Web page or FTP site. Future developments, such as ISDN telephone service and fiber optic cable TV connections, will eventually bring fast Internet access to home users as well.

Internet Addresses

Even if you have already used Internet mail addresses or FTP addresses and WWW addresses, it's always a good idea to understand how they work. All Internet addresses are based on the fact that every computer on the Internet has a unique name, called its *domain name*. Most domain names have three parts, separated by periods. For example, here's the domain name of the computer that I use for mail:

acpub.duke.edu

A domain name is made up of *subdomains,* and in the above example, three of them. The various subdomains identify a specific computer in a hierarchical manner that becomes increasingly more specific as you move from right to left. Thus the above domain name can be broken down as follows:

edu   An educational institution

duke   Duke University

acpub   The computer named "acpub"

In the United States, the last subdomain identifies the type of organization. Here are the most common ones:

edu   Educational

com   Commercial

gov   Governmental

org   Nonprofit

mil   Military

Net   Network

Outside the United States, the last subdomain almost always identifies the country. Thus, .nl is Netherlands, .ca is Canada, .es is Spain, etc. Why does the United States have priority? Simply because the Internet and the domain naming scheme originated here. The U.S. does have a geographical domain name ("us," of course), but it is not widely used.

The second subdomain from the right usually identifies the organization. In U.S. addresses, to my knowledge, it always does. Even in non-U.S. addresses, it often does, but is also sometimes used to identify the type of organization. For example, in the domain

history.oxford.ac.uk

the "ac" identifies Oxford as an academic institution.

Some domain names include only two parts. There are two possible reasons for this. A small organization may have only a single computer on the Net, so identifying the organization with the second–level domain name is all that would be necessary to identify the computer. At the other end of the scale, a large company may route all of its Internet traffic through a single *gateway* computer with a single domain name. Distribution of data to the various internal computers is handled by a program on the gateway computer. All the outside world needs to know is the domain of the gateway computer.

Just because an organization has an Internet address does not mean it has its own computer hooked up to the Net. Many smaller firms and individuals cannot afford the cost of obtaining and maintaining a direct Net connection. Instead, they contract with an Internet Service Provider. The provider does have a computer on the Net, and in effect rents space on the Net computer to its customers. Along with your rental you receive your own domain name, even though it doesn't really refer to a separate computer. Mail or other data sent to your domain name is routed to the service provider's computer, where it is identified as belonging to you. Periodically, you call the service provider with your modem to send and receive mail and so on.

How does the Internet itself—the router computers—know where to send a given message? There's no magic to it. You must register your domain name with the Internet address registry. This ensures that there are no duplicate domain names, and also provides the information necessary for the routers to identify your domain name with a specific physical location. As mentioned earlier in the chapter, each computer on the Net is identified by a unique 12 digit IP address. Each domain name is linked to a specific IP address by the Internet's Domain Name Service (DNS). This permits us humans to use the friendlier domain names, while the Net itself uses the numerical IP addresses.

Now that you understand domain names, the details of mail and Web addresses are easy. A mail address consists of a user identification (or user ID) followed by the @ symbol and a domain name. Your user ID is assigned locally, by the people who oversee your organization's Internet mail service. My mail address, for example, is paitken@acpub.duke.edu. The Internet only needs to know the domain name. My mail—and many other people's mail as well—is delivered to the computer identified by that domain name. A program on that computer, called a *mail server*, receives the message and stores it temporarily. When I log on, either via a direct connection or a modem, the mail client on my computer asks the mail server, "Do you have any mail for user paitken?" If I have the proper password, the mail is sent to my local computer for me to read.

Note that my user ID is of no interest at all to the Internet. It is only used locally by my mail server to identify me. There could be a hundred Internet users with the ID "paitken," and the Internet couldn't care less.

World Wide Web addresses are similar. They are referred to as Uniform Resource Locators, or URLs. (URLs are used for Internet services other than the Web, too). Here's a typical URL, pointing in this case to Netscape Communications Corporation's home page:

http://home.netscape.com/

I'm sure you can identify the domain name part of this address. But what about the http:// part? This identifies the Hypertext Transfer Protocol, another one of the many Internet data transfer protocols. In effect, this Web address says, "Go to the computer that has the domain name home.netscape.com and get me information using the Hypertext Transfer Protocol." But what information? It will be a hypertext file, but which one? HTTP specifies that if a file is not identified, then the file named INDEX.HTML in the specified directory will be retrieved. Since neither a file name nor a directory is specified in the above address, the file INDEX.HTML in the computer's top directory is the target. Here's another example:

http://www.ebay.com/aw/

This is the address for the Auction Web site. While a file name is not given, a directory is–in this case, /aw/. The target, therefore, is the file INDEX.HTML in the directory /aw/ on the specified computer. Here's a final example:

http://american.recordings.com/American_Artists/Love_And_Rockets/ loverox_home.html

Here we have not only a directory (/American_Artists/Love_And_Rockets/), but also a particular HTML file (loverox_home.html) specified.

Internet Services

The Internet provides a wide variety of services to its users. You are probably familiar with some of these, with Internet mail and the World Wide Web being the most popular. You may or may not have heard of the others. From the material presented earlier in this chapter, you should be aware that each Internet service is really a specific protocol that permits information to be exchanged in a certain manner.

The World Wide Web

The World Wide Web, or WWW, is perhaps the main factor in the Internet's exploding popularity. With the Web, you can bring an astounding array of material to your computer screen. Not just text, but pictures, animations, and sounds can be part of the experience.

The Web is based on the concept of *pages*. Each Web page consists of a hypertext markup language (HTML) document, or file, located on a computer that is hooked up to the Net. The HTML file can contain text, pictures, sounds— and perhaps most importantly, it can also contain links to other documents. The linked documents may be located on the same computer, or they may be on a system located halfway around the world. Each Web page, or document, is uniquely identified by its URL.

The beauty of the Web is that it permits you to follow a trail of ideas easily and seamlessly without regard to where the information is located. In your quest for information about, say, Java programming, you may visit pages in New York, Berlin, Canberra, Toronto, and Tel Aviv. You have no idea where each page is (although you may be able to figure it out from the URL)—and furthermore, you don't care. It's irrelevant with the Web; where you are located has no effect on your ability to obtain or provide information.

Mail

We've already covered a number of the details of Internet mail earlier in the chapter. Internet mail has become so important to most users that the term "mail" generally refers to it rather than regular postal service. Most Internet mail systems have become so sophisticated that they permit you to send not only messages, but picture, entire files, and so on. Regular postal mail is somewhat derisively referred to as snail-mail.

FTP

FTP stands for File Transfer Protocol. It is used to transfer files from one computer to another. FTP is another of the many protocols that are subsumed under the TCP/IP designation. To use FTP, you first log on to the remote computer using an FTP program. Logging on requires you to know the proper user ID and password. You can then view the remote computer's directory structure and file listings, and copy files back and forth to your local computer. When you're finished, log off and the process is complete.

Anonymous FTP is a popular technique that is used when someone wants to make a selection of files available to anyone who wants them. An anonymous FTP site allows anyone to log on using "anonymous" as the user ID. Often a password is not required; if one is, it will usually be either "guest" or your email address. You can then download files freely. An anonymous FTP site will not let you upload files, nor will it allow you to retrieve files from off-limit directories.

Usenet

If you've heard of news groups, you've heard of Usenet. This is an Internet protocol that permits messages, sometimes called articles, to be distributed all over the world. Rather than being sent to specific recipients, the messages are *posted* to a specific news group. News groups are organized by subject matter, and anyone who is interested can visit a news group, read posted messages, and post their own messages. When you *subscribe* to a news group, it simply means that your news–reader program will automatically download a list of that news group's new messages each time you log onto the news server. The Netscape Navigator browser includes a news–reader program (select Netscape News from the Windows menu).

News groups are named to reflect their topic. Like domain names, news group names are hierarchical, except that they work in left-to-right order. For example, the news group rec.collecting.stamps is in the broadest category of rec (for recreation), the narrower category of collecting, and the final category of stamps. There are thousands of newsgroups, some moderated and others pretty much a free-for-all. Topics range from humanities.languages.sanskrit to alt.sex.orgy, so there's a lot to choose from!

In order to access news groups, you must have access to a news host or news server. Your Internet service provider or network administrator can tell you the domain name of this computer.

Telnet

Telnet is an Internet protocol that lets you log onto a remote computer and use it just as if you were sitting in front of it. A scientist at a small college, for example, could use Telnet to log onto a supercomputer at Harvard and use it for calculations. Generally, you will use Telnet only if you have a specific need and also have been given permission and the required log-in information by the managers of the remote system. A few systems have set up anonymous Telnet accounts which permit anyone to log in and use a restricted set of the system's capabilities.

Gopher

The gopher system has certain similarities to the World Wide Web. You use a client program to locate and view information located on servers across the Internet. The difference lies in how the information is organized. The sum of all information available via this method is referred to as *gopherspace*.

Whereas the Web uses hypertext to organize information, gopherspace uses a system of menus that are organized hierarchically. Each gopher server (a computer that is part of gopherspace) has a main menu. Each item on the main menu can lead to a sub-menu, to a menu on another server, or to a resource. Resources include text, pictures, and so on. When you select a menu item, your gopher client will fetch the resource and display it for you.

Gopherspace is gradually being eclipsed by the World Wide Web with its richer content and flashier interface. Even so, a huge amount of information remains available in gopherspace, so it pays to know how to use it. The Netscape browser supports gopherspace. In fact, you may not even be aware that you have moved from the Web to gopherspace unless you notice the gopher:// protocol specifier in the link's URL.

Veronica and Jughead

Veronica and Jughead are tools for helping you to get the most out of gopherspace. Both are used to search the menus in gopherspace for one or more keywords that you specify. Veronica searches all the menus it can find, while Jughead searches a specified subgroup of menus. In either case, when the search is finished, you see a new menu containing all of the items that matched. You can then use this menu to retrieve information from the various gopher sites.

Archie

Archie does a job similar to that accomplished by Veronica and Jughead, but it works with FTP servers. It helps you to locate an FTP server that contains a copy of a particular file that you want. An Archie client, which is located on your computer, must work in conjunction with an Archie server. There are a number of Archie servers scattered around. Each one contains a regularly updated database of files available by anonymous FTP. Once the Archie server has identified one or more FTP sites with the desired files, it's a simple matter to fetch them.

Mailing Lists

Yes indeed, there is junk mail on the Internet, and mailing lists are how you get it. Typically, mailing lists revolve around a specific topic. Messages relating to the topic are gathered from a variety of sources and then mailed to the recipients on the list. Each mailing list is maintained by an individual or organization that has some connection with the topic. The details of maintaining the list are almost always handled by computer. You will typically subscribe to a mailing list by sending a specific message to a certain address. The mailing list program will intercept you message, determine that it's a subscription request, and add your email address to the subscription list. Unsubscribing is usually handled the same way.

One of the best way to find out about mailing lists is by means of a news group on the same subject. Mailing lists can be useful if you must keep up with everything that's going on, particularly in a computer-related area, but if my experience is any guide, you'll find that only about 1% of the messages you receive are of any real value. Of course, if you get a warm, fuzzy feeling from firing up your computer in the morning and finding a long list of messages in your in–box, mailing lists are definitely the way to go!

Talk and Chat

Talk lets you communicate in real time with other people on the Internet. In other words, you type something and they see it on their screen right away; they type an answer and you see it right away. Until recently all "talk" was actually "type" of the sort just described, but new hardware makes it possible to really talk and listen (both systems must have a sound card and microphone, and you need special software). All sorts of variations on talk are possible—private one-on-one conversations, restricted group meetings, or public free-for-alls.

Chat, or more precisely Internet Relay Chat, is a talk facility that can be used by anyone, anytime. Chat has several simultaneous channels. Each channel carries a conversation related to a specific topic. You can join existing channels at will, or create your own channel if desired. There's no end to the topics discussed in chat rooms, nor is there any limit to the amount of time you can waste.

Muds and More

Have you heard of the multi-player role–playing game called Dungeons and Dragons? The first Mud was an on-line version of D & D, which is where it received its name: Multiple User Dungeon. The main idea here is interacting with other players in a completely imaginary setting, with the players adopting fictional identities. From the original D & D–based Mud, a whole slew of similar "imaginary interaction environments"—or whatever you want to call them—have developed. Variations have arisen, too, with names such as Mushes, Moos, Mucks, and Muses. I can't tell you how to find or use Muds, because I've never been tempted myself. To be honest, it sounds about as interesting as listening to tapes of Bob Dole speeches—but to each his own!

Here are the details on the software provided on the CD-ROM.

What's On The Disk?

The JavaScript folder contains the JavaScript code examples that I developed in the book. You'll find each major project in its own folder, and you should be able to find what you're looking for by the folder name. Smaller projects and miscellaneous files are located in the MISC folder. The VBScript programs are located in the VBSCRIPT folder.

The Tools folder contains a variety of Web-related programs and utilities. These value-added tools are listed below, with brief descriptions of what they do. Keep in mind that only some of these programs are "freeware." Most of them are either shareware or limited-period evaluation copies where you are required to pay a fee, usually modest, to the program's creator if you use it regularly. Please note that all of these programs are provided on an "as-is" basis with no guarantee or warrantee of any sort. I have tried them all, but of course it was impossible for me to test all of them thoroughly. They all appeared to do what they claimed to do; they did not crash my system, and they were reported as virus-free by my virus scanning program. Even so, you're on your own.

375

Most of the programs are supplied in compressed form as either a ZIP or EXE file. For ZIP files, you should use PKUNZIP (provided on the CD-ROM in the \TOOLS directory) to decompress the file into a temporary directory on your hard disk. You'll then find INSTALL.EXE or SETUP.EXE, which you can execute from Windows to install the program. If the CD-ROM contains an EXE file, copy to its own temporary directory and execute it. In some cases, the EXE will decompress to create the installation files, including SETUP or INSTALL. In other cases, running the EXE will start the Windows installation process. In any case, follow the installation program instructions as displayed on your screen.

NAME

CMED

Description

A nicely executed HTML editor from down under (G'day, mate). For Windows 95/NT only. Differentiates between HTML 2, HTML 3, Netscape extensions, and Microsoft extensions.

Author(s)

Chad Matheson

Web Site

http://www.iap.net.au/~cmathes/

Location on CD-ROM

\TOOLS\CMED

Name

HTMLJive

Description

An HTML editor written in JavaScript. Simply load the HTML file into your browser and edit away! Not as full-featured as most stand-alone HTML editors;

it cannot save to disk (you must use the Clipboard), but it's still an excellent demonstration of advanced JavaScript use. May also have some specialized uses.

Author(s)

Ray Daly

Web Site

http://www.cris.com/~raydaly/htmljive.html

Location on CD-ROM

\TOOLS\HTMLJIVE

Name

EasyHelp/Web for Word for Windows 6/7/NT

Description

An add-on for the Microsoft Word word processing program that partially automates the task of creating HTML documents.

Author(s)

James Holroyd and Jeff Hall of Eon Solutions Limited

Web Site

http://www.eon-solutions.com

Location on CD-ROM

\TOOLS\EASYWEB

Name

WebEdit

Description

Yet another HTML editor, but one of the finer ones. There are two versions on the CD-ROM. WEBEDIT.ZIP is the release version 1.4, and is a 16 bit program. WEPRO2B3.ZIP is a beta of version 2, a 32 bit application. Even though it's a beta, it is very stable and feature-complete. By the time you read this, the release version should be available. These downloads are 30-day evaluation copies. If you like the program, after 30 days you must purchase the software

Author(s)

Kenn Nesbitt

Web Site

http://www.nesbitt.com/index.html

Location on CD-ROM

\TOOLS\WEBEDIT

Name

MAPEDIT

Description

An editor for client-side image maps. If you don't know what these are, you'll discover that they are definitely cool. Have you ever visited a Web site where clicking on different parts of an image takes you to different links? That's what a client-side image map does. There are two versions of MAPEDIT, one for 16 bit Windows and one for 32 bit. These are 30-day evaluation copies; it's $25 after that.

Author(s)

Boutell.com

Web Site

http://www.boutell.com/

Location on CD-ROM

\TOOLS\MAPEDIT

Name

NETCOLORZ

Description

NetColorz v1.0 provides a quick method of choosing and testing colors in your HTML Web pages, and displays their RGB hexadecimal codes. It easily integrates with your favorite HTML editor. NetColorz may also be used any other time you require an RGB hexadecimal red-green-blue triplet to specify colors. Color sliders and/or a palette are used to chose your colors. NetColorz is freeware.

Author(s)

PolyVision

Web Site

http://www.flinet.com/~muniz/

Location on CD-ROM

\TOOLS\NETCOLOR

Name

FindRGB

Description

A utility that helps with the pesky problem of finding the RGB combination that creates a particular color. You can choose from a color palate or create colors using scroll bars. In addition, you can choose color from another application that is running on your screen. Windows 95 shareware with a $19 registration fee.

Author(s)

Shetef Solutions

Web Site

http://ourworld.compuserve.com/homepages/dascalu/

Location on CD-ROM

\TOOLS\TESTRGB

Name

WinExpose

Description

Not a Web-related tool, but so useful that I decided to include it anyway. WinExpose tracks all file operations of all running programs. You receive a log of all disk operations specifying the program, the disk operation requested, and the file accessed. WinExpose can be very useful in debugging certain bugs and errors. This is Windows shareware with both Windows 95 and Windows 3.1 versions.

Author(s)

Shetef Solutions

Web Site

http://ourworld.compuserve.com/homepages/dascalu/

Location on CD-ROM

\TOOLS\WINEXPOS

Name

Keyboard Express

Description

This is another utility that is not directly Web-related, but it is a real time-saver. Keyboard Express is a keyboard macro utility that lets you define sequences of keystrokes that can be played back at the touch of a hot key. What's neat is that the keystrokes are sent to whatever application is currently active. For example, I have defined Ctrl+Alt+E to play back my email address, and I can easily insert it into anything—a Word document, an email message, or an HTML document I might be editing. The program on disk is the 16-bit version, but it works fine with Windows 95, too. A 32-bit version is in the works.

Author(s)

Insight Software Solutions

Web Site

http://www.smartcode.com/iss

Location on CD-ROM

\TOOLS\KBEXPRS

NAME

DIGITS.ZIP

Description

A zipped file containing images of digits for use in counters, clocks, and the like. All sorts of images, you won't believe the selection! The main ZIP file contains a whole mess of smaller ZIP files, one for each digit style. Have fun!

Author(s)

Various

Web Site

http://cervantes.learningco.com/kevin/digits/

Location on CD-ROM

\TOOLS\DIGITS

NAME

ACLIST

Description

A Microsoft utility that greatly simplifies the use of ActiveX controls in VBScript (and other scripting language) code. Once installed, this program compiles a list of all the ActiveX controls that are available on your system. You can then select a control from the list, and ACLIST places the required <OBJECT...> tag on the Windows clipboard, complete with that annoying CLASSID identifier. Paste it into your HTML file, and you're set.

Author(s)

The Microsoft Gang

Web Site

http://www.microsoft.com/INTDEV/

Location on CD-ROM

\TOOLS\AXLIST

NAME

Paint Shop Pro

Description

One of the most impressive shareware packages around. Paint Shop Pro provides powerful image creation and manipulation tools, including photo retouching, TWAIN scanner support, image processing filters, and support for some 30 file formats.

Author(s)

JASC Incorporated

Web Site

http://www.jasc.com

Location on CD-ROM

\TOOLS\PAINTSHOP

Name

Programmer's File Editor

Description

A freeware editor designed specifically for programmers. Light years ahead of Notepad, with multi-file capability and lots of programming-specific features. The CD-ROM contains the Win95/Win NT version and you can get other versions at the Web site.

Author(s)

Some talented folks in jolly old England.

Web Site

http://www.lancs.ac.uk/people/cpaap/pfe/pfefiles.htm

Location on CD-ROM

\TOOLS\PFE

Name

HotMetal

Description

Yet another Windows HTML editor. Personally, I haven't used this one much, but have heard good things about it from associates.

Author(s)

SoftQuad Inc.

Web Site

http://www.sq.com/

Location on CD-ROM

\TOOLS\HOTMETAL

Name

Internet Assistant for Microsoft Word

Description

An add-on for Microsoft's word processor that provides tools for HTML file creations. The version on the CD-ROM works with Word 7.0 for Windows 95. There's a Windows 3.1 version available on the Web site.

Author(s)

The gang in Redmond.

Web Site

http://www.microsoft.com/msword/internet/ia/

Location on CD-ROM

\TOOLS\WORDIA

Index

Symbols and characters

-, 73
—, 74
!, 83
!=, 80
%, 73
&, 47, 76, 83
&&, 78, 83
?:, 83
*, 73
+, 73, 74
++, 74
^, 76, 83
_, 68
/, 73
/* */, 89
//, 88
\, 71–72
|, 76, 83
||, 83
<, 80
<=, 80
=, 73
==, 80
>, 80
>=, 80
>>>, 78

—A—

<A>...</A>, 32, 123, 214
Abort button, 331–32
abs, 136, 155, 158, 320, 327
Absolute value, 320
acos, 136, 155, 158
Active Label, 311, 356
Active Label control, 310
ActiveX, 309, 356
  controls, 258, 279, 310–12
  objects, 309
  timer control, 357
ActiveX Control Lister, 312
Addition operator, 73, 83, 293
Adjust links, 59
Adobe Photoshop, 52
alert, 156, 159, 243
Alert dialog box, 134
ALIGN, 39
  settings, 30
Alignment, 48
All-at-once verification, 241–43
Alphabetizing, 333
ALT, 29
Ampersand (&), 47
Anchor, 32, 145, 155, 159
Anchor object, 122–23
Anchor-text, 33
AND, 76, 78, 296
Angle brackets, 18, 55, 78
Apostrophe, 284
appCodeName, 144
Applets, 4, 257, 279
  parameters, 260
Application modal, 331
appName, 144
appVersion, 144
Arc cosine, 158
Arc sine, 160
Arc tangent, 160, 320, 323
Arguments, 91-92
  passed by reference, 93
  passed by value, 93
  separating by commas, 305
Arguments array, 271
Arithmetic expressions, 72
Arithmetic operators, 73, 293–94
ARRAY1.HTML, 97
Arrays, 95, 279, 288, 336

deleting, 291
subscript, 96
Asc, 320, 327
ASCII, 320, 327
  files, 21
  values, 81
asin method, 136, 155, 160
Assignment, 293
  operators, 73, 75, 83, 293
  statement, 73
atan, 136, 155, 160
Atn, 320, 323
Automatic outliner, 215–29, 232

—B—

<B>...</B>, 26, 162
back, 143, 155, 160
Backgrounds, 34–38
Backslash, 71–72
Backspace, 71
Bandwidth, 280
Barry, Dave, 61
Bartlett's Familiar Quotations, 61
Base 10 logarithms, 324
BGCOLOR, 36
big, 145, 154, 161
<BIG>...</BIG>, 26
Binary, 76
Binary notation, 76
Bitwise AND (&), 76, 83
Bitwise exclusive OR (^), 76, 83
Bitwise OR (|), 76, 83
Bitwise shift operators, 77
blink, 145, 154, 161
<BLINK>...</BLINK>, 161
blur method, 113, 121–22, 162
BlurHandler, 116, 120–21
<BODY>...</BODY>, 25, 107, 140